Elara

The Prince of the House of David

or

Three Years in the Holy City

by Rev. Prof. J.H. Ingraham

Zoe Publications
PO Box 1361
Clemmons, NC 27012

ISBN 0-89841-003-7

Table of Contents

We wish to express our appreciation to the restoration team headed by J. S. Jackson, project leader and C. Brown, without their dedication and attention to detail this project would not have been possible.

The illustrations were contributed by Bjorn van Dongen.

INTRODUCTION TO THE

LETTERS OF ADINA.

Adina, the writer of the following letters, was the only child of Manasseh Benjamin, who, though an Israelite of the tribe of Judah, was a native of the Greeco Romano city of Alexandria. His ancestor was the learned David Esdras Manasseh, one of the Septuaginta (or LXX) appointed by Ptolemy Philadelphus in the year 277 BC to translate the Bible from the original Hebrew tongue into Greek. Esdras, with his companions, having accomplished this important work, was invited by the king to remain in Egypt, where he died at an advanced age, holding an office of trust and honor. His descendants for five generations where eminent men, and shared the confidence of the rulers of Egypt, under whom they accumulated riches which were finally inherited by Manasseh Benjamin, a man not unworthy of so eminent an ancestry. He was revered in Alexandria for his integrity, wisdom and rank, as well as for his learning and wealth, and was honored with the friendship of the Roman Pro-consul, Rufus Lucius Paulinus. His love and veneration for the land of his fathers, for the Holy City and Temple of Jehovah, were not lessened by his nativity as an Egyptian Jew, and as he had been in his youth sent to Jerusalem by his father, to be educated in the laws of Moses, so he resolved that his daughter should share the same privileges, be taught as beseemed a Jewish woman, and the inheritress of his name and wealth.

After a tedious journey of seventeen days by the way of Gaza, the lovely Adina at length came in sight of the walls and tower of the city of Zion. The caravan halted upon the ridge, and the Jewish travelers composing it alighted and prostrated

5

themselves in adoration before the city of David, and the mountain of Moriah, made sacred by the footsteps of Abraham. The maiden unveiled and bowed her head with sacred awe. It was her first sight of Jerusalem -- the city of her fathers, the birthplace of her parent, of which, from her earliest childhood, she heard him speak with the profoundest reverence. As she gazed upon it, she thought of Isaac, who had been bound upon an altar on yonder height, now glittering with walls overlaid with marble and gold; of Isaiah, who had been sawn asunder in the gloomy valley at her feet; of David and his glory; of Solomon and his wisdom; of the host of Prophets who had trod its streets or wandered upon its hills. Rapidly her memory brought to her mind the history of the mighty past, of the sieges the city had withstood against the Assyrians, the Persians, the Egyptians, and the nations of the earth: of the carrying away into captivity of her countrymen; of the demolition of its walls and of its Temple; and its rebuilding by Ezra. But most of all she dwelt with holy fear upon the thought that the presence of God, of Jehovah, had dwelt there century after century, visibly, in unbearable Fire, within the inner sanctuary of the Temple; and that there He had spoken with man, as it were, face to face. She thought also of the Ark of the Covenant, of the Tables of Stone, of Aaron's budded rod, and of the brazen serpent which were laid up in the Temple and her heart beat with emotion such as she had never felt before. Lower, and with more awful veneration, she bent her head in grateful reverence to Him who had so distinguished above all nations her nation, above all cities the city of her fathers and of the Prophets! Then she raised her eyes in pride that she was a Jewess, and looked around proudly upon the noble landscape which, in her imagination, it seemed must be as familiar to the eyes of angels as to men, so closely had Heaven connected itself with that chosen spot.

The Arabs her attendants, had also bowed and kneeled in the presence of the sacred towers; but it was in honor of Abraham and the patriarchs, their ancestors through Ishmael, who they believed lay with Isaac and Jacob in sepulchres upon Mount Zion.

Adina's proud glance around was arrested by the sight of a cohort of soldiers that came galloping up the ridge from the city, with a glittering eagle carried in advance.

"The Romani! The Romani!," cried the guides, and rising from their knees they remounted in haste, and used every exertion to leave the road open to the approaching troop of horse. An Israelitish muleteer, a few rods below in the path, who could not get out of the way soon enough, was over-run and thrown to the ground, and the cavalcade swept onward to the summit of the hill, disregarding him.

The cheek of Adina paled at the sight, but it was not from fear. All her pride died away in her heart; and she forgot the glory of the past, in the sense of the present degradation. In the first exultation of her emotions at fastening her eyes upon Jerusalem, she had forgotten that the land of the Prophets and of kings anointed by God, was now a conquered Roman province. But the sight of the Roman cohort brought this painful reality to her mind, and veiling her face, she was overcome by the deepest sadness.

The troops passed her and her escort like a whirlwind of war, with ringing spurs, jingling bits, clashing shields, and the noise of the tramp of five hundred hoofs. She could no longer gaze upon the city with joy and pride. The words of Jeremiah rose to her lips:

"How hath the Lord covered the daughter of Zion with a cloud in his anger! Is this the city that men call the perfection of beauty, the joy of the whole earth? The Lord has cast us off from being a nation, and the name of Israel is remembered no more!"

Tears, free and bountiful, relieved the fullness of her heart, and like a true daughter of Jerusalem, she mourned over the departed glory of her people.

Once more they rode on, winding down around a hill covered with tombs, one of which was pointed out to her by a Jewish Rabbi, under whose care she was journeying, as that of the prophet Jeremiah. Leaving this tomb on the left, they crossed a small valley, green and beautiful with groves, fountains and terraces, and thronged with a mixed multitude, both men and women who seemed to be enjoying a promenade there, outside the city walls; there were also booths arranged on one side of the shady walk, where merchants from all parts of the earth were selling. The Rabbi accounted for this concourse by informing her that they had arrived at Jerusalem on a great feast day. Avoiding this multitude they moved on their way to the right, and ascended a low eminence from which Jerusalem, in another point of view, burst upon them in all the splendor of its still unconquerable magnificence: for with all its vicissitudes of misfortune, in wars, sieges and desolation, the Jerusalem of the Romans was still a majestic metropolis, and, in a great degree, meriting its appellation of the "Queen of the nations."

"How beautiful!" exclaimed Adina, unconsciously reining up her camel.

"Men cannot destroy the city of God," said the Rabbi, with haughty confidence, "She will stand forever."

"Point out to me, good Rabbi Ben Israel, the prominent places. What is that frowning castle beyond the Temple which looks so strong and warlike?"

"That is the City of David," the castle of the kings! It protects the Temple and town. David fortified himself in it, and so did the noble Maccabees. It was built by Melchisedec, the king of Jerusalem and the friend of our father Abraham. It is now garrisoned by a thousand Roman soldiers."

The Jewish girl sighed, and then her eyes being attracted by a graceful tower which the sunbeams of the west burnished like gold, she inquired what it was.

"The one with the palm growing by its side and nearly as lofty?" asked the Rabbi, who seemed to take pleasure in gratifying the curiosity of his lovely protege.

"Yes, the same."

"That is David's Tower. Upon it David's watchman stood when he was looking for tidings from Absalom; and the wood you see far to the northeast is the wood of Ephraim, wherein Prince Absalom was slain."

"And what palace is that which the setting sun lights up so brilliantly, as if it were covered with plates of silver?"

"That is the palace of the Roman Governor, Pontius Pilate, who reigns in Jerusalem as a king. But why do you shudder?" he asked, as he beheld her change countenance; but following the direction of her eyes to their right, he beheld, not far distant, a score of crosses bristling upon a small eminence opposite the city gate; and two of the crosses held bodies nailed to them, while a guard of soldiers and a crowd of people stood near looking on and watching the writhing of the victims. The groans and execrations of one of them distinctly reached the ears of Adina.

"That is the Hill of Calvary, daughter," said the Rabbi with a look of outward indifference. "It is where the Romans execute their malefactors. Two have suffered today. It is a cruel punishment, not so mild as stoning to death; but the Romans have little feeling. Let us ride on."

On the left they wound round the wall of a garden that seemed to be open to the public, as in some places the enclosure was thrown down. Several persons were seen within, walking up and down, or reclining under the shade of olive trees. "That is Solomon's garden, now called Gethsemane," said the Rabbi "it is now like all the royal woods, desolate."

"Yet beautiful in its desolation. How majestically the walls of the temple rise heavenward, seen from this valley! What noble hill, partly covered with trees, is this behind the garden?"

"Olivet, also a portion of the king's garden in the days of Israel's glory. The village beyond it is Bethlehem."

"What, the Bethlehem of Judah out of which the prophet says shall come a Ruler over Israel?"

"The same! and we look one day to have that prophecy fulfilled. It cheers us with the assurance that Jerusalem shall not forever be trodden down of the nations, but one day have a king and governor of the royal seed of David."

"And do any of the family of David now exist?" asked Adina, fixing her eyes earnestly upon the bearded face of the Rabbi.

"Yes, or the prophecy could not be accomplished. But they are, as far as known, poor and humble; but I have no doubt that in some part of the world among the nations, exists some of the sacred stock who are reigning princes, as Daniel and Joseph reigned in Persia and Egypt, from whence they shall come as conquerors to rule over Israel."

"How then can they spring from yonder little village of Bethlehem?" asked the maiden.

The Rabbi looked a little embarrassed, and was about to make some reply to this difficult question, when their road was blocked up by a flock of sheep, mingled with a drove of cattle, being driven into the city for the altars of sacrifice. It was with some delay they made their way through these obstacles and came to the gates of Damascus. Here they were detained by the Roman guard and made to show their passports, and to pay thirty sesterces for every camel, and half as many for each mule in the caravan.

The scene in the streets was quite bewildering to Adina; who had been journeying so many days through a desert; but as the dwelling of the relations of her father was near the gate, she was soon in the arms of her friends, who, though they had never seen her before, received her affectionately, as much for her father's sake, who had commended her to their protection, as for her own prepossessing loveliness.

Just entering her seventeenth year, the daughter of the rich Alexandrian was in the prime of female charms. Her hair was an auburn brown, long, and shining like gold; her face oval, and transparently olive in its color, tinted with the least perceptible roseate; her eyes large, and of the most splendid light and glory of expression; her nose straight and finely outlined, and her mouth exquisitely shaped with an expression of heavenly sweetness.

Having been kindly welcomed, and finding every preparation made for her comfort and happiness, she gave a few days to repose, and then, on the return of the caravan, addressed the following letter to her father. This letter was followed by many others, all of which it is our intention to give to the reader, as they are written at a period the most interesting of any other of which history takes record. The first letter is dated, according to the Jewish chronology, three years before the crucifixion of our Savior.

LETTERS FROM ADINA.

LETTER I.

My Dear Father: My first duty, as it is my highest pleasure, is to comply with your command to write you as soon as I arrived at Jerusalem; and this letter, while it conveys to you intelligence of my arrival, will confirm to you my filial obedience.

I will not fail to write you by every caravan that leaves here monthly for Cairo; and if there are more frequent opportunities, my love for you, dear father, and sympathy for you in your separation from me, will prompt me to avail myself of them.

My journey hither occupied many days, Rabbi Ben Israel says seventeen, but although I kept the number up to ten, I soon became too weary to keep the account. When we traveled in sight of the sea, which we did for three days, I enjoyed the majesty of the prospect, it seemed so like the sky stretched out upon the earth. I also had the good fortune to see several barges, which the Rabbi, who was always ready to gratify my thirst for information, informed me were Roman galleys, bound some to Sidon and others into the Nile; and after one of these latter, as it was going to you, I sent a prayer and a wish. Just as we were leaving the seashore to turn off into the desert, I saw a wrecked vessel. It looked so helpless and bulky, with its huge black body all out of the water, that it seemed to me like a great sea monster, the Behemoth, stranded and dying; and I felt like pitying it. The Rabbi gave me to understand that it had come from Alexandria, laden with wheat, bound for Italia, and been cast ashore in a storm. How terrible a tempest must be upon the sea! I was in hopes to have seen a Leviathan, but was not gratified in the wish. The good Rabbi, who seemed to know all things, told me that they seldom appear now in the Middle Sea, but are seen beyond the pillars of Hercules at the world's end.

At Gaza we stopped two days. We entered the gateway of which Samson carried away the gates, and I was shown the hill two miles to the southeast where he left them. Many other places of interest were shown me, especially the field, which our path led across, where he put to flight the Philistine hosts with much slaughter. A lion's cave was also pointed out to me, out of which came the lion which Samson slew, and upon which he made his famous riddles.

The dry well into which the ten Patriarchs lowered the Prince Joseph, their brother, was also shown me by our Arab guide, and the rock on which the Ishmaelites told down the pieces of silver. I fancied the old Arab related the occurrence with more elation than was needful, as if he took pride in perpetuating the fact that our noble ancestor had once been the purchased slave of theirs. I noticed, several times during the journey, that the Ishmaelites of Edom in our caravan took every occasion to elevate their own race to the disparagement of the sons of Israel; indeed, Aben Hussuff, our white-bearded chief of the caravan, in a wordy discussion with Rabbi Ben Israel at Isaac's well, where we encamped, would have it that Isaac was the son of the bondwomen, and Ishmael, the true heir, but disinherited and cast out through the wiles of the bondwoman, who would have her owns son the inheritor. But, of course, I was too well instructed in the history of my fathers to give heed to such a fable; though the Arabs all took part with their chief, and contended for the truth of what he asserted as warmly and zealously as the learned Rabbi did for the truth of his own side.

The morning of the last day of our journey we caught sight of the Sea of Sodom and Gomorrah, at a great distance to the east. How my pulse quickened at beholding that fearful spot so marked by the wrath of Jehovah! I seemed to see in imagination the heavens on fire above it, and the flames and smoke ascending as from a great furnace, as on that fearful day when they were destroyed, with all that beautiful surrounding plain, which we are told was one vast garden of beauty. How calm and still lay now that sluggish sea beneath a cloudless sky! We held it in sight many hours, and once caught a glimpse of the Jordan north of it, looking like a silver thread; yet, near as it appeared to be, I was told it was a good day's journey for a camel to reach its shores.

After losing sight of this melancholy lake, the glassy sepulcher of cities and their countless dwellers, our way lay along a narrow valley for some time, when, all at once, on reaching an eminence, Jerusalem appeared, like a city risen out of the earth, it stood before us so unexpectedly; for we were still, as it were, in the desert; yet so near on the side of our approach does the desert advance to its walls, that it was not two miles off when we beheld it.

I cannot, my dear father, describe to you my emotions on beholding the Holy City! They have been experienced by millions of our people -- they were similar to your own as you related them to me. All the past, with its mighty men who walked with Jehovah, came up to my mind, overpowering me with the amazing weight. The whole history of the sacred place rushed to my memory, and compelled me to bow my head, and worship and adore at the sight of the Temple, where God once (alas, why does He no longer visit earth and His Holy House?) dwelt in the flaming Shechinah, and made known the oracles of His will. I could see the smoke of the evening sacrifice ascending to the skies, and I inwardly prayed Jehovah to accept it for thee and me.

As we approached the city several interesting spots were pointed out to me, and I was bewildered with the familiar and sacred localities which I had known hitherto only by reverential reading of the Prophets. It seemed to me that I was living in the days of Isaiah and Jeremiah, as places associated with their names were shown me, rather than in the generation to which I properly belong. Indeed, I have lived only in the past the three days I have been in Jerusalem, constantly consulting the sacred historians to compare places and scenes with their accounts, and so verify each with a holy awe and inward delight that must be felt to be understood; but, dear father, you have yourself experienced all this, and therefore can understand my emotions.

We entered the city just before the sixth hour of the evening, and were soon at the house of our relative Amos, the Levite. I was received as if I had a daughter's claim to their embraces; and with the luxuries with which they surrounded me in my gorgeously furnished apartments, I am sure they meant to tempt me to forget the joys of the dear home I had left.

The Rabbit Amos and his family all desire to be commended to you. As it is his course to serve in the Temple, I do not see much of him, but he seems to be a man of piety and benevolence, and greatly loves his children. I have been once to the Temple. Its outer court seemed like a vast caravansera or marketplace, being thronged with the men who sell animals for sacrifice, which crowded all parts. Thousands of doves in large cages were sold on one side, and on another were stalls

13

for lambs, sheep, calves, and oxen, the noise and bleating of which, with the confusion of tongues, made the place appear like anything else than the Temple of Jehovah. It appears like desecration to use the Temple thus, dear father, and seems to show a want of that holy awe of God's house that once characterized our ancestors. I was glad to get safely through the Bazaar, which, on the plea of selling to sacrificers victims for the altar, allows, under color thereof, every other sort of traffic. On reaching the women's court I was sensible of being in the Temple, by the magnificence which surrounded me. With what awe I bowed my head in the direction of the Holy of Holies! I never felt before so near to God! Clouds of incense floated above the heads of the multitude, and rivers of blood flowed down the marble steps of the altar of burnt offering. Alas! how many innocent victims bleed every morning and evening for the sins of Israel! What a sea of blood has been poured out in the ages that have passed! What a strange, fearful mystery, that the blood of an innocent lamb should atone for sins I have done! There must be some deeper meaning in these sacrifices, dear father, yet unrevealed to us.

As I was returning from the Temple I met many persons walking and riding, who seemed to be crowded out of the gate on some unusual errand. I have since learned that there is a very extraordinary man -- a true prophet of God, it is believed by many, who dwells in the wilderness, fifteen miles eastward, near Jordan, and who preaches with power unknown in the land since the days of Elijah and Elisha. It is to see and listen to this prophet that so many persons are daily going out from Jerusalem. He lives in a cave, feeds on plants or wild honey, and drinks only water, while his clothing is the skin of a lion; at least, such is the report. I hope he is a true prophet of Heaven, and that God is once more about to remember Israel; but the days of the Prophets have long passed away, and I fear this man is only an enthusiast; but his influence over all who listen to him is so remarkable, that it would seem, and one has almost the courage to believe, that he is really endowed with the Spirit of the Prophets.

Farewell, dear father, and let us ever pray for the Glory of Israel.

Your affectionate daughter,
ADINA.

14

LETTER II.

My Dear Father: The excellent Rabbi, Ben Israel, has just made known to me his intention of returning to Egypt tomorrow, and has waited upon me, to inquire if I had any commands to entrust him with, for my friends in Alexandria. Instead of this letter, which he will be the bearer of to you, I would rather commit myself a second time to his care, and instead of placing this parchment in your hand, let him lay your child again upon your bosom. But it is by your wish, dear father, that I am here, and though I sigh to behold you once more, I will try to be content in my absence from you, knowing that my discontent would cause sorrow to bow down your gray hairs.

So far as a daughter can be happy from the home of her youth, I have everything to render me so. The good Rabbi Amos in his kindness recalls your own mild and dignified countenance, and Rebecca, his noble wife, my cousin, is truly a mother in Israel. Her daughter Mary, my younger cousin, in her affectionate attachment to me, shows me how much love I have lost in never having had a sister. It is altogether a lovely household, and I am favored by the God of our fathers in having my lot, during my exile from my home on the banks of the beautiful Nile, cast in so peaceful and holy a domestic sanctuary.

The street in which we dwell is elevated, and from the roof of the house, where I love to walk in the evening, watching the stars that hang over Egypt, there is commanded a wide prospect of the Holy City. The stupendous Temple, with its terraces piled on terraces of dazzling marble, with its glittering fountains shooting upward like palm trees of liquid silver, with its massive yet beautiful walls and towers, is ever in full sight. The golden arc, that spans the door which leads into the Holy of Holies, as it catches the sunbeams of morning, burns like a celestial coronet with an unearthly glory. I dare not gaze steadily upon that holy place, or imagine the blinding splendor within, of the visible presence of Jehovah, in the Shechinah once present there.

Yesterday morning I was early on the housetop, to behold the first cloud of the day-dawn sacrifice rise from the bosom of the Temple. When I had turned my gaze toward the sacred summit, I was awed by the profound silence which reigned

over the vast pile that crowned Mount Moriah. The sun was
not yet risen; but the east blushed with a roseate purple, and
the morning star was melting into its depths. Not a sound
broke the stillness of the hundred streets within the walls of
Jerusalem. Night and silence still held united empire over the
city and the altar of God. I was awe-silent. I stood with my
hands crossed upon my bosom and my head reverently bowed,
for in the absence of man and his voice I believed angels were
all around in heavenly hosts, the guardian armies of this
wondrous city of David. Lances of light now shot upward and
across the purple sea in the east, and fleeces of clouds, that
reposed upon it like barks, catching the red rays of the yet
uprisen sun, blazed like burning ships. Each moment the
darkness fled, and the splendor of the dawn increased; and
when each instant I expected to see the sun appear over the
battlemented heights of Mount Moriah, I was thrilled by the
startling peal of the trumpets of the priests: a thousand silver
trumpets blown at once from the walls of the Temple, and
shaking the very foundation of the city with their mighty
voice. Instantly the house-tops everywhere around were alive
with worshipers! Jerusalem started, as one man, from its
slumbers, and, with their faces toward the Temple, a hundred
thousand men of Israel stood waiting. A second trumpet-peal,
clear and musical as the voice of God when He spake to our
father Moses in Horeb, caused every knee to bend, and every
tongue to join in the morning song of praise. The murmur of
voices was like the continuous roll of the surge upon the
beach, and the walls of the lofty Temple, like the cliff, echoed
it back. Unused to this scene, for we have nothing like this
majesty of worship in Alexandria, I stood rather as a spectator
than a sharer, as it became thy daughter to have been, dear
father. Simultaneously with the billow-like swell of the
adoring hymn, I beheld a pillar of black smoke ascend from
the midst of the Temple, and spread itself above the court like
a canopy. It was accompanied by a blue wreath of lighter and
more misty appearance, which threaded in and out, and
entwined about the other, like a silvery strand woven into a
sable cord. This latter was the smoke of the incense which
accompanied the built sacrifice. As I saw it rise higher and
higher, and finally overtop the heavy cloud, which was
instantly enlarged by volumes of dense smoke that rolled
upward from the consuming victim, and slowly disappeared,
melting into heaven, I also kneeled remembering that on the

wings of the incense went up the prayers of the people; and ere it dissolved wholly, I entrusted to it, dear fathers prayers for thee and me!

How wonderful is our religion! How mysterious this daily sacrifice, so many hundreds of years offered up for the sins of our fathers and of ourselves! How, I have often asked myself since I have been here, how can the blood of a heifer, of a lamb, or of a goat, take away sins? What is the mysterious relation existing between us and these dumb and innocent brutes? How can a lamb stand for a man before God? The more I reflect upon this artful subject, the more I am lost in wonder. I have spoken to Rabbi Amos of these things, but he only smiles, and bids me think about my embroidery; for cousin Mary and I are working a rich gold border in the phylactery of his next New Year's garment.

The evening sacrifice, which I witnessed yesterday, is, if possible, more imposing than that of the morning. Just as the sun dips beyond the hill of Gibeah, overhanging the valley of Aijalon, there is heard a prolonged note of a trumpet blown from one of the western watch-towers of Zion. Its mellow tones reach the farthest ear within the gates of the city. All labor at once ceases! Every man drops the instrument of his toil, and raises his face toward the summit of the house of God. A deep pause, as if all held their breath in expectation, succeeds. Suddenly the very skies seem to be riven, and shaken with the thunder of the company of trumpeters that rolls, wave on wave of sound, from the battlements of the Temple. The dark cloud of sacrifice ascends in solemn grandeur, and sometimes heavier than the evening air, falls like a descending curtain around the Mount, till the whole is veiled from sight; but above it is seen to soar the purer incense to the invisible Jehovah, followed by a myriad eyes, and the utterance of a nation's prayers. As the daylight faded, the light of the altar, hidden from us by the lofty walls of the outer court of the Temple, blazed high and beacon-like, and lent a wild sublimity to the towers and pinnacles that crowned Moriah.

There was, however, my dear father, last evening, one thing which painfully marred the holy character of the sacred hour. After the blast of the silver trumpets of the Levites had ceased, and while all hearts and eyes were ascending to Jehovah with the mounting wreaths of incense, there came from the Roman castle adjoining the City of David a loud martial clangor of brazen bugles, and other barbarian war-instruments of music, while a smoke, like the smoke of sacrifice, rose from the height of David's fortified hill. I was told that it was the Romans engaged in worshiping Jupiter, their idol God! Oh, when, when shall the Holy City be freed from the reproach of the stranger! Alas, for Israel! Her inheritance "is turned to strangers, and her houses to aliens." Well said Jeremiah the Prophet, "The kings of the earth and all the inhabitants of the world would not have believed that the adversary and the enemy should have entered into the gates of Jerusalem." How truly now are the prophecies fulfilled, which are to be found in the Lamentations: "The Lord hath cast off His altar, He hath given up into the hands of the enemy the walls of her palaces: they have made a noise in the house of the Lord, as in the day of a solemn feast." For these things I weep, my dear father even now, while I write, my tears drop on the parchment. Why is it so? Why does Jehovah suffer the adversary to dwell within his holy walls, and the smoke of his abominable sacrifices to mingle with that of the offerings of the consecrated priests of the Most High? Surely, Israel has sinned, and we are punished for our transgressions. It becomes the land "to search and try its ways and turn unto God," if perhaps He will return and have mercy, and restore the glory of Israel. Our kings are the servants of the Gentiles. Our laws are no more. Our prophets no longer see visions. God has gone up in anger, and no longer holds discourse with his chosen people. The very smoke of the daily sacrifice seems to hang above the Temple like a cloud of Jehovah's wrath.

Nearly three hundred years have passed since we have had a prophet -- that divine and youthful Malachi! Since his day, Rabbi Amos confesses that Jehovah has ceased from all known intercourse with His people and holy house; nor has He made any sign of having heard the prayers or heeded the sacrifices that have been offered to Him in His time! I inquired of the intelligent Rabbi, if this would always be thus? He replied, that when Shiloh came there would be a restoration of all things -- that the glory of Jerusalem then would fill the whole earth with the splendor of the sun, and that all nations should come up from the ends of the world to worship in the temple. He acknowledges that we are now under a cloud for our sins; but that a brighter day is coming when Zion shall be the joy of the whole earth.

May conversation with Rabbi Amos, dear father, a conversation which grew out of the subject of the Roman garrison occupying the citadel of David, and offering their pagan sacrifices by the side of our own smoking altars, led me to examine the Book of the Prophet Malachi. I find that after plainly alluding to our present shame, and reproaching the priests, "for causing the people to stumble," and thus making themselves "contemptible and base before all nations," he thus prophecies; "Behold, I will send my messenger, and he will prepare the way before me, and the Lord whom ye seek shall suddenly come to his Temple; and he shall sit as a refiner and purifier of silver, and he shall purify the sons of Levi, and purge them as gold and silver, that they may offer unto the Lord an offering in righteousness. Behold," adds the divine seer, "I will send you Elijah the prophet before the coming of the great and dreadful day of the Lord."

These words I read today to Rabbi Amos -- indeed, I was reading them when Rabbi Ben Israel came in to say that he departs tomorrow. The excellent Amos looked grave, graver than I had ever seen him look. I feared that I had offended him by my boldness, and, approaching him, was about to embrace him, when I saw tears were sparkling in his eyes. This discovery deeply affected me, you may be assured; dear father and, troubled more to have grieved than displeased him, I was about to ask his forgiveness for intruding these sacred subjects upon his notice, when he took my hand, and smiling, while a glittering drop danced down his snow-white beard and broke into liquid diamonds upon my hand, he said, "You have done no wrong, child: sit down by me and be at peace with thyself. It is too true, in this day, what the Prophet Malachi writeth, Ben Israel," he said sadly, to the Alexandrian Rabbi: "The priests of the Temple have indeed become corrupt, save the few here and there! It must have been at this day the Prophet aimed his words. Save in the outward form, I fear the great body of our Levites have little more true religion and just knowledge of the one God Jehovah, than the priests of the Romish idolatry! Alas, I fear me, God regards our sacrifices with no more favor than He looks upon theirs! Today, while I was in the Temple, and was serving at the altar with the priests, these words of Isaiah came into my thoughts and would not be put aside, "to what purpose is the multitude of your sacrifices unto me?" saith the Lord; "I am full of the burnt offerings of rams, and the fat of fed beasts; and I delight not in the blood of bullocks, or of lambs, or of he goats. Bring no more vain oblations; incense is an abomination unto me; I am weary to bear them; yea, when ye spread forth your hands I will hide mine eyes from you; yea, when ye make many prayer I will not hear; your hands are full of blood! Wash you; make you clean. Cease to do evil; learn to do well!"

"These terrible words of the prophet," added Rabbi Amos, addressing the amazed Ben Israel, "were not out of my mind while I was in the Temple. They seemed to be thundered in my ears by a voice from heaven. Several of the younger priests, whose levity during the sacrifice had been reproved by me, seeing me sad, asked the cause. In reply, I repeated, with a voice that seemed to myself to be inspired, the words of the prophet. They turned pale and trembled, and thus I left them."

"I have noticed," said Ben Israel, "that there is less reverence now in the Temple than when I was in Jerusalem a young man; but I find that the magnificence of the ceremonies is increased."

"Yes," responded Ben Amos, with a look of sorrow, "yes, as the soul of piety dies out from within, they gild the outside. The increased richness of the worship is copied from the Roman. So low are we fallen! Our worship, with all its gorgeousness, is as a sepulcher white-washed to conceal the rottenness within!"

You may be convinced, my dear father, that this confession, from such a source, deeply humbled me. If, then, we are not worshipping God, what do we worship? If Jehovah of Hosts, the God of our Fathers, Abraham, Isaac, and Jacob, hides his face from our sacrifices, and is weary with our incense, whom does Israel worship? NOUGHT! We are worse off than our barbarian conquerors, for we have no God; while they, at least, have gods many and lords many, such as they are! Alas, alas, the time of the judgment of Jerusalem seems to be at hand. The Lord must suddenly come to his Temple, and as a refiner! I am deeply impressed with the conviction that the day is very near at hand! Perhaps we shall see it in our lifetime, dear father!

Since writing the last line I have been interrupted by Mary, who has brought to see me a youth, son of a noble Jewish ruler, who was slain by the Romans for his patriotic devotion to his country. He dwells near the Gaza gate, with his widowed mother, who is a noble lady, honored by all lips that discourse of her. Between this young man and Mary there exists a beautiful attachment, not ardent enough to be love, but sincere enough for the purest friendship; yet each day their friendship is ripening into the deepest emotion. He has just returned from the vicinity of Jericho, where he has been for some days past, drawn thither by curiosity, to see and hear the new prophet, alluded to by me at the close of my last letter, whose fame has spread fair and wide, and who is drawing thousands into the wilderness, to listen to the eloquence that flows from his mouth. The young man had been giving Mary so interesting an account of him that she desired me also to be a listener! In my next I will write you all I heard; and I trust, dear father, you will patiently bear with me in all things; and believe that, however I may, from the investigating character of my mind, venture upon sacred mysteries, I shall never be less a lover of the God of our Father Abraham, nor less the affectionate and devoted Adina to thee! Adieu.

ADINA

LETTER III.

My Dear Father: This morning, as I was coming from the Temple, whither I had gone to worship and witness the imposing ceremony of the presentation of the First Fruits, I noticed a vast pile of edifices crowning the opposite rock, which I was told was the Tower of Antonia. It seemed to frown sternly down upon the Temple; and upon its battlements glittered, at intervals, numerous Roman eagles. I had so often heard you relate historical events connected with this celebrated castle, that I regarded it with peculiar interest. You, who had so frequently described it to me, seemed to stand by my side as I gazed upon it. The four towers, one at each corner, are still as they stood when you fought from the northernmost one, and defended it single-handed against the Romans. But now these barbarians throng its courts, and their bugles, which have sounded from the conquered walls of every land on earth, are ever heard in the ears of the citizens of Jerusalem. The insolence and power of the Roman garrison have made the beautiful walk about the base of the Tower almost deserted; but of this I was not aware; and, attended only by my Ethiopian slave, Onia, I lingered to admire the splendor of the cloister once surrounding the treasure-house of the Temple, with its terraces supported by white marble pillars, fifteen cubits high, when two Roman soldiers coming from one of the city gates, approached me on their way back to the castle. It was then that I saw I was alone, the company who left the Temple with me being gone far in advance of me. I drew my veil closely, and would have passed them with a rapid step, when one of them placed himself in my path, and catching hold of my veil, tried to detain me. I left it in his grasp and was flying, when the other soldier arrested me. This was in full view of the castle, and at my shrieks the barbarians in the castle laughed aloud. At this crisis appeared a young Centurion, who was on horseback, coming down the rocky path that ascends the Rock of Zion, and calling aloud to them, he galloped forward, and with his sword put the men, who were drunk with wine, to immediate flight, and rescued me, at the same time sending the two soldiers under arrest into the castle. He then addressed me in the gentlest manner, and apologized for the rudeness I had met with at the hands of his men, saying that they should be severely dealt with. I was struck with his manly beauty, his civility, and his air of patrician command, although he could not have been more than eight and twenty. In order to escort me safely to the streets below, he alighted from his horse, and leading him by the rein, walked by my side. I confess to you, dear father, I had not reached the house of my relative before my prejudices against the Romans were greatly modified. I had found in one of them as courteous a person as I had ever met with among my own countrymen, and for his sake I was willing to think better of his barbaric land and people. He saw through my prejudices, and how I shrunk from him as he walked by me; and while we descended the height, he spoke eloquently in defense of his native land, of its fair daughters, of its wise men, its brave chiefs, its power and glory, and its dominion over the whole earth!

When I heard him use these last words, I sighed deeply, for Judah, it is prophesied, should have dominion over the whole earth, and these Romans, therefore, hold the dominion that rightfully belongs to our people. How is this, dear father? How is it that these barbaric men are permitted by Jehovah to hold the scepter that is the rightful heritage of the Lion of the tribe of Judah? How many times in a day, since I have been in Jerusalem, have I been reminded of the degradations of my people? How is it that these enemies of Jehovah, these worshipers of false gods, stand in the Holy place, and usurp the power that God has given to us?

I put these questions to Amos, the good priest, after I had returned home; for my account of my adventure naturally led to a conversation upon the Roman dominion over the earth. It appears that this noble Centurion is not unknown to Rabbi Amos, who speaks of him as one of the most popular Roman officers in command in the city. I am glad to hear this. He also gave me warning not to approach again near the garrison points of the town, as the soldiers take pleasure in giving annoyance to the citizens.

While I was writing the above, a commotion without, as if something unusual was occurring, drew me to the lattice which overlooked the street that goes out of the gate to Bethany, one of the most frequented thoroughfares in the city.

The sight that met my eyes was truly imposing, but made my heart sink with shame. It was a pageant with banners, eagles, trumpets, and gilded chariots! but not the pageant of a king of Israel, like those which dazzled the streets of Jerusalem in the days of Solomon and King David! not the triumphant passage of an Israelitish prince, but of the Roman Governor! Preceded by a cohort of horses, he rode in a gilded war-chariot, lolling at his ease beneath a silken shade of blue silk, fringed with gold. The horses were snowy-white, and covered with silver mail, and adorned with plumes. He was followed by another body of cavalry, chiefly composed of richly attired young men, and at the head of them, looking more like a ruler and prince than the indolent Pilate; I beheld the generous Centurion who had aided my escape from the two soldiers. His eye sought the lattice at which I stood, and I drew back, but not before he had seen me and saluted me. Certainly, father, this youth is noble and courteous enough to be a Jew, and should any providence cause us to meet again, I shall try and convert him from his idolatry to serve the living Jehovah. I was not pleased with the appearance of the governor. He is a dark, handsome man, but too fleshy, and with the countenance of a man given to much wine; and I learn that he is naturally indolent and luxurious, and deficient in decision of character. He is a particular friend of the Roman Emperor, and to his partiality he owes the governorship here. It is, however, better to have a table-lover and idle man for our master, than a cruel and active tyrant like his predecessor, in an insurrection against whom was slain that eminent man, the father of John, the cousin of Mary, of whom I spoke to you in my last letter.

And this reminds me that I had something to relate to you. You will remember, dear father, that I alluded to an excitement that is increasing every day, in reference to a new prophet, who is preaching in the wilderness of Jericho, and whose life is as austere as was that of Elijah! For three weeks past several parties of citizens have been to the valley of Jordan to see and hear him, and have so far been carried away by him, as to have been baptized of him in Jordan, confessing their sins. Among these is John, the cousin and betrothed of Mary, who, having heard much said of the power with which this man spoke, by those who had returned, also went to satisfy his curiosity, and, as he says, with a secret hope that God had again remembered Israel, and sent to us a prophet of reconciliation. Upon his return we saw that his countenance was animated beyond its wont, for he is usually of a sad and gentle aspect, and that his fine eyes beamed with an ardent hope, that seemed newborn in his soul. He thus recounted to us his visit to the prophet of Jordan:

"After leaving the gate and crossing the brook and valley of Kedron, I encountered a large company ascending the road that winds over the south side of Olivet. These were men, women, and children, and they were provided with food in baskets, and travel as our people do, when they come up to the Feast of the Passover. I found on joining them that they were directing their steps also toward the wilderness, in order to hear the great prophet, whose fame was in all men's mouths. Among them were priests and judges, Sadducees, and Pharisees, and Esenes, and even men of no faith; for even in Judah we have many ten thousands who believe in no God, so long has it been since Jehovah hath visited his people!

Passing on ahead of this company, I being well mounted, and they traveling slowly, I at length reached the summit of the hill, from which I obtained a distant view of the valley of the Jordan, and even thought I could make out the town of Jericho, though the distance was thirty or more miles. I looked back to take a parting glance at the city. How like the "City of God" it crowned its lordly hills! All the glory of Jerusalem, of the past came before my memory, and I sighed that that glory had departed, not in the destruction of edifices, for Jerusalem is still magnificent and imposing, but in the downfall of its power. I heard, distant as I was, the strains of the Roman bugles, echoing over the valleys where the prophets, priests and kings lay buried; and reverberating from the Temple walls, the sacred echoes of which, aforetime, had been awakened by the voice of God! Gethsemane, the fair garden of Solomon, where he tried to create a second Eden, lay at my feet, its walls broken, and its walks wild and overgrown; here and there a fig or an olive, or a palm tree only, remaining to tell the passing traveler that "here was the delight of gardens, the abode of pleasure and of mirth, from which were excluded all who were sorrowful, that no tears might fall upon its enameled floors, dedicated to voluptuous joy." This description of it, given by our poets, passed through my mind, as I beheld its melancholy and deserted aspect -- looking more like a place of tears than joy, as if its shades would invite the sorrowful to weep in them, rather than the silvery feet of the dancer!

"I soon reached the pretty town of Bethpage, where, at the inn, I beheld several horsemen just mounting to go in the direction of Jericho. Several of them I knew, and, on joining the cavalcade learned they were for the most part drawn out of Jerusalem on the same errand of curiosity with myself. But one of them, however, a wealthy young noble of Arimathea, was actuated by the same holy desire that burned in my bosom, a desire that we might, in the prophet who was called John, discover a man sent from God. The others were bent on commerce, on pleasure, on mere idle curiosity, to see one of whom everyone talked in all the land of Judea. As Joseph of Arimathea and I rode together, we conversed about the man we expected to see, and the different reports which were noised abroad respecting him. My companion seemed to believe that he was a true prophet, for being very well read in the scriptures, he said that the seventy weeks of Daniel were now about completed, when the Messiah was to come. I then asked him if he believed that the Messiah, who was to be a "Prince and King, and have dominion from the sea to the ends of the earth," would come in the wilderness, clad in the skins of wild beasts? To this he replied, that he could not regard this prophet as the Messiah, for when the Christ should come, he was "suddenly to come to the Temple," and that we should doubtless first see him there but that he was greatly in hopes that the prophet we were going to see, would prove to be the forerunner, foretold by Malachi. Having a roll of the Prophet Daniel with me, for I took the prophets along to compare what I should hear the preacher of Jordan proclaim with them, I saw to my surprise, that not only the seventy weeks had about reached their completion, but that the expiration of the "thousand two hundred and ninety days" drew presently nigh! We were both surprised at this coincidence with the advent of this new prophet; and joy and fear trembled in our hearts, tempered with hopes we dared not utter.

"Those who have heard him," said Joseph, as we rode into the village of Bethany, "say that he publicly proclaims himself the forerunner of the Messiah. The opinion of the more ignorant who have listened to him is, that it is Elijah himself, risen to life! while others assert that it is Enoch, comedown from heaven; and not a few believe him to be Isaiah."

"In this manner, conversing, we crossed the hill of Bethany, where, tradition says, stood the Tree of the Knowledge of Good and Evil, and also, where rested the foot of Jacob's

Ladder; and from which place, it is believed by many, all good men after the resurrection shall ascend into the third heaven; for it is the common belief that the throne of Jehovah is directly above it."

"At length, after a long day's ride, during which we had overtaken and passed many large companies hurrying forward to hear the prophet, also meeting many returning, spreading wonderful accounts of his eloquence, wisdom and power, we came in sight of Jericho. The city is very stately, with its Roman towers and palaces, it being the favorite summer resort of the governors. Its situation, in a green valley, was refreshing to the eyes, after our dreary ride all day over the broken and barren hills. On our left, a mile before you come to the town, we passed the ruins of the tower and house of Hiel, who rebuilt Jericho in the days of the Kings. To the right was the field where the Chaldean army defeated our fathers in battle, and took King Zedekiah captive; it was now covered with beautiful gardens, and smiled as if peace had ever dwelt in its sweet shades. On an eminence, to the north of us, about half a league off, Joseph, who had often traveled this way, made me take notice of the ruins of Ai, and of the hill of ambush, where lay the warriors of Joshua, who surprised and cut off the city. As we approached the city, I could not but recall the period when Israel's hundred thousands, shod with the sandals they had worn forty years in the wilderness, marched seven times around it. In imagination I heard their martial tread shaking the very earth, and beheld the princely Joshua, standing aloof on an eminence near, directing the solemn march. I heard again the thunder of the trumpets of the hosts of God seven times sounded, and saw the proud wall of the city fall, darkening the whole heavens with the clouds of dust that rolled over the heads of awe-struck Israel. But how different was the reality! The setting sun was gilding the firmly standing towers, turrets, pinnacles and battlements of the Roman city, lending to it a splendor that moved the soul to admiration; and the blue sky bent serenely without a cloud above it; and the circling vale, instead of echoing to the tread of an armed host, for whom Jehovah fought, was now filled with Roman knights and ladies on gay parties of pleasure, and processions of maidens moving to the cemetery of the tombs, clad in snow-white vestments, casting flowers in their path, and chanting sacred songs; for it was the day in which the daughters of Jericho celebrate the hapless fate of the lovely daughter of Jephtha, by visiting her sepulcher; for she was born and buried in this city, where Jephtha long dwelt."

"At the gate we were stopped by a Roman soldier who demanded our passports and the traveler's tribute, which humiliating affair settled, we rode into the city, for it was our intention to pass the night there, and early in the morning walk to the banks of the Jordan, where we understood the prophet was teaching and baptizing."

At this point of the narrative of the cousin of Mary, dear father, I will close this letter. We had all listened with the deepest attention, not so much for the interest it contained in itself, as on account of the admirable manner in which he recited what he had seen; his face being calmly beautiful, hill eyes soft and expressive, his voice musical, and his whole aspect the true and expressive manifestation of the intelligence, gentleness, amiability, and noble ardor of piety which belong to his whole character. In my next I will resume his narrative, dear father, for when I have given it to you wholly, I have many things to ask you to which it gives rise in my mind. May the blessing of the God of Israel be upon thee, my dear father!

ADINA.

PRINCE OF THE HOUSE OF DAVID

LETTER IV.

My Dear Father: I have had the pleasure today, not only of hearing from you, but of being assured of your continued welfare. The messages of parental affection contained in your letter are cherished in my heart. The costly gifts of your generous love, sent by you with the letter, and which where safely delivered from your hand into mine, by your faithful servant Elec, will be worn by me with all a daughter's pride. I regret to hear of the death of Rabbi Israel, while I rejoice that the high office he held with so much dignity has been bestowed upon you by the Proconsul; for though you may not need its emoluments, dear father, such selection is a flattering proof of the estimation in which you are held by the Roman Governor.

You need not fear, my dear father, that I shall be carried away from the faith of Israel by any strange doctrines; I will take counsel by your wisdom, and be cautious how I adventure in my inquiries upon too sacred ground. I have freely written to you for your advice, and I trust that you will not look upon my inquiries as expressions of doubt, but as searchings after what is true. I know you are read in the law above all Jews, and that any difficulties I may meet with in observing things here in Jerusalem, especially in the worship and ceremonies of the Temple you will remove for me.

In my last letter, which will not reach your hands for some days yet, I commenced writing you the narrative of John, the cousin of Mary, who went down into the wilderness to see and hear the prophet of Jordan. I will not take it upon myself to decide or form an opinion upon anything yet, dear father, but state facts, and let your wisdom instruct me into the truths that

31

may grow out of them. One thing which your letter states gratifies me, and gives me confidence; it is these words. "Do not fear that the integrity of the laws of Moses, or of the worship of the Temple, or the predictions of the Prophets, can be moved by any investigations that man can make into them. They are founded in truth, and will abide forever. The worship of Israel fears nothing from inquiry. But while you ask and question about sacred things, remember that they belong to God, and must be inquired into with awful reverence and profound humility. Any inquiries made into the prophecies with an eye to search out their day of fulfillment, are proper and useful; and as this day seems to be that of fulfillment rather than that of prediction, your studies may be suggested and directed by heavenly wisdom, and, if so, they will be guided to their true issue. As I am so far removed from you, I cannot judge concerning this prophet your first letter named as being in the wilderness; yet I should not be surprised if the fullness of time indicated by Isaiah were near at hand, for the events you enumerated seem to proclaim its approach, such as the lax worship in the Temple; the worship of the Roman idols on Mount Zion; the profanation of the altar; and the rule of the heathen over the empire of David. Let us fervently pray, my child, for the fulfillment of the prophecies, which promise Messiah to our stricken people! Let us supplicate for the rising of the Star of Jacob, the Prince of Peace, who shall erect his throne on Mount Zion, and whose scepter shall be a scepter of righteousness; under whose wide dominion Israel shall lift up her head and rule the nations. My daily prayer, with my face toward Jerusalem, is that I may live to behold the hope of Israel, and with my eyes see the splendor of the glory of Shiloh." These words of yours, my dear father, give me, courage. I believe, with you, that the day of fulfillment of the Prophets is dawning; and perhaps is nearer than we believe. When I have completed the history of John's journey to Jordan to hear the prophet, you will understand why I speak with such hopeful confidence; and you will agree with me that this preacher of repentance is not one of the class of false prophets, against whose chimeras your letter so properly cautions me.

"We arose at dawn," said Mary's cousin, in continuation of his interesting narrative, "and, leaving the inn, we took our way out of the city by the eastern gate, which we easily found, in as much as a quarter of the city was in motion, and moving in the same direction. Here we were detained by the Gentile guards for full half-an-hour, till the multitude had become so immense as to tread one upon another, and fill the whole street. Nevertheless, we had to wait till the indolent Captain of the Gate chose to be disturbed in his morning repose, and then bathe his dainty limbs, and then break his fast, all which he did very deliberately, before he would suffer the gate to be opened! Such slaves are we to such masters! Oh, when shall arrive the day when, as saith Isaiah, "our gates shall be opened continually; they shall not be shut day nor night, that men may bring unto thee the forces of the Gentiles, and that their kings may be brought captives to our feet."

Having passed out of the gate, my friend of Arimathea and myself separated a little from the crowd, and crossed the plain toward Jordan, which was about a mile and a half off. The morning was balmy; the sun made all nature glad. The dew reflected a myriad lesser suns, and the earth appeared strewn with diamonds. For a little way the road lay between fields of corn and gardens; but soon it crossed the open plain, on which were droves of wild asses, which lifted their small, spirited heads on our approach, eyed us with timid curiosity, and then bounded off to the wilderness southward with the speed of antelopes. As the great body of the people took their way obliquely across the plain, we knew the prophet must be in that direction, as it proved; for we at length found him on the banks of the Jordan, full half a league below the landing and ford, which is opposite Jericho, on the great caravan road to Balbec and Assyria, that long and weary road so often traveled by our forefathers when they have been led into captivity -- the road which so many kings have watered with their tears! We gazed upon it with emotion of sadness, and with tearful prayers that Jehovah would return and visit once more the remnant of his people, and not be angry with us forever! After we had approached the Jordan some distance above the ford, we beheld the multitude listening to the prophet far to the south of us, on the edge of the desert, which approaches in this quarter very near Jericho. As we traversed the banks of the flowing stream, we came all at once upon a pillar of stones partly in the water. "This," said my companion, stopping, "is the Mount of Twelve Stones, which Israel set up to commemorate the passage of Jordan. Here they crossed on dry ground."

"I counted them, and found but nine of them remaining.

What vicissitudes, I reflected, had not Israel passed through since the hands of our fathers placed that heap together! Generations of judges and long lines of kings; captivities succeeding captivities; wars, conquests and defeats, and subjection, finally, till we are no longer a people; having a king, indeed, but whose scepter is a mockery -- a Herod, holding his crown at the courtesy of the Imperial Monarch of Rome. Alas, with the end of the reign of such a king, the scepter will forever depart from Judah! he added bitterly.

"Then will Shiloh come!" exclaimed my cousin Mary, with animation.

"Yes, Judah must be abased to the lowest step, before she can rise, and with Shiloh king, her glory will fill the whole earth," responded John, with hope once more beaming in his eyes. At length we drew near the dark mass of human beings which we had beheld afar off, assembled around a small eminence near the river. Upon it, raised a few cubits taller than their heads, stood a man, upon whom all eyes were fixed, and to whose words every ear was attentive. His clear, rich, earnest tones, had reached us as we approached, before we could distinguish what he said. He was a young man not above thirty, with a countenance such as the medallions of Egypt give to Joseph of our nation, once their Prince. His hair was long, and wildly free about his neck; he wore a loose sack of camel's hair, and his right arm was naked to the shoulder. His attitude was as free and commanding as that of a Caucasian warrior, yet every gesture was gentle and graceful. With all his ringing and persuasive eloquence there was an air of the deepest humility on his countenance, combined with an expression of the holiest enthusiasm. The people listened eagerly to him, for he spake like the Prophets of old, and chiefly in their prophetic words! His theme was the Messiah:

"Oh, Israel, return unto the Lord thy God, for thou hast fallen by thine iniquity," he was saying, as we came up, as if in continuation of what had come before, "Take with you words, and turn unto the Lord, and say unto Him: Take away all iniquity and receive us graciously. Behold, He cometh who will heal your backsliding, and will love you freely! He will be as the dew unto Israel! He shall grow as the lily, and cast forth his roots as Lebanon! His branches shall spread, and his beauty shall be as the olive tree, and his fruit shall be for the healing of the nations! They that dwell under his shadow shall return and dwell evermore; and it shall come to pass that whosoever shall call on the name of the Lord shall be delivered, for besides him there is no Savior."

"Of whom speaketh the prophet these things?" asked one who stood near me, of his neighbor, and then of me, for by this time we had taken places as close to the prophet as we were able; for I did not wish to lose one word that should fall from the lips of a man who could thus empty cities, and people the wilderness with their inhabitants.

"Of Messiah -- listen!" answered him a Scribe near, as if not pleased to have his attention interrupted by his side talk. "His words are plain. Hear him."

"Blow ye the trumpet in Zion, for the day of the Lord cometh!" continued the prophet, in a voice like that of a silver trumpet; "For, behold, the day is at hand when I will bring again the captivity of Judah. Put ye in the sickle, for the harvest is ripe! The day is at hand when the Lord shall roar out of Zion and utter his voice from Jerusalem."

"Art thou not Elias?" asked one, aloud.

"I am he of whom it is written, the voice of one crying in the wilderness, make straight a highway for our God. The day of the Lord is at hand. I am but the herald who is sent before to prepare the way of the Lord!"

"Art thou not the Messiah?" asked a woman, who stood near him, and seemed to worship his very lips.

"He who cometh after me is mightier than I, whose shoes I am not worthy to bear," he responded, in the deepest humiliation of manner. "He who cometh after me hath his fan in his hand, and he will thoroughly purge his floor and gather the wheat into the garner; but will burn up the chaff with unquenchable fire. Therefore, repent ye, repent ye, take words and return unto the Lord your God. Repent and be baptized for the remission of your sins; for the day cometh which shall burn as an oven, and take heed that ye be not consumed! The ax is laid at the root of the tree; therefore, every tree that bringeth not forth good fruit shall be hewn down and cast into the fire."

"Master," said a Levite, "dost thou speak these things to us, who are of Israel, or to these Gentiles and Samaritans?" For there were not a few Roman soldiers among the multitude, drawn hither by curiosity, and also many people from Samaria, nay, even from Damascus.

"Go and cry in the ears of Jerusalem, saith the Lord, for my people hath committed two evils; they have forsaken me, the fountain of living waters, and hewed them out cisterns, broken cisterns, that can hold no water. The Lord hath made me this day an iron pillar and brazen wall against the whole land -- against the kings of Judah, against the princes thereof, against the priests thereof, and against the people of the land! and yet thou sayest, O Israel, thou hast not sinned. Thine own wickedness shall correct thee, and thy backsliding shall reprove thee. Repent and do works meet for repentance, every one of you, for ye have polluted the land; neither say, where is the Lord that brought us up out of the land of Egypt? I am provoked to anger every day by your hardness of heart and stiff-neckedness. Amend, amend your doings! Trust not in lying words, saying, The Temple of the Lord, The Temple of the Lord, The Temple of the Lord! Ye have made it a den of robbers! Your sacrifices therein are become an abomination to the Lord!"

"This would touch us who are priests, masters," said a priest, with a crimson brow, "We are not robbers!"

"Thus saith the Lord," answered the youthful prophet, as if it were God himself, speaking from Horeb, so that we trembled as we heard him: "Woe be unto the pastors that destroy my sheep; I will visit upon you the evil of your doings. How is the gold become dim -- how is the most fine gold changed! The precious sons of Zion, comparable to fine gold, how are they esteemed? Her priests were purer than snow! they were whiter than milk; they were more ruddy in body than rubies; their polishing was of sapphire! Their visage is blacker than coal; they feed the children of my people with ashes for bread! Woe to Zion, for the sins of her prophets and the iniquities of her priests. Run ye to and fro through the streets of Jerusalem, and seek in the broad places thereof, saith the Lord, if you can find a man that executeth judgment, that seeketh truth! Though they say the Lord liveth, surely they swear falsely. Hear ye this, O priests, and harken, ye house of Israel! Woe unto you, ye priests, for ye have transgressed! I have seen in the prophets of Jerusalem a horrible thing; they commit adultery and walk in lies, saith the lord. My people have transgressed, for the lack of knowledge! Therefore, I will reject thee, saith the Lord; thou shalt be no priests to me since thou hast forgotten the law of thy God. Like people, like priests! Therefore doth the land mourn, and everyone that dwelleth therein languisheth. Therefore do swearing and lying, and killing and stealing, and committing adultery, break out in the land, because there is no truth, nor mercy, nor knowledge of God in the land. Woe unto you, ye priests!" Many of the Levites then turned and left him, and went away greatly murmuring; and they would gladly have done the prophet a mischief, but they feared the multitude, who said he had spoken only the truth of them.

"But the elders of Israel, who are not priests, and who spring from Abraham, shall be saved by Abraham, master?" asserted, or rather inquired, a rich ruler of our city, after the tumult caused by the withdrawal of the Levites had a little subsided. The youthful prophet rested his dark eyes, like two suns, upon the old man's face, and said impressively, "Begin not to say within yourselves, we have Abraham to our father, for I say unto you," he added, pointing to the pebbles at his feet, "that God is able of these stones to raise up children unto Abraham. He is of Abraham who doth righteousness; therefore repent, and bring forth fruits meet for repentance."

Here was heard some murmuring among a group of many Pharisees and Sadducees at these words, when, sending his lightning glance toward them, as if he could read their very hearts, he cried:

"O generation of vipers! Who hath warned you to flee from the wrath to come? The day cometh when he who is to come shall sit as a purifier by his furnace. Bring forth, therefore, fruits meet for repentance. Wash thy heart from wickedness, that thou mayest be saved. And ye, daughters of Judah, repent you of the vain thoughts that lodge within you," cried he, addressing many females in rich apparel and plaited hair, "gird ye with sackcloth, lament and howl; put away these abominations out of my sight, and fear the Lord. Though thou clothest thyself with crimson, though thou deckest thyself with ornaments of gold, though thou rentest thy face with painting, in vain shalt thou make thyself fair; for I hear the voice of the daughters of Zion bewailing themselves, spreading forth their hands in the day when they are spoiled and despised for their iniquities. Repent ye, for the kingdom of heaven is at hand!"

"Hear, O Israel! Am I a God at hand and not a God afar off, saith the Lord. Hear ye the message of the Most High, for the day hath come when Jehovah shall once more visit the earth and talk face to face with his creatures. Behold the day hath come, saith the Lord, that I will raise unto David a righteous branch, and a king to reign and prosper, who shall execute judgment and justice on the earth."

"Behold the day hath come, saith the Lord, in which Judah shall be saved, and Israel shall dwell safely, when I will set up shepherds over them, who shall feed them, and they shall lack nothing!"

"Arise! shine, for thy light is come! Hear, O Israel, for Zion's sake I will not hold my peace; I will not rest until the righteousness thereof go forth as brightness, and the salvation thereof as a lamp that burneth. Arise, shine, for thy light is come and the glory of the Lord is risen upon thee! Darkness covereth the earth, and gross darkness the people, as saith Isaias; but the Lord shall rise upon thee, and his glory shall be seen upon thee. The Gentiles shall come to his light, and kings to the brightness of his rising. He shall be called The Lord Our Righteousness, and shall be a crown of glory in the hand of the Lord, and a royal diadem in the hand of thy God. The Spirit of the Lord is upon me to proclaim the acceptable year of his coming. He hath set me a watchman upon thy walls, O Israel, and I may neither hold my peace day nor night, nor keep silence, nor seek rest, till he come, who hath sent me forth his messenger before his face. How can I refrain from my message of joy? How shall I not speak of his fame? His sons shall come from afar, and his daughters shall be nursed at his side. The people of the nations shall fly as a cloud, and as doves to their windows, to behold, fall down, and adore him. The isles shall wait for his law, and kings shall minister unto him, even unto the Holy One of Israel. Saith he, I, the Lord, am thy Savior and thy Redeemer, the mighty one of Jacob. Say ye to the daughters of Zion, Behold thy salvation cometh; behold, his reward is with him, and his work before him. Ho, everyone that thirsteth," he now cried, raising his voice like the chief of a host, till the farthest heard, "come ye to the waters; yea, come buy wine and milk, without money and without price. Incline your ear and come unto him. Hear, and your soul shall live. Repent, keep justice; and judgment and prepare a contrite heart to offer to him, when thou shalt behold him; for thus saith the High and Lofty One that in habiteth eternity, whose name is Holy, I dwell in the high and holy place with him, also, that is of a contrite heart and humble spirit. Peace, peace to him that is afar off, and to him that is near, saith the Lord.

"Sing unto the Lord a new song, and his praise from the ends of the earth; for thus saith God the Lord, he that created the heavens and stretched them out; he that spread forth the earth, and that which cometh out of it; he that giveth breath unto the people upon it, and spirit to them that walk therein: Behold my servant whom I uphold -- mine elect in whom my soul delighteth. I have put my spirit upon him; he shall bring forth judgment to the Gentiles; a bruised reed shall he not break, and the smoking flax shall he not quench. I, the Lord, saith Jehovah, addressing the only begotten, I have called thee in righteousness, and will hold thy hand and keep thee, and will give thee for a covenant of the people, for a light on the Gentiles, to open the blind eyes, to bring out the prisoners from the prison. I am the Lord, that is my name, and my glory will I not give to another; yet have I made him my first-born, higher than the kings of the earth. Look unto him, and be saved, all the ends of the earth; for unto him every knee shall bow, every tongue shall swear. Our Redeemer, the Lord of Hosts is his name, the Holy one of Israel!"

All this was spoken with an enthusiasm and fire that made every pulse bound.

"Such," said John, "was the extraordinary style of this mighty prophet's preaching, and to those who read the books of the Prophets, every word shone with the brightness of the sun. I fancied I had only to look around to behold the Messiah! The immense multitude stood awed and silent when he had ceased. I gazed upon him with the most adoring reverence. My heart filled with holy joy; for I believed and knew that God had remembered Zion, and was about to display his wonders more remarkably on earth than ever had been witnessed before. Leaving the eminence, he said, and I thought he fixed his eyes on me, "Ye who desire to be baptized for the remission of sins, that your hearts may be cleansed for the visitation of this Holy One of God, follow me to the river side! Thousands obeyed, and I one of the first. I trembled all over with a sweet pleasure, when he took me by the hand, and asked me if I believed in Him who was to come, and would prepare the way for His abode in my heart by being baptized, which rite also was to be a sign and pledge that when I should behold the Shiloh rising, I should acknowledge Him. Not less than one thousand were baptized by him that day in Jordan, confessing their sins, and hopes of pardon through the name of the unknown One, who was soon to come. Among these were Pharisees and Sadducees, rulers and lawyers, and one gray-headed Roman soldier. Joseph of Arimathea was not baptized, as he said he wished to examine into the extraordinary subject fully before he could believe.

"After the baptism, the whole company dispersed in groups, and the prophet returned into the wilderness till the cool of the evening, where his repast was the wild honey of the desert, and the locust-berry of the ravines. When he reappeared, he again spoke to an increased multitude. In this second sermon, he explained more clearly the application of the glittering chain of prophecies he had given utterance to in the morning as to Messias, and thus enabled me to see more clearly the true character of the expected Messias than I had before done."

With this remark of his, dear father, I close my long letter. I make no comments. I will only say, that my expectations are actively awake, and that I am looking, with thousands of others, for the near advent of the Messiah.

Your daughter,
ADINA

LETTER V.

My Dear Father: Although but three days have elapsed since I completed my last letter to you, I am so solicitous to have your judgment and counsel upon the remarkable events now occupying the public mind of Israel, that I cannot withhold giving you the further relation of the remaining circumstances connected with the visit of Mary's cousin, John, to the divine prophet of Jordan. In as much as his words have made a deep impression upon my mind, and moved me to believe with him in the truth of this prophet's words, it is proper that you should know with me all that he has told me and which has influenced my feelings and opinions, in order that you may judge of the weight and value at which all I have heard is to be estimated; and be assured, dear father, that I am ready to be governed in all things by your wisdom and learning. Listen, then, with your usual goodness, to the residue of this young man's narration.

"After the prophet had ended his second discourse, and baptized two hundred more in the sparkling waters of Jordan," resumed the eloquent cousin of Mary, "he sent them away to the city to lodge and buy meat; for few, in their eagerness to hear him, had brought provisions with them. Many, before leaving him, drew near to receive his blessing of love, and it was touching to see venerable men, with locks shining like silver, and leaning upon a staff, bend their aged heads before the youthful Elias, as if in acknowledgment of his divine commission. Mothers also brought their infants, that he might bless them; and youth and maidens knelt reverently at his feet in tears of love and penitence. Calmly he stood upon the green shores, like an angel alighted upon earth, and blessed them in words all new to our ears, but which thrilled to our hearts with some secret power that agitated us with trembling joy."

"In the name of the Lamb of God, I bless thee!" What can be

the meaning of these words? asked Mary, with her gentle earnestness. Her betrothed could only reply, that he knew not.

"At length, one after another, the multitude departed, save a few who encamped beneath trees on the banks of the river. Joseph of Arimathea and I were left almost alone, standing near the prophet, and regarding him with reverential curiosity. The sun was just disappearing over the distant towers of Jericho, and painting with the richest purple the hills between the river and Jerusalem. Jordan, catching its reddening radiance, rolled past like a river of liquid gold embanked in emerald. The brow of the prophet, lighted up by a sun ray that shone between the branches of a pomegranate tree, seemed like the face of Moses when he came down from Sinai, a glory of light. He appeared rapt in heavenly meditation, and we stood silent and gazed upon him, not daring to speak. At length he turned toward us, smiled, and saluting us, grasped the crook or staff on which he had been leaning, for he was weary and pale with his labors of the day, and slowly walked down the shore in the direction of the wilderness. He had not advanced many steps when I felt an irresistible impulse to follow him. I burned to talk with him -- to sit at his feet, and ask him questions about the great things I had heard him utter in both of his discourses! I wished him to explain and unfold what had seemed mysterious, and yet teeming with mighty revelations. I panted for light -- -for knowledge. I yearned to have him open the Scriptures to me, and give me that illuminated understanding of them which he possessed. I therefore said to my companion:

"Let us follow him, and learn more of these great things, which we have this day heard."

"Joseph, like myself, being anxious to hold converse with him, at once assented, and we proceeded slowly after him, as he moved in a contemplative mood along the desert path. The sun had already gone down, and the full moon rose on the opposite shore, and the prophet stopped as if to gaze upon its autumnal beauty. We drew near to him. He beheld us, but did not avoid us; seeing which I advanced with timid confidence, and said,

"Holy prophet of the Most High God, wilt thou permit two young men of Israel to speak to thee, for our hearts yearn toward thee with love?"

"And we would fain keep thee company in the desert, Rabbi," added Joseph, "for it does not seem well for thee to dwell thus alone."

"But chiefly," said I, "we would inquire of thee touching the advent of the Mighty Personage whose near coming thou dost foretell."

"Friends," said the prophet, in a calm and serene manner, "I am a dweller in the desert, and alone from choice. I approach men only to proclaim my message. The delights of earth are not for me. My mission is one. Its duration is short. Its aim worthy the greatest prophet of God, yet am I the least of them, not worthy to be called a prophet; and before the splendor of Him whom I announce to the world, I am the dust of the balance. If thou hast sought me to search after knowledge, come and sit down with me upon this rock, and let me hear what thou hast to say, that I may answer thee and go my way."

"This was said softly, gently, almost sadly, and in a tone that made me love him more and more. I could have cast myself upon his bosom and wept there; for I was deeply touched that one should be chosen by Jehovah to become his prophet to earth, and yet show such lowliness of heart and sincere humility. We seated ourselves, one on either side of him, for he refused to permit us to place ourselves upon the ground at his feet, saying reproachfully, as he did to those whom he had seen kneel to him, "I also am a man!" The scene and the hour were well fitted for such a converse as we were about to hold. The broad disk of the moon poured a flood of orange-tinted radiance full upon us, and lent a hallowed softness to the divine countenance of the youthful prophet. The Jordan, dark as India's dye, darted swiftly past at our feet, between its deeply shaded banks, sending up to our ears the faintest murmur of its pebbly passage. Above our heads swelled the vaulted arch of the Temple of Jehovah, with its myriad of altar fires. To our left lay Jericho, just visible, looking like a black mass of castellated rock, unilluminated save by a single watch-fire which burned upon its loftiest tower. Behind us stretched the desert waste, cheerless and yet grand, in its desolate distances. Afar off rose upon the air, and was borne to us at intervals, the voice of a singer in one of the camps; and near us, upon an acacia tree, sat a solitary bulbul, which ceaselessly sang its sweet and varied hymn to the listening moon.

"All things praise God -- shall we be silent?" said the prophet. "Let us sing the evening hymn of the Temple." He then commenced, in a rich, melodious chant, such as I had never heard from the priests, our sacred psalm to the whole

43

creation of God. We joined our voices with his, and the tide of praise floated over the waters, and echoed and re-echoed from the opposing shores, as if the banks and stream, trees, hills and sky, had found voice as well we:

Praise! praise! praise ye the Lord!
Praise Him in the heights! Praise Him in the sea!
Praise Him men of Israel! Praise ye the Lord!
　For He exalteth high His people,
　　And reigneth evermore!

Praise Him all ye angels! Praise Him all ye hosts!
Praise Him sun and moon, and all ye stars of light!
Praise Him fire and hail! Praise Him storms and snows!
　For He judgeth the earth in righteousness,
　　And reigneth evermore!

Praise! Praise! Praise ye the Lord!
Praise Him winged fowl, and herds, cattle and all beasts!
Praise Him kings and people, princes, priests and judges!
Praise Him youths and maidens, old men and young children!

Praise the name, let them praise the name,
Praise the name of the Lord God of Hosts!
For His name alone is excellent,
His glory above the heavens:
Israel is His first born -- a people well-beloved!
Praise! let Israel therefore, praise Him!
　Praise Him evermore
　　Evermore,
　　　Ever, evermore.

"Never shall I forget the effect produced upon my inmost being by this hymn, sung at such a time, and in such a place, and in such company. The prophet sang as if he was leading a choir of angels. My heart leaped at the chorus, as if it would break out, take wing, and leave the earth! When we called on the winds and the fowls of the air to praise Jehovah with us, it may be fancy, but the thrilling voice of the bulbul seemed to pour from its throat a wilder, richer, more joyous tide of song, and the audible wind bent the adoring trees, and mingled its mystic whispers with the psalm of men! Surely, thought I, it is good for me to be here, for this is none other than the gate of Paradise!

After a few moments' silence, the prophet spoke and said: "You sought me, brethren of Israel, can I do aught for you?"

"We would hear more, great prophet, touching this mighty man, if man he may be termed, who is to come after thee," said Joseph.

"I can tell thee but little, my brethren, save what thou hast heard from me this day. The future is veiled. I hear a message, indeed, but I may not break the seal and read. I am but the

courier of God to man. To you it will be given to know what is
now unknown to me. Happy, thrice happy are ye who will
behold face to face the Divine One whom I can only behold
afar off. If it be permitted me to see him, it will be but for a
brief space, for when he cometh I depart, my errand is done.
Blessed are those who live to witness his glory, and to hear the
gracious voice of God that proceeds from his anointed lips."

"When will be his advent, and with what form and power
cometh this Divine Being?" I asked.

"As a man, but not with comeliness of form that men should
desire him. His appearance will be humble, lowly, and meek.

"Yet, you say today, Rabbi," I continued, "that his power
should be infinite, and that of his kingdom there should be no
end. You spoke of the glory of his dominions, and the
humiliation of Gentile kings beneath his scepter."

"This I cannot explain -- it is a mystery to me! I speak as God,
by whom I am sent, gives me utterance. I know that He who
cometh after me is greater than I, the latches of whose shoes I
am not worthy to unloose!"

"You taught us this evening that he would be the Lord from
Heaven; and yet that Isaias saith he will be despised and
rejected of men, wounded for our transgressions, and bruised
for our iniquities!"

"The spirit of God teaches me that these words apply to
Shiloh; but I cannot comprehend how these things can be," he
answered, with deep sadness.

"May I remind you, good Rabbi," said Joseph, "that you taught
us how that this Divine personage should die, though Lord of
Life, and be numbered in his death with transgressors, though
the Holy One of God!"

And such will be the events that are ordained to happen; but
seek not to know what no man hath had revealed to him. The
Divine Messiah himself must be his own interpreter. Blessed
will be the eyes that behold Him, and listen to the wisdom of
His mouth, and keep the law of His lips!"

"May I ask you, holy prophet of the Lord," said Joseph, "how
is it that He whom you are sent by God to bear witness to can
be the Deliverer of Israel, when you predict for Him so sad a
fate? Messiah is to restore Jerusalem, and the glory of the
Temple, and the splendor of its worship, so saith Esaias, so say
Ezra and Jeremiah. He is called a Mighty Prince, a King, the
Redeemer of Israel, who shall rule the nations and have
dominion from sea to sea, and from the river to the ends of the

earth! We, therefore, in the Messiah of the Prophets, have looked for a powerful potentate, who shall reign in Jerusalem over the whole earth, and subdue all nations, bringing their kings captive at his foot-stool, and binding their princes with chains; before whom every knee shall do homage -- a monarch who shall not leave a heathen sandal to tread on the sacred soil of Judea, and who shall establish the worship of Jehovah in every place where now rises a temple of idolatry."

"His kingdom is not of this earth," answered the prophet impressively.

"How, then, can we interpret the Prophet David, who maketh the Lord to say: I have set my King upon my holy hill of Zion. Also, how shall we interpret those sayings of Esaias, who, prophesying of the blessed Christ of God, hath these words:

Of the increase of his government and peace there shall be no end, upon the throne of David, and upon his kingdom, to order it and to establish it with judgment and with justice, from henceforth, even forever?"

"I know not. These secrets are with God. I can reveal nothing. I am but the trumpet through which Jehovah speaks; I know not the words I utter. This I know, that the least child and lowliest hireling that liveth in the day of Messias is greater than I. I am the last of the prophets. I stand on the threshold of that glorious kingdom, the greatness and brightness of which they saw afar off, like some heavenly, indistinct vision. Nearer than they, I am permitted to catch clearer glimpses of its glory, and it may be vouchsafed to me to see more than I now see; but of this I have no certain revelation. It is for me to open the last door that leads out from the night of prophecy into the glorious dawn of the day of fulfillment; but I am not permitted to enter beyond the threshold, or share in its blessings. All who come after me will be preferred before me. But the will of Jehovah be obeyed! I am his creature, and to murmur becomes not dust. Rather let me rejoice that the day-star is about to rise, though his beams shine on all the earth but me!" This was said with the most touching pathos.

"We were both deeply moved, I, myself, even to tears, at hearing these words spoken by him. My heart yearned toward him with the most sacred sympathy. I sank on my knees, and kissing his hand, bathed it with my tears.

He gently raised me, and said in a sweet voice:

"Brother beloved, thou shalt see Him to whom I bear

witness, and He will love thee, and thou shalt repose in His bosom! At this saying," continued the cousin of Mary, whose voice as tremulous with lively sensibility as he spoke hereof, "I burst into tears; and, rising, I walked a little ways apart, and lifting up my eyes toward heaven, I prayed the God of our fathers that I might be found worthy of this blessed honor."

"And shall I also behold this mighty Son of God?" asked Joseph, with solicitude.

The prophet took his hand in his, and fixing upon him his eyes of prophetic brightness, said slowly, and in tones awe-inspiring and painfully sorrowful:

"Thou shalt one day bear Him in thy arms, and lay him upon a couch, which thou hast prepared for thine own repose. Thou knowest not now what I say, but thou shalt remember it when it cometh to pass!"

"When he had thus spoken, he rose, and waving his hand to us both, he walked rapidly away toward the desert, and was soon lost to the eye in the obscurity of the darkness which hung over it."

"Didst thou hear him?" at length, after some minutes pause, asked Joseph of me. "What can his words mean? they are prophetic of some fearful event. His eyes betrayed some terrible meaning. My heart is troubled."

"And mine rejoiceth," I answered. "We shall see Him! I shall be near Him! Oh, if he be like this sweet prophet of God, I shall love him with all my soul's being. How wonderful that we are to be thus associated with this Divine Person! Welcome the hour of his blessed advent!"

"Wilt thou welcome the advent of a sufferer?" said a voice so near that it startled us by its abruptness; and, looking round, we saw, standing within the shadow of a wild olive tree, a young man who was a stranger, but to whom I afterward became deeply attached. His face was pale and intellectual, and his form slight, but of the most symmetrical elegance. His question at once made me sorrowful, for it recalled the sad prophecies of Esaias.

"He is also to be King and Monarch of the world, and infinitely holy and good," I said. "If thou hast been near, thou hast heard the glorious things the prophet has spoken of Him."

"I have been near -- I was reclining beneath this tree, when you seated yourselves there. Be not deceived. The divine man who is to come is to be a man of sorrows and acquainted with grief. He is to be rejected by Israel, and despised by Judah.

Those whom he comes to bless will despise him for his lowliness and obscurity. His life will be a life of tears, and toil, and heaviness of heart, and he will at last be cut off from among the living, with the ignominy due only to a transgressor. Dost thou welcome the advent of a sufferer?"

"But how knowest thou this? Art thou a prophet?" I asked, with surprise and admiration.

"No, brother, but I have read the Prophets. I heard, more over, the words of this holy man, sent from God, and he dwells more on the humility of Christ than on his kingly grandeur. Believe me, the kingdom of Shiloh is not of this world. It cannot be of this world, if such is to be his life and death; and that it is to be his life, Esaias clearly states. Let me read to you his words." He then took a roll of parchment from his bosom, and read by moonlight that mysterious and inexplicable passage, which beginneth with the words: Who hath believed our report? When he had ended, and perceived the assenting impression he had made upon our minds, he resumed: This is not the history of a prosperous earthly monarch, but rather the painful record of a life of humiliation, of shame, and of contempt."

"But, thou dost not say, brother," said Joseph, with some warmth, "that the sacred person borne witness to by this prophet is to be an object of contempt?"

"Does not Esaias say that he will be despised, beaten with stripes, rejected of men, imprisoned, and put to death as a transgressor of the law?"

"There can be no question but that Esaias speaks of the Messiah," I remarked.

"This prophet of Jordan now bears full testimony to Esaias, and plainly maketh application of his words to Him whom he has come beforehand to proclaim," answered the young man, with singularly graceful eloquence in all he said. "Let us, who have been baptized this day for the remission of our sins, expect a Messiah of sorrows, not a conquering prince. Let us behold one who is to humble himself beneath the yoke of human infirmities, that he may be exalted, and draw all men after him to a kingdom in the heavens."

"But, the throne of David," -- objected Joseph ---

"Is at the right-hand of God."

"But Jerusalem, and its rule over the nations ---"

"Jerusalem that is above, is above all."

"But his kingdom that is to be everlasting --"

"Is where life is everlasting. How can he rule an everlasting realm here on earth, without living forever, and his subjects also? Read not the prophets so. As Adam fell and lost Paradise, so Messias, like a second Adam, must, as man, humble himself in human nature, to atone for our guilt; and having made full atonement for us by his life and his death, he will purchase the kingdom of Paradise for the race of man; but he restores it to us not on earth, but translated on high, where the angels still guard it in the kingdom of God. It is this kingdom which this prophet proclaims as being at hand, and the path to which our leader and king can only tread through the mire of Adam's sin, which spreads through this world; but without taint of sin upon his robes. He being the bearer of our iniquities, we shall thereby escape their chastisement. Healed by his stripes, we shall be free from the penalty which our sins demand. Laid upon him will be the transgressions of the world; and by one mighty sacrifice of himself, thus laden, as a sin-offering, he shall make atonement for the great family of Adam, and restore our race to reconciliation with Jehovah. Such is to be our looked-for Messiah. Alas, while we look for him, let us mingle tears with our gladness, and humble ourselves, that one so holy and excellent should be destined to endure these things for our sakes; and when we behold him, let us sink at his feet in grateful adoration of his love and charity, of his mercy and goodness, of his noble self-denial and voluntary upgiving of himself as a sacrifice for us; for there could be no higher or more valuable victim than he in the universe of God; therefore, he hath offered himself, according to the words of the prophet, recording his offer, Lo, I come to do thy will, O God!"

"When the young man had spoken, he walked away. Impelled by an unconquerable impulse. I followed, and took him in my arms, and embracing him, said: "Of a truth thou art a prophet! Thy words come home to my heart like the echo of ancient prophecy."

"Nay. I have learned these things from the study of the Scripture," he said, with angelic candor and modesty. "But I have been aided, how much I have no words to tell thee, by one who both wisdom and truth abiding in him above all men, and whom it is my happiness to have my bosom friend, as he is near my own age. If I am wise, or virtuous, or good, or know the Scriptures, it is that he hath been my counselor and teacher."

"What is his name?" I asked, "for I also would go and learn of him."

"He withdraws from the public eye, and hath little converse with but few, and shuns all notice. Without his permission I could not take thee to him. Yet I will ask him, if you desire it."

"What is his appearance, and where doth he dwell?" I inquired, more deeply interested.

"He abides at present at Bethany, my own city. He is so beloved by us, that we detain him as our guest. But he dwelleth at other times with his mother, a holy widow of great sanctity and matronly dignity, living at Nazareth, in humble condition, and he contributes by labor to her support, with the most exemplary filial piety; thus setting an example to the young men of Judah, who in this age make amuck of parental restraint, and under the evil practices which the free license of the weekend custom of Corban giveth, neglect them, and no more do aught for their father or mother. Indeed, no person ever approaches and speaks with him, without leaving him a wiser and better man."

"Verily," said both Joseph and I together, "you have only increased our desire to behold him. His appearance must be noble."

"He possesseth neither beauty of form nor comeliness to strike the eye; but there sits upon his brow a serene dignity, tempered with mildness, that commands the respect of age, and wins the confiding love of childhood. His eyes beam with a light, calm and pure, as if shining from interior holy thoughts, and they rest upon you, when he speaks, with a tenderness of love that is like the dewy light of the young mother's gaze, when she bends in silent happiness and tears over the face of her first-born. He never smiles, or rather his face is one soft sunshine of smiling rays, tempered in an indescribable manner with a settled look of sadness, an almost imperceptible shade of permanent sorrow, that seems to foreshadow a life of trial and suffering. When he reads from the Prophets, and unfolds to us with a wisdom that we can regard only as given him from heaven, the great truths that relate to the long-looked-for, and, as we now believe, the near-present Messiah, he seems to speak by inspiration, yet without emotion, but calmly and naturally, in a low-toned voice, that is never lifted up at any time, nor ever heard in the streets."

"He must be another prophet," said Joseph, with deep earnestness.

"He does not prophesy, nor preach," answered the young man.

"What is his name?" I asked.

"Jesus, the Nazarene!"

We both promised to remember this name and as our way to Jerusalem lay through Bethany, we wished much to call and see him: but this step the young man mildly objected to, until he, having made known our wishes to him, he then might, if he desired to see us, send into Jerusalem for us to go to Bethany.

"As the young man was then about to move away I asked him his name, as he had greatly drawn out my heart toward him, and I felt that if I could be his friend, and the friend of the wise young man of Nazareth, who sojourned with him, I should be perfectly happy, and have no other desire -- save, indeed, to live till the Messiah came, that I might behold him, and lay my head upon his sacred bosom.

"My name is Lazarus, the Scribe," he answered, as he took his leave.

"What," interrupted Mary, when her cousin had spoken this name, "then I know him well. It is the brother of Mary and Martha, both my friends at Bethany, where I passed a week last year, just before the Passover."

"I am glad to hear that," said John, "for this will be a closer bond of friendship between us. The next day we renewed our acquaintance, and after three days, departed together homeward. Upon arriving at Bethany, he learned that his friend had gone to Cana, in Galilee, on a visit with his mother, to the house of one of her kinsfolk, whose daughter is in a few weeks to be married."

Having now, my dear father, communicated to you all that John related to us, you will see what grounds there are to look upon the prophet of Jordan as a man sent from God, or to believe that he is the true Elias, whom Malachi hath foretold, and who, as the most learned of the Scribes say, must first come to proclaim the approach of the Prince of Peace, the Shiloh of Israel's hopes. My emotions, my ideas, my opinions, at present, are conflicting and full of indecision. On one hand, I am ready to become one of John of Jordan's disciples, and be baptized of him, looking with faith unto Him who is to come after. On the other hand, I tremble lest all should be a delusion, for it does not seem possible that it is my lot to live in that blessed age when Messiah cometh, a period toward which all the patriarchs and prophets have looked, desiring to see His day, but died without possessing the promise, beholding it only afar off. The infinite greatness of this privilege is all that causes me to doubt. Instruct me, dear father; open to me the treasures of your wisdom. Thou art read in the prophets. Doth the youthful prophet of the wilderness truly use their predictions in their application to Messiah? Is it that the intellectual Lazarus truly drew the sad portraiture of His dark career on earth? How are the opposing prophecies to be reconciled in another manner than the young man of Bethany has unfolded them? Explain to me one other interpretation, dear father: how he can be both king and a prisoner! Lord of life, yet suffer death! With a kingdom boundless as the world, yet despised and condemned of men!

The account brought by John has set Rabbi Amos to studying the Prophets, and, indeed, all men are looking into them with interest unknown before; for the multitudes that go away from the new prophet noise his predictions abroad, throughout all the land. May God be, indeed, about to blest his people, and remember his inheritance!

ADINA.

LETTER VI.

My Dear Father: Health and peace to thee, and all my friends honored and beloved in Alexandria! -- I have again seen the excellent Ben Israel, with whom, four months ago, I came from Egypt, to sojourn in Jerusalem. He not only delivered to me your letters, with the acceptable gifts you kindly sent by him, but also assured me of your welfare in all things. He is at present absent at Damascus, whither he went soon after his arrival here, in order to buy the celebrated Syrian blades of that city, which he takes down to Egypt at a great profit, with other merchandise. He assures me that he is gaining much wealth by his caravans of commerce, at which I rejoice, for he is an amiable and worthy man. His entreaties, that I would return to Alexandria with him, would nearly have overcome my resolutions of remaining here, but for the commands you have laid upon me to avail myself of the peculiar privileges which Jerusalem affords for improving the mind; and were it not I am deeply interested in the issue of the great expectation of Israel. Your letter, dear father, commands me to banish this "novelty" from my mind; and continue humbly to worship Jehovah after the manner of our fathers. I trust this I shall ever do, my dear father; and did I discover in this prophet any disposition to bring in a new faith, opposed to the ancient faith of Abraham, I should tremble to entertain it for a moment. You say that this man must be "a false and base prophet," or he would not herald a master so low and despised as he professes will be the Christ he bears witness to. "There have been many false Christs and false prophets, my child," you add, "and Israel has run after them, as they now run after this John of Jordan, and the result has been, that they have either perished in the wilderness or been cut to pieces, with their deceiver, by the jealousy of the Roman Governors, who looked upon such assemblies as seditious. Hold fast, my child, to the religion of our fathers, and be not carried away, as I fear you are in danger of being, by this wild preacher of repentance. The kingdom of Messias is not a kingdom of repentance and of humiliation, but one of victory, of glory, and dominion. Touching those prophecies of humility and abasement which this prophet of Jordan applies to Messias, they have no application to our expected Shiloh and Prince. They either apply to some lesser prophet, who will be the forerunner of the true Christ (for that he will have a forerunner, the Scriptures speak too plainly for doubting), or, as some say and believe, especially do the Pharisees, there are to be two Messiahs, one who shall come in humiliation and suffering to the Gentiles, as an atonement for the expiation of their sins, and one to come to us in regal power, and in circumstances of glory and splendor, such as no potentate hath ever manifested, and who shall make Jerusalem the metropolis of the globe, and the kings of the earth tributary at his feet. Such is our Messiah, whom the Lord of Hosts send us speedily, to lift Judah from the dust of her humiliation! If the base person this prophet of the desert heralds be a Messiah, he is one to the Gentiles only, whose great iniquities need the self-immolation and humiliation of one come from God, in atonement herefor; but he is not a Messiah to Israel, nor the mighty Prince who shall sit in David's seat on the throne of Zion. Therefore, my child, you, as a daughter of Israel, have no interest in this novelty that cometh out of the wilderness, and after which half the land hath foolishly run mad. Wait, be patient, the day of Israel's glory shall truly arise and shine, and all nations shall see it and rejoice. Think no more of what thy cousin hath told thee. When Messias cometh, He will be heralded by a more glorious and eminent person than a young man of thirty, clothed in skins, and for food eating locusts and wild honey, whose origin and authority no man knoweth. Believing that your good sense and sound judgment, my Adina, will at once lead you to adopt my views, I shall not urge them further, as if I seriously feared your defection from the house of your fathers, an event which would bring my gray hairs down with sorrow to the grave. It is my belief that this prophet preaches only himself, and, under the mysterious and deceitful notions of another to come after him, is but gathering an expectant multitude around him, to wield them as instruments for his own ambitious ends; and by the time you write me again, I expect to learn from you that he openly proclaims himself the Christ, after all; or that he, with all who are led by him, will be destroyed by the swords of the Roman legions."

How can I write to you, my dear father, that which is now rushing to my pen, after such an expression of your sentiments as you have made in the extract from your letter? But I know you are wise, and will not evade truth, in whatever form it may offer itself to you, and I therefore, with confidence in your justice and wisdom, will faithfully make known to you the events relating to the prophet which have transpired, and may take place in Judea during my abode here. Hear me always with candor, and judge without partiality; for this is, without doubt, a day of wonderful revelations. I fancy that I can now see your brow darken, and that you say, "enough of this. Are we to have more of this new prophet?" Yes, my dear father, more still, and more extraordinary circumstances I am about to relate than I have yet written; for the very priests of the Temple have become believers in the youthful Seer.

You will remember how that John, Mary's cousin, stated that many priests and others were offended at the plain preaching of the prophet, whom they went out into the wilderness to see. When they returned to Jerusalem, and made known to the other members of the House of the Priests what had been spoken against them, by the application to them of the words of Esaias and Jeremias, and other Prophets, there arose at once a great outcry against him. Many of the Levites even forgot their duties in the Temple, in holding discourse with the Scribes and Pharisees, and others, in the streets, in the arches of the gates, and in the market-places, touching this new prophet, and his bold denunciations of them, being so much the more grieved at them because they were, alas, but too well merited by the looseness of their lives. At length, Annas, who is High Priest with Caiaphas, sent two of the most learned men of the Temple, Levites of weight of character, to invite the prophet to Jerusalem; for Annas is a wise man, and not easily carried away by popular feeling; and, as Rabbi Amos hath told me, he is disposed to look upon the preaching of John, for such is his name, with a serious and reverential eye. The messengers returned after the fifth day, and made their report openly in the Court of the Temple, where the High Priests sat to receive them, expecting to behold the prophet in their company. At length, the assembly being convened, the two learned and venerable Levites both rose up, and declared that they had delivered the message to John, the son of Zacharias, the prophet of Jordan, and that his answer was given with the reverence due to the station of the High Priest who had sent to him:

"Go and say to the noble High Priest," said he, "that I am the voice of one crying in the wilderness, as it is written in the book of the words of Esaias, the Prophet, who, foreseeing my day, saith, "The voice of one crying in the wilderness, prepare ye the way of the Lord, make his paths straight." All flesh will soon behold the salvation of God. My errand is not to city nor temple, nor into any house of Israel will I enter. He who would hear my testimony to Him who is to come after me, let him seek me in the wilderness, whence only I am commanded to lift up my voice till Shiloh come."

When the priests heard this answer, they were greatly enraged, and many fiercely cried one thing, and many another; some that he should be sought out and stoned to death for defying the High Priest (which he did not do, as it was for him to obey God rather than man); others, that he should be accused to the Procurator, Pontius Pilate, Governor of Judea, as a seditious and dangerous person, and fomenter of insurrections. Caiaphas was of the latter opinion, and wrote, from his tribunal, an epistle to the Roman ruler, making accusation hereof against the prophet of the desert, and recommending him to secure his person, lest further mischief should come of it; adding, that Tiberius Caesar, hearing of the matter, would conceive it to be a movement of the whole Jewish nation, desirous of casting off the Roman rule, under a new chief; and thus bring down an army upon the land, utterly to destroy it. But the milder Annas viewed the whole matter in a different light, and said:

"Men and brethren -- let nothing be done hastily. If this man be a false prophet, he will soon perish with his lies and we shall hear no more of him. If, peradventure, as it would appear, he is sent from God, let us not make haste to do him a mischief, lest, haply, we be found fighting against the Lord of Hosts."

This moderation found favor with but few, but of these few, Rabbi Amos was one. But if the priests who thronged the outer court, in presence of the High Priest, were deeply moved at the report of the prophet's answer, their excitement became well-nigh uncontrollable, when both Melchi and Heli, their messengers, rose up, waving their hands for silence, and declared that, after having listened to the prophet to whom they had been sent, they were convinced of the truth of his words, and of his divine commission, and been baptized of him in Jordan, confessing their sins.

Only the sanctity of the Temple prevented the five hundred priest rushing upon them, and smiting them when they heard this. They were at once placed under arrest by order of the High Priest Caiaphas, for acting in a manner unbecoming a priest of the Most High God: "For," said he, "this is to degrade the Temple to the feet of a wandering impostor, and is an open acknowledgment that virtue hath left the worship of Zion, and must be sought for in deserts of Jordan. "Which," he called aloud, "which, men of Israel, is the greatest, the altar of the Lord, or the waters of Jordan? -- the Priest of the Most High, or he of the wilderness? Away with these recreant blasphemers, to be tried and adjudged according to our sacred laws." The people who had heard John preach hereupon were only prevented from rescuing the two priests by the presence of a guard of Roman soldiers, for which Caiaphas promptly sent.

From this account, my dear father, you can form some idea of the excitement which the preaching of this new prophet is producing among all classes. The poorer sort of people are his advocates, and the rich and the rulers, the priests and the great men of the nation, oppose him, save a few among the best and the wisest. Of these few is Rabbi Amos, who is engaged all the time he is not on duty in the Temple, in searching the Scriptures, to see if these things are so; and at every prophecy he reads, he is more and more convinced that the day of Messias is at hand, and that this prophet is, without doubt, he who was to be sent from God in the "spirit and power of Elias," to prepare the way before him. Every evening there are assembled at our house from twelve to eighteen of the chief men of the Jews, who often pass half the night in warm discussions upon these great things; those among them who have heard John being disposed to give him the high rank he claims, as forerunner of Shiloh. Among these is Stephen, a man whose father was High Priest, and who is himself a lawyer and student of no mean repute. He has not yet heard John, the prophet, but he openly said last night that, after the most careful examination of all the Prophets, he was firmly of the opinion that the day of their fulfillment was close at hand; and that, for his part, he was willing to hail the prophet of Jordan as the true herald of Messias. Hereupon, two-thirds of the company said the same thing, but the others doubted, and cautioned the rest not to be too rash; that it was time enough to believe in Messias when he himself should come in his own person.

Such, my dear father, is the present condition of the mind of people of Jerusalem. If the Prince of Glory should, indeed, suddenly appear, there could be scarcely more excitement, though it would be of a different nature. There is something sublime to see a young man, who dwelleth alone in the wilderness, poor and unknown, thus moving great heart of a nation; surely, his power must be divinely derived. You ask me, and so is the question constantly put by the Scribes, and Pharisees, and Pharisees, and Priests, to the disciples of John: "Does he perform miracles? Show me a miracle, and I will believe in him; for this is the only test of a true prophet's Divine commission." No, dear father, he has performed no miracle, unless it be one continuous miracle, whereby he keeps in the wilderness a multitude, daily enlarged, from the outpouring gates of every city in Judah, listening to his words, and bowing their heads to the scared waters of his penitential baptism.

As next week Rabbi Amos does not serve in his course in the Temple, and as he will have some affairs that will take him to Gilgal, where he has three fields now ripe for the sickle, he has yielded to the desire of his daughter Mary and myself to accompany him; for he does not conceal from us that he shall make it a point to visit and hear the prophet, as it will be but two hours' travel from Gilgal to the place where he preaches. You will, I fear me, object to this journey. But if the worship of our fathers has nothing to fear from falsehood, it surely has nought to fear from truth; and in either case I, as a true daughter of Israel, have nothing to fear. If the prophet teach what is false, I shall remain true; and if he teach what is true, shall I not be the gainer? I hear you say this is but feeble and womenly argumentation. But as you have given me the credit of, more than once, declaring it to be your belief, that I am old and wise enough to judge for myself in most matters, I beg you will suffer me to hear the prophet with my own ears, in order that I may decide whether I ought to give heed to his predictions, or reject them as the visions of a dreamer. One thing is clear -- if the Christ that John prophesies be the true Son of the Highest, and is, in reality, to make his appearance ere long, in humiliation and poverty, his rejection by the High

Priests, and by the rich and powerful Judah, is certain. May
God, then, remove blindness from our eyes, that if this be very
Messias indeed, Israel may recognize their king, and not do so
fearful a thing in their pride as to reject him openly! In this
case, who will stand between God and our ill-fated race?
Therefore, my dear father, it behooves every man in Israel to
examine this matter with a sober and humble mind, and move
with caution in opposition to what may prove the dearest
hopes of our people. When I shall have returned from the
desert, whither we are to travel on litter and mules, I will
write you all that I have heard.

You will remember the young Roman Centurion, to whose
courtesy I was indebted in rescuing me from the rudeness of
the two Gentile soldiers. He has preserved, since then,
acquaintance with Rabbi Amos, who speaks of him with
respect; and as he has of late expressed some interest in
knowing what the studies are which occupy the Rabbi so
constantly when he calls to see him, which he has done
frequently, a copy of the Prophets was placed in his hands; but
as he professed he was not learned enough to read Hebrew,
the good Rabbi, who believed he saw in him a hopeful convert
to the faith of Judah, called in Mary to read and interpret to
him. But her knowledge of the Roman tongue did not prove
sufficient, and at her request, the Rabbi sent for me, to come
into the marble hall of the corridor, where they sat by the
fountain, under the shade of the acacia, which Amos says you
took, with your own hands, from Isaiah's grave, and planted
here, many years ago, and which I therefore call "my father's
tree."

"Come hither, Adina," said my uncle, in his benevolent tones:
"here you behold a noble Roman youth whom you must be too
generous to have forgotten." I bowed, and scarcely lifted my
eyelids from the tessellated floor; for there was a fire in the
glance of the handsome youth that they could not encounter.
He said some words of salutation, but I only heard the voice,
which fell upon my heart with a strange vibration like the
effects of music. Surely, these barbarians of Italia have the
richest language of all men; compared with it, our Hebrew is
harsh, and strangely guttural. "The Roman Centurion,"
continued Amos, "hath desired to know something of the
sacred books of our nation, of which he saith he hath heard
much; and of the prophecies, from which he believes the
famed Sibylline books were composed." "I have studied the

sacred books of Etruria, of Gaul, and those of the Goths and the Druids, of Egypt, and of Persia, as well as of my own people," said the Centurion modestly, "but in all these I find rites and ceremonies, doctrines and laws, that are unworthy to emanate from the supreme Jove of so vast a universe. We, Romans, in the multiplicity of our Gods, in deifying everything, in reality deify nothing! Everything we call God, but we realize God nowhere."

"Then thou hast well directed thy inquiries touching this book," answered Amos, with warmth, and looking on the Roman with respectful compassion. "Here is to be found the true and only revelation of Jehovah to men. Here is developed a divine character, worthy of the Creator of the universe. Here are laid down laws and ceremonies, rites and doctrines, commands and precepts, that are worthy to emanate from the Father and God of all men. Thou shalt hear and judge for thyself. I am but imperfectly skilled in the Roman tongue, save for daily intercourse, but here is an Egyptian maiden who can interpret for thee in the idiom of Grecia, or of Italia, and I will place the sacred scroll in her hands, while I listen. Come, Adina, open and read the beginning of the Book of Moses."

I obeyed, as I would have obeyed you, dear father, and, seated at the feet of Amos, I read and translated aloud into Greek, which the Roman youth had said was even more familiar to him than his native tongue (as it is to all educated persons in the world), the first five hundred lines. These, as you know, give an account of the creation of the world, and of man, of his defection, and his expulsion from Paradise; of the promise of Messias to restore what he had lost; of the curse denounced upon the creation, and the slaying of the Patriarch Abel, with the population of the earth, its wickedness, and destruction by the flood.

To this the youthful warrior listened with the profoundest respect and attention; and when he had thanked me, and asked permission to come and be further taught from pages which he said seemed, indeed, to be written with the finger of the Supreme Lord of the universe, he asked if the Messias had yet come who was to restore all things? and if not, when was he to be looked for? This inquiry led to a conversation upon the preaching of John in the wilderness, and his predictions of the near advent of Shiloh. Rabbi Amos, seeing that he became deeply interested in the subject, made me turn to the particular prophecies of Daniel, Esaias, David, and others, and read them to him: both those which described, in golden words, the glory and dominion of his power, and those which represented him as despised and rejected. After I had read all which the Rabbi directed me to read, the young man remained some time very thoughtful. At length he said, with animation: "I can now comprehend why men run into the wilderness. I should like to hear this prophet."

When Amos told him that he contemplated journeying to Gilgal the next week, and intended to visit the desert to hear him, he at once asked permission to be of his company; but when I remarked that Mary and I were also to go, his dark eyes beamed with pleasure, and he immediately said:

"I will accompany you with a squadron of horse, as the roads are not safe, for no longer than yesterday we received a rumor that the celebrated robber chief, Barabbas, at the head of a large band, has made his appearance again on the hills, between Ephraim and Jericho, and had robbed not only two caravans, but many of those who were traveling to hear this prophet. I will make an expedition against him, after seeing you safely in Jericho."

When we heard of this robber, we were not a little disposed to decline our journey; but Rabbi Amos thanked him, and said he would gladly accept his escort, "inasmuch," he added, smiling, "as I know you Roman knights here in garrison have but little to employ your time, and would esteem it a privilege to have an excursion of this kind. Moreover, you say you must go against this bandit; so we do not so much draw on your courtesy as take shelter under your duty."

It is therefore, decided, dear father, that we leave early next week for Jericho and Gilgal, and go also into the wilderness, to see and hear the prophet. On my return, I shall not fail to write you without delay. Till then, withhold your judgment, and have confidence in mine. With holy aspirations for the coming of the kingdom of David, and the restoration of his throne in Zion, I remain, with filial love, your daughter,

ADINA.

(John, cousin to Mary, who I erroneously told you in my second letter was the son of the rich matron whose husband was slain by the Romans, and is only her nephew, as doubtless, you are aware, has gone to the Lake of Galilee, where his father and brother have ships, and many servants, engaged in fishing, in order to look after their welfare. He may meet us at Gilgal.)

61

LETTER VII.

My Dear Father: My trembling fingers scarcely hold the light reed with which I am about to write you concerning the extraordinary things I have seen and heard; but they tremble only with joy. Oh, my father, my dear, dear father, Messias has come! I have seen him! I have heard his voice! He has truly come! Oh, joy, joy! My eyes have beheld him. Of whom Moses and the Prophets did write! But let me not anticipate. In order that you may believe at I believe, though you have seen Him not, I will give to you an account of those events which have happened since my last letter was sent to you. I will try to write free from emotion, and keep my bounding heart still, and my hand calm, while I set in order all that has taken place, that your understanding may judge of them with that candor and wisdom which makes men see in you the wisest Israelite in the land of Egypt.

You will recollect that in my last epistle, which went by the Cairo caravan, I mentioned that Rabbi Amos, taking advantage of the recess in his duties at the Temple, the course of the venerable Elihud being now waiting upon the altar, made up his mind to pay his annual visit to the wheat fields which he has in charge, near Jericho, and which, as you know, are not his own lands, but are in trust to him for the heirs of Manasseh, of the tribe of Benjamin, who was slain in trying to rescue Jericho from the Romans. Rabbi Amos also felt no little curiosity to hear John of Jordan, as he is called, whose fame has spread far and wide. At the request of Mary and myself, he consented that we should accompany him. John, the young man who is betrothed to my cousin, having gone to the sea of Galilee to see about certain ships which were there in charge of his brother James and his father, was to meet us at Gilgal, and accompany us to Jordan; for he thinks and speaks of nothing now but the prophet of the wilderness, from whom he feels that he suffers great loss to be absent, even for a day.

The road from Jerusalem to Jericho had become recently unsafe, on account of the boldness of an insurrectionary chief called Barabbas, who a year ago made insurrection against the Romans, but was defeated, and his band dispersed into the mountains south of the sea of Sodom; but, at last, driven to famine, he has taken to robbing caravans; and since the number of travelers has increased so much between Jerusalem and Jordan, to hear John, and be baptized of him, he has fallen upon large parties of them and taken from them all their goods and money. On this account Rabbi Amos accepted the courteous offer of the escort of young Centurion, who had been ordered by the Procurator, Pontius Pilate, to keep the road open between Jerusalem and Jericho; for even the Roman couriers were stopped by this fearless robber and slain by him. The pride of Rabbi Amos shrunk from this dependence upon a Roman arm, in making a peaceful journey through his own land; but there is, alas! dear father, no one now among the seed of Abraham to assert their rights. We can only bow our heads to the yoke the Lord God has placed upon our neck.

It was faint dawn when we rose from our couches to prepare for the journey. The mules upon which we were to ride were brought into the court by the two swarthy Gibeonite serfs, whom Rabbi Amos holds in his service, and caparisoned with rich saddles covered with Persian saddle-cloths, embroidered with gold. The two pack mules were also made ready, on one of which was the traveling equipage of my cousin Mary and myself, which Rabbi Amos smilingly said, took up more space than the goods and traveling wares of a Damascus merchant. At sunrise, after we had kneeled upon the house-top, in view of the Temple, and sent up our prayers with its sacrifices and cloud of ascending incense, we descended to the courtyard to mount for the road. There was a stout mule for good Rabbi Amos, though the Centurion sent him a handsome Persian horse to ride; but my uncle said that he had never trusted himself on so uncertain an animal as a horse in his youth, and he thought he should scarcely adventure such a feat in his old age; so he preferred his mule.

Having got ourselves seated upon our cushioned saddles, and our veils ready to draw over our faces, we expected each moment the arrival of the Centurion and his cohort of horse; but a Numidian slave came running, and, bowing to the ground before Rabbi Amos, said that the Centurion would meet us at the corner of the two ways, beyond the walls, at Absalom's Pillar. Whereupon we all mounted, and took our way toward the East Gate. We were five persons in all, Rabbi Amos, my cousin Mary and myself, and the two Gibeonites, both of whom were young men, whose fathers for many centuries had been servants in the family of Amos, even from the time of Joshua, when this people deceived him by their craftiness, and were doomed to perpetual servitude. I am much struck with the appearance of this singular race of men. They have very dark faces, eagle-beaked noses, flashing black eyes, and slender, lithe forms. They look cunning and treacherous, but seem to be cowardly, and easily controlled by firmness. They are incapable of any attachments, and gratitude seems to be thrown away upon them. I heard a singular tradition about them from one of the Levites, who often visits Rabbi Amos; which is, that they are descended from the servants of Noah, who were saved with him in the ark, but who, as being of an inferior rank, were not included in the record of Noah's family. But, doubtless, you have heard the same tradition.

The morning was bright and cheerful, with the golden sun pouring its light over temple and tower, cattle and roof, wall and rampart, hill and grove, valley and brook, one and all of which were lighted up with the glory of his morning beams. As we turned the street leading to the Sheep Gate, we passed the house of Caiaphas, the High Priest, whom I saw standing upon the marble porch of his superb palace. He was not arrayed in his sumptuous robes, with the breastplate of dazzling stones, and kingly cap, as I had seen him in the Temple; but was dressed in a flowing black robe, over which was thrown a scarf of white linen; and upon his snow-white locks he wore a scarlet hood, a dress common to all the priests, so that if I had not recognized him by his tall and commanding form, and flowing white hair, and piercing eye, as he surveyed us, I should not have known that it was the High Priest. He spoke to Rabbi Amos, who did him reverence, and lowly did I bend my own head before the majesty of the representative of God on earth.

A little further on, we met a party coming from the country beyond Kedron, with large cages upon their mules, laden with turtle-doves and young pigeons, which they were carrying to the Temple, to be sold there for sacrifices. My heart pitied the innocent things, whole blue, pretty heads were thrust by the dozen through the rough bars of their prison houses, as they cast their soft eyes up at me, as if asking me to deliver them from their bondage. And when I reflected that they were to offer up their innocent lives for the sins of the men and women of Israel, my cheek burned with the blush of shame, that we were so guilty before the Lord God, that the innocent must die for us. As Mary was riding behind me, in order to let the laden mules pass with their immense cages, one of the turtle-doves, affrighted by the noise of the streets, extricated itself from between the bars, and, spreading its wings, flew into the air, and then taking its flight for the country, soared far above the city walls, and disappeared in the distance. I felt rejoiced at the innocent bird's escape, and sent my good wishes for its safe return to its lodge in the wilderness. Just before we reached the Sheep Gate, by which we were to gain the Jericho road, we met a poor blind man leading a lamb, or rather, being led by a tame lamb. He also had two pigeons in his bosom. He was asked by Rabbi Amos, who knew him, whither he was going. He answered that he was going to the Temple to sacrifice them: "Nay," said Amos, with surprise, "thou wilt not sacrifice thy lamb, Bartimeus!"

"I have promised them to God, Rabbi Amos, and I may not break my promise without sin."

"But thy lamb leadeth thee everywhere. It is eyes to thee. Thou canst not do without it."

"God will provide me another lamb, he answered, his face beaming with hope."

"But thy doves? Thou earnest by them many a mite in a day, they are so well taught in cunning and pleasant tricks to please children. If thou must sacrifice according to thy vow, spare these so needful to thee, and here is money to buy doves and another lamb," answered my benevolent uncle.

"Hear what I have to say," answered Bartimeus, "My father became sick, and was likely to die, and I vowed a vow to God that if he would heal the old man, my father, I would sacrifice unto him one of my doves. The next day my mother, who has nourished my childhood, and loved me, though I was born blind, with all her heart, was also taken sick. I then vowed my other pigeon. The same night my little daughter, my little blind daughter, whose face I never saw, and who never saw her father's face, was sick nigh unto death. Then it was that I vowed all that remained to me, even the lamb of my bosom, whom I love next to my child! My father, my mother, my child, are restored, and in my joy I am on my way to the Temple to offer these gifts of God to him. It will be hard, sir, to part with them, I shall miss them so much; but shall I not perform my vow? It will be hard but God will not let blind Bartimeus suffer, since He will see that he offereth, in offering his two little doves and his lamb, all that hath?"

With these words he moved on, the lamb, obeying the string which he held, softly moving on before: while I could see the sightless eyes of the righteous son and father trickle tears, as he kissed, and kissed again, the doves that lay in his bosom. This little occurrence made me sad; yet I honored the resolute piety of this poor man, whole eyes, though they saw not men, seemed to see God and feel his presence. There is still humble piety in the land, my dear father, and finding it not among the proud and splendid priests, we must look for it in the hearts of the poor and humble, like Bartimeus.

Upon reaching the Sheep Gate, we were not detained by the Roman captain, who kept others, examining their passports, and taking gate-money from those who were without them; for though foot passengers may pass in and out free, yet from those who ride horses or mules is exacted money, unless they have passes signed by the Procurator. But the captain of the gate no sooner saw us, than he, with great civility, made us pass through the gate in advance of others who were ready to go through, saying that the young Centurion, whose name, I think, I have not told you, is Aemilius, had given him orders not to detain us. The stern, iron-cased Roman soldiers that stood about the gate, struck me as having just the aspect and forms of men who would conquer the world. When I reflected that there was not a city on the earth, at whose gates did not stand just such men as these, armed, and clad, and bearded like them, I could not but respect the universal power of the Roman empire, while I feared it.

Once outside of the gates, the air blew fresh from the hills of olives, laden with fragrance. After being so long confined within the walls and narrow streets, it seemed to me that I had just broken out of my cage, like the pretty, blue-headed turtle-dove, and I felt like winging my way, too, to the free deserts, if wings of a dove, so ardently longed for by King David, could only have been given me. On our right, not far from the gate, Rabbi Amos pointed out to me the pool of Bethesda, and turning my eyes toward it, I beheld a most touching spectacle. All the five porches were filled with sick and impotent folk, the lame, halt, blind, and withered, waiting, as my uncle told us, for the moving of the waters; for, at certain seasons, he said that God sends an angel down into the pool to trouble the water, when, who so ever steps in first, is made whole of whatever disease he may have. I could not but stop my mule to regard so remarkable a sight as this congregation of miserable people, of whom there must have been no less than four hundred; some leaning, pale and haggard, against the columns, some creeping about in helplessness, like brutes trying to get nigher the pool, from which the stronger thrust them back; some reclining patiently upon their beds, in humble waiting for God's time and others being borne hither on the shoulders of men. Suddenly, as I was about to ride on, and shut out this painful sight, one of the most extraordinary scenes that human eyes could witness took place. The surface of the pool, which was hitherto perfectly placid, all at once became agitated, as if it were boiling, and began to swell, rush, or rather swing from side to side, in a remarkable manner. No sooner was this seen, then there arose from the throng of wretched invalid who crowded its steps, a cry of four hundred voices all at once, shrieks of joy, shouts of wonder, words of amazed exclamation, while a simultaneous movement took place of the whole mass of human bodies, which became as wildly tossed to and fro as were the waters. Those nearest plunged madly in, while those behind rushed down, some wildly shrieking in their agonizing haste, and some uttering the most fearful curses, as they found their way obstructed by the impenetrable masses before them. The most weak and impotent being most eager, and being farthest off, made superhuman exertions to gain the pool, howling, and climbing with hands and feet, over the backs of others, to be hurled to the ground and trampled upon by others who were behind them. Some strong men who tried to open the way for one they were carrying, drew knives, and proceeded to cut their way through the haggard and mouthing wretches who crowded the way, which violence being seen by the Romans from the gate, they went down, some score of them, with drawn swords, to quell the tumult; for the whole pool was in an uproar. Unable to endure the dreadful scene, we rode rapidly on, but I afterward heard that before quiet was restored, several men were slain, and that five of those who had got into the pool were drowned beneath the feet of those who recklessly leaped in, over the heads of others, upon them.

"Is it possible," I asked Rabbi Amos, after we had reached the borders of Kedron, "that it is the act of an angel that can produce all this confusion and out-break of the worst of human passions?"

"There is no doubt that the troubling of the waters is a miracle," he answered. "The act of the angel is good. His touch gives a healing power that cures diseases; and shall his benevolence be answerable for these dreadful and disgusting consequences which we have just witnessed?"

I was silent; but I sighed for the wickedness of man, that can make even God's gifts curses in the reception of them.

We now turned a little to the right, for as the bridge by which the road of Jericho is usually gained was being solidly rebuilt by the Romans, we had to follow the brookside till we came near Absalom's Pillar, at the sight of which the whole history of that misguided young prince came before me. How wonderful, that the glorious head of golden hair, of which he was vain, and of which the poets of that day speak more than once, should have been the instrument of his death! There were ancient oak trees in sight, which the Rabbi said were old enough to be part of the forest through which he rode so fatally, and, doubtless, were. He showed me the pit into which the ten young men who slew Absalom cast him, heaping great stones upon him. It is close beside the pillar. This prince must have been as brave as he was beautiful and disobedient, that when hanging by his hair in the oak, and incapable of doing them harm, it should require "ten young men to compass him and smite him." How interesting to me is every spot about Jerusalem! I seem to live in the ancient days, when I see the scenes where have been enacted the great events which constitute the history and glory of our nation.

We had hardly reached the place where the two roads meet, when we heard to the west the sound of the galloping at a large body of horse, and the next moment the young Roman Centurion came in sight, by the road from the Horse Gate, riding at the head of a troop of horse, whose martial appearance, with the ringing of their armor, and the melody of their bugles, made my blood leap; and I am sure, if I could have seen my eyes, I should have discovered in them a martial fire. Aemilius looked like a Prince, and his burnished armor shone in the sun like armor of fire. At his side rode a youth, who bore the eagle of his band; but the Centurion himself carried in his hand only the badge of his rank, which was a vine-rod bound with rings of gold. He saluted us with that courtesy which distinguishes his every motion, and then dividing his troop into two bodies, half of whom trotting on ahead, led the van, and the other half, falling behind, served as a rear-guard. He then gave the word to move forward. The Centurion himself rode either by the side of Rabbi Amos, or near our bridles, but he did not so far occupy himself with us as to forget his duty as captain, which he fulfilled with the utmost vigilance, especially after we passed the village, and entered upon the desert space that lies beyond Bethany. Farewell, dear father, till my next, when I will resume my narrative of the events which have taken place since I left Jerusalem. The God of our father Abraham be your defense and shield.

Your affectionate daughter,   ADINA.

LETTER VIII.

My Dear Father: The very kind manner in which you have received my communications respecting the extraordinary prophet now drawing all Judea after him into the wilderness, and the assurance that I can obtain from your wisdom, learning and piety, a solution of all difficulties, and a true guide to the truth, prompt me to continue freely, and in detail, the relation of events that have passed under my experience. I shall, in my accounts of the marvelous occurrences that I have witnessed, and may yet witness, not only convey to you the impressions made upon my own mind, but upon the minds of many others, of the wise, and learned, and great, who also have heard and seen these things. Thus you will have the weight of many testimonies, which you will doubtless hold in respect in proportion to the dignity, and wisdom, and rank of the persons.

My last letter ended with an account of the Roman escort, under the authority of the young Roman Centurion, who, as I have before written to you, with so much courtesy proffered its protection to our little party. The day was yet early, the sun not having got more than an hour and a half high above the Arabian hills, and the air was of that buoyant elasticity so agreeable to breathe, and which strikes me as one of the peculiar blessings of this holy land of our fathers. In Egypt there is a want of life in the torrid air at this season, that we do not here experience; and as I rode along, I felt as if I would gladly mount the Arabian of the desert, and fly across the sandy seas of Edom, with the fleetness which amazes me whenever I see the children of the desert ride; for a band of thirty came near us from a gorge as we approached Bethany, and, after watching us a few moments, scoured away

71

into the recesses of the hills, like the wind, as a detachment of a score of our Roman escort was ordered to gallop toward them. Upon this, Rabbi Amos said that we were fortunate in having such strong protection, for this party of the children of Esau would otherwise have attacked and plundered us, as they are wont to do every party of Israelites they fall in with; and the recent concourse of so many people to Jordan, has drawn them boldly near Jerusalem, says the Roman Centurion, in great numbers, to lay in wait for, and rob them. Thus, the hostility which began between the patriarch Jacob and the patriarch Esau, has never yet been healed, but rankles in the bosoms of their descendants even to this day; and still, "Esau hateth Jacob, because of the blessing wherewith his father blessed him." The Romans greatly admired the horsemanship of these children of Esau, and, upon their heavy horses, armed with their iron armor, it would have been vain to have followed them to their retreats.

We soon afterward reached Bethany, from which we had a gorgeous view of the Holy City of God, with its lofty Temple glittering in the sunbeams, like a mountain of architectural silver. The tower of Antonia darkly contrasted with its splendor, and the citadel of David frowned over the walls with a warlike majesty that deeply impressed me. Ah, how could I gaze upon the scene, my dear father, without emotions of awe, wonder, adoration, and gratitude! I drew rein, and entreated Rabbi Amos to delay a few moments, while I surveyed Jerusalem, which, familiar as it might be to him, and to all the rest of our cavalcade, was new to me; but he was too far ahead to hear me, for I had already been lingering for some seconds; and the Centurion, riding up to my side, stopped respectfully, with a portion of his command, and said he would await my leisure. I could not but thank him for his civility, and then turning to the city, I was soon lost to all else but the awful contemplation of it. Irresistibly, as I gazed, I went back, in memory, to the time when our father Abraham was met before its gates by Melchisedec, its king, who received regal homage from him. I saw again, David coming forth from its lofty portals, at the head of armies, to conquer the surrounding nations. I beheld the splendid trains of Oriental monarchs, of the kings of the South, and the kings of the North, and of Sheba, the queen at happy Arabia, winding through its pleasant valley, and entering in to prostrate themselves before Solomon, the prince of wisdom, glory, and power, the fame of whose wisdom and greatness filled the whole earth. Alas! the whole earth is now filled with the story of the shame and bondage of Israel! But the day cometh, dear father, when she shall lift up her face from the dust, and put on regal garments, and God shall place a crown upon her head, and her glory and dominion shall be without end. This certainty quenched the tears that burst into my eyes, as I contrasted the present with the past. In memory, as I continued to gaze, I saw the armies of the Assyrians, and the armies of the Chaldeans, the armies of Egypt, and of Persia, of Cyrus, and of Greece, all, each in its turn, encompassing the Holy City, and conquering it, even though God dwelt therein in the mysterious fire of the Shechinah. But the presence of Jehovah, in a city or in a heart, will not save it from its foes, if the city or the heart be not with God; and we know from the Prophets that the hearts of our fathers were far from God; and, therefore, were they delivered up to their enemies to be scourged. Oh, my dear father, that our people of today would learn the fearful lesson that the past teacheth them!

"You should see Rome," said the Centurion, who had watched my emotion evidently with surprise. "It is a city of grandeur unequaled. It covers six times more space than this city, and it contains three hundred and sixty-five temples, while Jerusalem contains but one!"

"There is no God but one," I answered impressively.

"We believe that there is one God, who is the author of a great multitude of lesser gods, and to each we erect a temple." Upon this, touched with pity that one so noble in mind and person should be so ignorant of the truth, I began to show him from the Prophets that God was one, and that all things were made by Him. But he, plucking a blossom from a tree which was within reach, said:

"It is beneath the dignity of the Father of the gods, the great Jove, to descend to make a flower like this; or shape a crystal; or color the ruby; or create that golden-dyed humming-bird which flutter among those fragrant blossoms. He made the sun, and moon, and stars, and earth, but left the lesser works to inferior deities. Talk to me of thy One God, and prove to me, maiden, that He made all things, and is One, and thy God shall be my God."

It was then no time for me to endeavor to combat this error, but I have reserved to myself the first convenient opportunity to endeavor to instruct him in the truth as it is revealed from Heaven to our favored people. He has already manifested an inquiring spirit into our holy faith, and Rabbi Amos has taught him many things from the books of Moses, but sufficient only to lead him to desire to know more; but not to eradicate from his heart his pagan superstitions. The gentleness of his nature, his sound judgment, the frankness of his character, the ingenuous temper of the whole man, inspire me with great confidence that he will be ultimately convinced of his errors, and embrace the faith of Israel.

We now rode forward through the principal street of Bethany, and soon came to the house of your former friend, Rabbi Abel, who died many years ago at Alexandria, when he went there with merchandise, and after the welfare of whose children you desired me to make inquiries. They are now, as you are aware, grown to the full estate of manhood and womanhood, and still dwell at Bethany. Being friends of my cousin Mary, it was decided that we should stop there to rest half an hour before proceeding on our way. It was a plain and humble dwelling, before which Rabbi Amos assisted me to alight; but there was an air of sweet domestic repose about it that at once came home to my heart, and made me love the place even before I had seen the inmates, who had come out to receive, and gone in with my cousin; but on hearing of my arrival, there came out a fair young girl of twenty-two, with the most amiable expression of affectionate welcome and, approaching me, with mingled respect and love, she embraced me, while Rabbi Amos pronounced our names to each other. I felt immediately as if I were in a sister's arms, and that I should love her always. Next came forth a young man of about thirty years of age, with a countenance of exceedingly interesting expression, full of intellect and good will. He was pale and habitually thoughtful, but a fine friendly light beamed in his dark, handsome eyes, as he extended his hand to welcome me. You have already had a full description of him, and of his character, in one of my former letters, and need not be told that it was the son of your friend. At the threshold, Martha, the eldest sister, met me, but with more ceremony, and made an apology for receiving into so lowly a dwelling the rich heiress of Alexandria, as she termed me but I embraced her so affectionately, that this feeling passed away instantly. I was much struck with this whole family. Each member of it possessed attractions of a peculiar kind; and in all three I seemed to have found two sisters and a brother. Martha busied herself at once to prepare refreshments for us, and soon set before us a frugal but agreeable repast, more than we desired; for we all insisted that we needed nothing, as we had not been long in the saddle. Mary, in the meantime, and Lazarus, sat on either side of me, and asked me many questions about Alexandria, and particularly if I had ever seen their father's tomb. And when I told them that at my father's request I had kept the flowers fresh about it, they both pressed my hands and thanked me so gratefully, that tears in my own eyes answered to the tears in theirs.

How shall I describe to you the loveliness of the person of Mary, and yet not so much the perfection of feature as the soul which animates them, and lends them a charm that I cannot adequately convey to you? Her eyes are of that remarkable color so seldom seen among our people, and when it is, is of a richer and more cerulean tone than is found in the azure-eyed natives of the north. They are as blue as the skies of Judea, and yet possess all the starry, torrid splendor of the eyes of the Hebrew maids. Her hair, which is a soft, golden brown, is worn knotted in wavy masses about her superbly molded neck. Her air is serene and confiding, and she has so little art that she lets you read all the secrets of her pure soul in the summer heaven of the sweet eyes I have spoken of. There is an indescribable pensiveness about her that is most touching, and at the same time pleasing.

Martha, the oldest, is of a more lively disposition, yet more commanding in her aspect, being taller, and almost queenly. Her eyes and hair are jet-black; the former mild, and beaming with intelligence, like those of her brother Lazarus, whom she resembles. She has a winning voice and a manner that leads you to feel strong confidence in her friendship. She seemed to take the whole management of our entertainment upon herself, which the quieter Mary left to her, as if a matter of course, preferring rather to talk with me about the land of Egypt, where our fathers were so long in bondage, and about which all our young people in Judea have such awful ideas. Mary asked me if I was not afraid to dwell there? if I ever saw the tomb of the Pharaohs? and if the seventy pyramids of the Nilus were not the work of our forefathers? Lazarus conversed chiefly with Rabbi Amos, who questioned him with much interest about the prophet John of the wilderness, to whom, you will remember, I wrote you Lazarus had paid a visit. After our repast, Martha showed me three beautiful bands of embroidery, which she was, working for the new veil of the Temple to be put up next year; for the sisters live by working needlework for the Temple, and Lazarus makes copies of the Law and Psalms for the priests. He showed me his copying-table, and the rolls upon it, some partly done, some quite complete. He also showed me a copy of the book of Isaiah, which he had just finished, and which had occupied him one hundred and seven days. It was exquisitely executed. Another incomplete copy was thrown aside, and was destined to be burned, because he had made a mistake in forming one letter; for if an iota be added too much, the work is condemned and burned, so strict are the priests that perfect and immaculate copies of the Law, and none others, shall exist. Mary, also, showed me a beautifully embroidered foot-tablet, which the wife of Pilate, when she was last from Cesarea, ordered for herself.

"I shall not receive coin for it," said Mary, "but present it to her for she has ever been very kind to us and when, last year, she and the Procurator Pilate, her lord, came up from Cesarea to Jerusalem, about the time of the Passover, she sent her own household physician to heal Lazarus, who was taken sick from over-much confinement to his tasks. She knew us only by inquiring who it was who worked the embroidering of the altar mantles, which she had much admired."

Seeing upon the table a richly worked bookcover of silk and velvet, with the letters "I. N." embroidered in olive leaves upon it, I asked her if that, it being so elegant, was not for the High Priest?

"No," answered Martha, with brightening eyes, speaking before her sister could reply, "that is for our friend, and the friend and brother of Lazarus."

"What is his name?" I asked.

"Jesus, of Nazareth."

"I have heard John speak of him," said my cousin Mary, with animation, and appealing to me, reminded me how John had repeated what Lazarus had spoken to him of his friend from Nazareth which I have written to you, "I should feel happy," added my cousin, "to know him also."

"And from what I have heard of him," said I, "it would be, indeed, a pleasure to see him."

The two sisters listened to us with pleasure, and Martha said:

"If you had been here a few days ago, you would have seen him. He left us, after being with us three weeks, to go to Nazareth again. But he requested to meet Lazarus at Bethabara, on the third day from this, for some important reason; and my brother will go, for he loves him so that he would cross the seas to meet him."

"Then," said Rabbi Amos to Lazarus, "if you are to journey so soon toward Jordan to meet your friend, you had best join our company, and share our escort." To this Lazarus, after some consultation with his sisters, consented.

What a happy family, thought I, is this! The sisters happy in each other's love, the brother happy in theirs, all three united as one in purest affection, and yet a fourth is added to the circle whose love for the three is equal to theirs for him! Humble in station, poor, and dependent upon the labor of their hands for their daily bread, yet their household is one that kings might envy, and which no gold or jewels could purchase.

I left this blessed abode of fraternal friendship with regret, and felt that I should be perfectly happy if I could be admitted as a fifth link in the wreath of their mutual love. Even the Roman Centurion had been struck with the air of peaceful repose reigning there, and spoke of it to me as we road away.

About noon we stopped at a caravansera, half the way to Jericho from Bethany. Here we overtook a friend of Rabbi Amos, the venerable and learned scholar and lawyer, Gamaliel. He was, he confessed, also riding to Jordan, to have an interview with the prophet, being persuaded to seek it on account of an extraordinary dream he had, which he repeated to his friend Rabbi Amos, but not in our hearing but the effect upon my uncle excited a good deal of my curiosity to know what it was, but he has been studiously silent upon the subject. Accompanying the lawyer, Gamaliel, was a young man who was his disciple, and who went with him as a companion by the way. His name is Saul; and I noticed him particularly, because I overheard the venerable lawyer say that he was the most remarkable young man who had ever sat at his feet to learn the mysteries of the law. This young law-disciple and Lazarus rode together, and talked long and earnestly by the way, the former thinking that nothing but mischief would come of the new prophet's preaching, while the latter warmly defended him and his mission as divine. To their conversation the Roman Centurion listened with the closest attention, for Saul was learned in the Prophets, and drew richly from its stores to prove that the true Messias can never be heralded by so mean a messenger as this preacher of repentance in the wilderness. Saul eloquently drew a gorgeous picture of Messias' coming, and the splendor of his reign, and that angels and heavenly signs, and not a wild man of the wilderness, with water baptism, should prepare the way before him.

At length, as the day closed, we came in sight of the walls and towers of Jericho, but succeeded in reaching the gates only after they were closed. But the presence of the young Centurion caused them to be immediately reopened, and we were admitted, with some hundreds, who, having reached the gate after it was shut, now begged and received permission to enter in our company.

The next day we proceeded to Gilgal alone, the road being perfectly safe, the courteous Roman having early the same morning issued from the gates, in haste to pursue the famous Barabbas, who had the last night attacked a caravan within four leagues of Jordan, and taken much booty, as well as slain many men.

"I now write to thee beneath the roof of the summer residence of Rabbi Amos. Tomorrow, early," says a passage which I copy from my journal, written there, we are going to Bethabara, a little village beyond Jordan, but on its banks, near which we learn John is now baptizing, he being no longer at the ford of Jordan, where my cousin Mary's betrothed, John, found him, and was baptized of him a few weeks ago. Lazarus has gone on with Saul, and the learned Gamaliel, with many lawyers and doctors in company, who desire to see and hear this prophet of the wilderness."

Indeed, dear father, the advent of a prophet is of so rare an occurrence among us, that the bare idea that John the Baptizer may be a true prophet of God has moved the great heart of Israel, and stirred up curiosity, hope, and marvel, in the highest degree ever known in the land. There seems to be but one subject, and but one thought. Every man says to his neighbor: "Have you seen or heard the new prophet? Is he Messias, or is he Elias?"

My next letter will give you a narration, my dear father, of what I witnessed at Bethabara, and will, perhaps, more deeply interest you than anything I have yet written.

That the hope of Israel may not the long deferred, and that we may receive the Messias, when he cometh, in humble faith, in honor, and in love, is the prayer of

Your affectionate daughter,

ADINA.

LETTER IX.

My Dear Father: In these letters to you which give you an account of my excursion with Rabbi Amos to the Jordan, I hope you will pardon the details which I enter into, for it is my earnest desire that you should see everything with my eyes, as if you had been present with me; in order that you may, though absent, be able to judge as if you had been an eye-witness of the remarkable events of which I have undertaken to give you a complete history. I know that your liberal mind, and your sense of equity and justice, will lead you to read all I have to write before you take upon you to make a reply to the facts which, with filial love and reverence, I present to your consideration.

After Rabbi Amos had reached the house in the wheatfields of Gilgal, where he intended to take up his sojourn for the two weeks of harvest, and had directed his servants what to do, he kindly told us that he was ready to accompany my cousin Mary and myself to the Jordan, to hear the prophet. It was with no little gratification, therefore, that my cousin and myself once more mounted our mules, and proceeded toward the place where we heard the prophet was baptizing. But we had not ridden a great way from the house. When we overtook two men on foot, with staves in their hands and wallets upon their shoulders. As we passed one of them raised his cap with respect to Rabbi Amos, who, from his rank as a priest, and his venerable appearance, always commands the homage of all men.

"Whither goest thou at such a pace, friend Matthew?" said Rabbi Amos, returning his salute, for he seemed to know him. "Canst thou leave thy tax-gathering these busy times to go into the wilderness?"

The person, who was a man of stout figure, with dark hair and beard, and a look of intelligence, but whose costume was plain and ill-worn, smiled, and answered:

"If a man would find the payers of tribute nowadays, good master, he must not stay at home, forsooth, but go into the wilderness of Jordan where all men have gone. Verily, this new prophet emptieth our towns, and we publicans must remain idle in our seat of customs, or go with the tide."

"Thy words are near the truth, friend Matthew," answered my uncle "but hast thou no other motive in thy heart than looking after thy Roman coins, in taking this journey from Jericho?"

"I have curiosity to see a man whom multitudes resort to from Galilee, and from Decapolis, and from Jerusalem, and from all Judea, and from beyond Jordan."

"And thinkest thou," continued my uncle, as the two men walked along by the side of his mule, "thinkest thou this prophet is a true son of the prophets?"

"He works no miracles, unless, indeed, the power of his preaching be a miracle," answered Matthew.

"This man is an impostor. There can be no prophet unless he proves his mission by miracles," suddenly said the companion of Matthew, speaking up abruptly in a sharp and unpleasing voice. Now neither Mary nor I liked the face of this man from the first. He was of good height, he was well-featured, and his attire was rich; but he had a haughty air, combined with a cringing deference to Rabbi Amos, that made me think he must be a hypocrite. He smiled with his mouth and teeth, but at the same time looked sinister out of his eyes. He had an air of humility which seemed to me to be put on to conceal the pride and wickedness of his character. He looked like a man who could artfully deceive to gain his selfish ends, and who would kneel to you to overturn you. The sound of his voice confirmed my first impression of him. Upon his speaking, Rabbi Amos fixed his eyes upon him, as if he did not like the manner of his breaking in upon the conversation, and then mildly replied:

"Moses performed no miracles. Aaron, or Aaron's rod was the instrument whereby these were done before Pharaoh. This prophet may be as Aaron to the great Prophet he foretelleth. What is thy companion's name, friend Matthew?" he asked, aside, as the other walked on ahead.

"His name is Judas, called Iscariot. He hath been engaged by me to bear the moneys I collect in the country villages; and as we are to gather taxes both at Gilgal and Bethabara, he cometh with me."

We now came in sight of the Jordan, but could discover no crowd upon its banks. While we were wondering at not beholding any signs of the multitude, we met a stranger who was riding a horse, and coming from the northward, who, seeing us apparently in perplexity, inquired with courtesy, if we were not seeking John the prophet. Upon Rabbi Amos replying in the affirmative, the horseman informed us that he had removed up the river, some two hours' ride, and was then baptizing at the little village of Bethabara, on the east bank of Jordan and he added, that not less than eight thousand people must be thronging the shore.

"Dost thou know this stranger?" asked of Matthew Rabbi Amos, who had gratefully thanked him for his intelligence, looking back after him, as he rode on. "I saw thee salute him."

"He is an officer of Herod the Tetrareh's household," was the response, "a Hebrew of great wealth, and he payeth more tribute-money to the emperor from his lands than any Israelite between Jericho and Jerusalem."

At length, dear father, after hastening the speed of our mules, and riding pleasantly for two hours along the verdant banks of Jordan, we came in sight of a square tower of stone, peering above the trees, which marked the site of the village of Bethabara. "That tower," said Rabbi Amos, "stands over a cave in which Elijah long dwelt, and in which Isaiah at one time concealed himself from his enemies. It is now called the "Tower of Elijah." From the summit of yonder hill, at the left, the prophet was caught up, and ascended to heaven upon the chariot of fire; and near where you see the single rock, Elisha divided Jordan, with the fallen mantle left him by the ascending prophet of God."

All these places, with many others, which the intelligent Rabbi Amos pointed out to us, were very interesting to me, for nothing commands my attention so profoundly as allusions to the scenes of the olden days of the prophets and kings of Israel. While my eyes were fixed upon the hill, and my imagination presented to me Elijah upon the chariot of heaven, disappearing amid the clouds, there was an opening in the wood before us, and all at once we beheld a scene that made my heart cease to beat, it was so new and wonderful. At that place the river takes a broad curve, and the opposite village of Bethabara lies in the hollow of it, forming the center of half a circle. This wide curving shore was alive with the human heads that filled it. Not a place could be seen where someone did not stand. And of this vast multitude every eye was concentrated upon the prophet, as from the crescent tiers of the amphitheater in Alexandria, all gaze at once upon the scenes passing in the arena. He was standing upon the opposite shore (for Jordan here was very narrow, and can be forded), on the verge of the water, addressing the countless assembly that stood opposite and half encircling him. Near him, behind, and on either side, sat his disciples, at least a hundred in number, chiefly young men. Behind, rose the Tower of Elijah, and receding farther from the shore lay the sweet village of Bethabara, with its green gardens and snow-white walls.

The clear voice of the youthful prophet of the wilderness fell distinctly on our ears, so great was the stillness of the vast audience. We could not approach very near on our mules, and, dismounting on the outskirts of the throng, we left them with the two servants, and on foot drew as near to the place where the prophet stood as we could. Many of the people, seeing and recognizing Rabbi Amos, made way for him, so that at length we stood directly opposite the speaker, with a full view of him, so that we could hear every word. To my surprise, I saw John, the cousin of Mary, standing close to the Prophet and listening with the deepest and most reverent attention to every word he uttered. The subject of the prophet's discourse was as before, and as always, the coming of the Messias. Oh, that I could give you, my dear father, the faintest idea of the power and eloquence of his words!

"There is no remission of sin without shedding of blood," he said earnestly. "The baptism of water with which I baptize you is unto repentance; but there must be blood outpoured ere sin can be washed away! Do you ask me if the blood of bulls and goats take not away sin? I answer and say unto you, that the Lord hath said that he delighteth not in these rivers of blood." "For what, then, great prophet," asked one of the chief Levites who stood near us, "for what, then, are the sacrifices ordained by the Law of Moses? For what, then, the altar and the Temple, and the daily sacrifice of the Lamb?"

"For what," repeated the prophet, with his eyes beaming with the earnest light of inspiration, "For what, but as types and shadows of the true blood--of the real and true sacrifice appointed by God from the foundation of the world! Think ye I can slay the lamb of my flock for the sin of my soul? If God demands thy life, shall he accept the life of a brute? Nay, men of Israel, the day has come when your eyes shall be opened. The hour is at hand when the true meaning of the daily sacrifice shall be understood. Lo! the Messiah cometh, and ye shall see and believe!"

There now came several persons toward him who desired baptism. While he was baptizing these persons, both men and women, I saw appear on the little mound near the tower from which Rabbi Amos had said Elijah ascended, Lazarus, the brother of Martha, accompanied by a man of about his own years, of an indescribable dignity and grace of aspect, combined with an air of benevolence and peace that at once attracted me.

"It must be the friend of Lazarus," said Mary to me; for she had discovered them at the same time. "See with what calm serenity he gazes upon the multitude, yet retiring in his manner, as if he shrank from the common eye!" He was wrapped in a vesture of dark blue cloth, which was folded about this form; his head was bare and his dark hair flowed down about his shoulders. He seemed so unlike all other men, in a certain majesty united with sweetness, that marked his whole air, that I could not withdraw my gaze from him.

The prophet, at the same moment, rested his eyes upon him, and as he did so, I saw a change come over his face, as if he had seen an angel. His eyes shone with unearthly brilliancy, his lips parted as if he would speak, yet had lost the power; and then, with his right hand stretched forth toward the noble stranger, he stood for a moment like a statue. All eyes followed his, and the direction of his stretched-out arm. Suddenly, he exclaimed, and oh, how like the trumpet of Horeb his voice rung:

"Behold!"

There was not a face in that vast multitude that was not directed toward the little eminence, where Lazarus, evidently amazed at the attitude and words of the prophet, and the gaze of all that way, stood by his friend.

"Ye have asked wherefore is slain the daily lamb," continued the prophet. "The day has come when the lamb of sacrifice, which can take away no sin, shall cease. Behold!" and here he stretched forth both arms toward the dignified stranger: "Behold the Lamb of God which taketh away the sins of the world. He it is who, coming after me, is preferred before me. He it is to whom I bear witness, the Messiah, the Son of the Highest! There stands the Christ of God! Behold the only true Lamb, whose blood can wash away the iniquities of us all! He hath stood among you -- He hath walked your streets -- He hath sat in your homes, and I knew him not, till I now behold above Him the sign of the Messiah, and, therefore, know I that it is He who is to redeem Israel!"

When the prophet had thus spoken in a voice that thrilled to every bosom, we beheld the august stranger advance toward the prophet. He moved on alone. Lazarus had fallen prostrate on his face when he heard that it was the Messiah with whom he had thus been on terms of friendship. As he continued to come forward, all was expectation in the immense multitude. The mass of heads swayed this way and that to get a sight of his face, which I could see was serene, but pale and earnest. John, the cousin of Mary, seeing him approach, lowly knelt, and bowed his head in reverential awe and love. Those who stood between him and the prophet moved apart, and left an open path for him to the water-side. He walked at a slow and even pace, with an air of humility, veiling the native dignity of his kingly port.

The prophet, on seeing him come near, regarded Him, as it seemed to me, with more awe than all others.

"What wouldst thou of thy servant, oh, Messiah, Prophet of God, mighty to save?" he said, in tremulous tones, as the Messiah came even some paces into the water toward him.

"To be baptized of thee," answered the Christ, in a still, quiet voice, that was heard to the remotest bounds of the crowd. Never, oh, never shall I forget the sounds of that voice, as it fell upon my ears!

"I have need to be baptized of thee, and comest Thou to me?" answered the prophet, with the lowliest humility and awe of manner, and with looks expressive of his amazement.

"It becometh us to fulfill all righteousness," answered Messiah mildly; and when He had said this, the prophet, though still with a manner of doubt, and with the holiest reverence, administered unto Him, in the sight of all the people, the same baptism which he had administered to his disciples.

And now, my dear father, comes to be related the most extraordinary thing that ever took place in Israel, and before human eyes, and which it must be clear to you bears unquestionable testimony, that Jesus of Nazareth, the noble stranger baptized in Jordan, and to whom John bore witness, is truly Messias, the Son of God.

No sooner did the baptized stranger go up out of the water, than there was heard above all our heads a noise of rolling thunder, although the sky was cloudless; and when we looked up we beheld a dazzling light, though it was noon-day, brighter than the sun; and from the midst of this celestial splendor there darted with arrowy velocity a ray of light, which descended upon the head of the Christ. Some of the people said it thundered; and others that it lightened; but judge the amazement and admiration of all, and the dread awe that shook every soul, when, amid the glory above his head, was seen the form of a dove of fire, with outspread wings overshadowing Him as it were, and from the heavens, what was supposed to be thunder shaped itself into the voice of God, which uttered these words in the hearing of every ear:

"This is my beloved Son, in whom I am well pleased. Hear ye Him." At hearing these words, a great part of the multitude fell on their faces. Every cheek was pale, and each man gazed on his neighbor in wonder and fear. When the majestic, yet terrible voice had given utterance to these words, the light disappeared, the dove reascended to the skies, and was lost to the sight; and Messias, who alone seemed unmoved and calm amid all this awful scene, went up from the river, and disappeared suddenly from my earnest gaze. At length, when men came a little to themselves, and would gaze on Him whom all knew now to be the Christ, no one could find Him, so effectually had he withdrawn himself from their homage. Your affectionate

ADINA

LETTER X.

My Dear Father: I will commence this letter by asking your dispassionate perusal of my preceding epistle, and entreating you not to let any prejudice unworthy of the wisdom and liberality by which you are distinguished among men, lead you to reject, without examination, belief of the events which have formed the subject of my recent letters to you, and to close your mind to the convictions to which they may give rise. Please, my honored and beloved father, please to consider impartially the things of which I have written: the preaching of John, and his baptism of Jesus, whom, before ten thousand people, he declared to be Messias, to whom he bore witness, and how the voice of God, as audible in the ears of all as that which shook Horeb, proclaimed from heaven that he was "His beloved son!" Think of all this, and ask yourself seriously, "Is not this the Christ?"

This question need not pass far on its way ere it finds a response from my lips and heart: "Yes, it is the Christ, and I will believe in Him!"

I can see your face, my dear father, change its expression of mild benignity, as you read this confession from my pen! I can see you look both displeased and grieved. But you have no reason to fear that I shall do or believe aught that will bring shame on your gray hairs, or your name. If thou art a Jew, and proud of being descended from the lineage of the Patriarchs who walked with the Lord, I am also equally proud of my nation and of my faith. In believing Jesus of Nazareth to be Messias of God, I do not make myself less a Jewess; but, without believing it, my dear father, I could not be completely a Jewess. Has not the Messias of our nation been the burden of Judah's prayer, and of Israel's hope, for ages? Does not the belief that Messias cometh, constitute one of the great characteristics of the Jewish race? Do the Gentiles look for the Christ? If not, then, and we alone look for him, and every mother in Israel hopes, tremblingly, with joy and doubt, that he may be found in her first-born son, is it that I am less a Jewess, or rather, that I am only a true Jewess, when I believe Jesus to be the Messias, seeing in Him all that a Messias could bring, even the voice of God, in testimony of His Mission? But I sincerely trust, my dear father, that I am defending my belief unnecessarily, and that when you come to read and compare, and examine well, you will rejoice with me that God has remembered Israel, and that He is about to take away her reproach among the nations.

I shall wait for your next parcel of letters with the deepest solicitude, in order that I may know what your decision is in reference to these extraordinary things which are coming to pass. You will not hear them only from my letters, dear father, for the report of these wonders is broadcast over the land, and men who witnessed the baptism of Jesus will, no doubt, report in Egypt what then took place, especially the voice of God rolling like articulate thunder along the cloudless sky, and the descent of the fiery dove upon the head of the new Prophet. Merchants of Damascus and of Cairo were present, leaving their trains of camels a little way off; and Arab horsemen sat in their saddles on the outside of the crowd; while Roman soldiers, strangers from Persia and Edom, and even the merchants from Media, with numerous people, Gentiles, as well as Jews, were seen mingled with the multitude. This thing, therefore, was not done in a corner. The voice I plainly heard, and understood every word! It seemed to me to come from the far blue depths of Heaven, at an immeasurable distance, but with the clearness of a trumpet, and the sonorous majesty of thunder. But the light which descended was the most dazzling that human eyes ever encountered and though when descending with the velocity of lightning, it seemed like a lance of fire; yet, upon reaching the bared head of Jesus, as He came forth out of the water, it assumed, as I before stated, the shape of a dove and, resting upon Him, overshadowed Him with its wings of light, and cast over his whole person a glittering splendor, like the sun. This lasted for full a minute, so that all eyes beheld it, and then came the voice from heaven! The brilliancy of the light from the dove was so resplendent that I could not behold it; and when I looked again it had disappeared; but a halo of softened luster shone still around the head of Jesus, and his face, like that of Moses, emitted rays of glory. While thousands either stood stupefied, or fell upon their faces in adoration and fear, He withdrew himself from the multitude, no one knew how, save two persons, whose eyes never wander from him. These were the cousin of Mary, John, and Lazarus, the brother of Mary and Martha.

The people, after recovering a little from their amazement and awe, were looking for Him, and inquiring whither he had gone, some gazing into the water, some toward the wilderness, some even gazing upward into heaven, of whom I was one, as if they expected to behold Him ascending upon a chariot of dazzling clouds toward the throne of his God and Father, who had acknowledged Him to be his Son. The general impression was, that He was taken up into Heaven; and some wept that a Prophet was sent to be taken so soon; while others rejoiced that the Lord had not forgotten to be gracious unto the house of Israel; some doubted, and called it magic and sorcery; and others, who were doubtless filled with their own wickedness, mocked, and said the voice was thunder, and the light lightning. But here they were disputed against, for said hundreds, "There is no cloud in the sky, then whence could come thunder and lightning?" But the majority believed, and greatly rejoiced at what they had seen and heard. The prophet John of Jordan appeared to me to be more surprised at what had taken place than any others. He looked constantly around for Jesus, and then, with his hands clasped together and uplifted, gazed heavenward, as if satisfied, with the thousands around him, that he had been received up into Heaven.

The excitement which the sudden disappearance of Jesus produced led to a universal separation of the multitude, who dispersed in all directions, some to seek for Him, some to spread the news of what they had seen, and all forgetting John, whom they had hitherto followed, in the greater splendor of the new Prophet, whose advent had been so remarkably accompanied by fire and voice from the sky.

Rabbi Amos and our party remained standing near the water, for he did not wish us to be lost in the retiring throngs, and he desired to speak with John, who stood alone in the midst of the water, precisely where he had baptized Jesus. Not one of his disciples remained with him. Rabbi Amos drew near, and said to him:

"Holy prophet, knowest thou what man, if man he may be called was just baptized by thee?"

The prophet, whose eyes had been steadfastly raised all the while, bent his looks with tearful tenderness upon Rabbi Amos, and said plaintively and touchingly:

"This is He of whom I said -- After me cometh a man which is preferred before me, for He was before me. And I knew Him not; but He that sent me, to baptize with water, the same said unto me, Upon whom thou shalt see the Spirit descending and remaining on Him, the same is He that baptizes with the Holy

Ghost. And I saw the Spirit descending like a dove, and I saw and bear record this is the Son of God!"

"And whither, oh, holy prophet of Jordan," asked Rabbi Amos, with deep and sacred interest, "whither has He departed?"

"That I know not! He must increase and I must decrease, whether He remaineth on earth, or be taken up into Heaven! My mission is now drawing to its close: for He to whom I have borne witness is come."

"And is He come to depart so soon forever?" I asked, with deep interest; "shall we behold Him no more?"

"The hidden things belong to God. I know not whence He came, for I knew Him not until the Spirit descendeth and abode upon Him, nor whither He goeth. Ye have heard my testimony that this is the Messias, the Christ, the Son of God!"

Thus speaking, he turned and walked out of the water, on the side toward Bethabara, and disappeared among the trees that fringed the bank. I now looked in the face of Rabbi Amos, upon whose arm Mary was tearfully leaning, still under the influence of the terror which the scenes she had been a spectator of had produced in her soul. His face was grave and thoughtful. I said, "Uncle, dost thou believe all that thou hast seen and heard?" "I know not what to say," he answered, "only that the things which I have beheld this day are evidences that God has not forgotten his people Israel!" He said no more. We left the banks of the Jordan in silence and awe, and remounting our mules, which the two Gibeonite slaves held for us in waiting, under a palm tree not far off, we returned toward my uncle's house at Gilgal. On the way, we constantly passed crowds of people who were riding and walking; and all were in high talk about what had taken place at the river. The impression seemed to be that Jesus had gone up into Heaven.

But, my dear father, it is with deep joy that I am able to tell you that this wonderful person is still on the earth, and doubtless permitted to remain for some great purpose. I stated that my cousin John, and Lazarus, the Secretary of the Scribes, had kept their eyes upon Him from the first, and that they had seen Him pass down the river, where some projecting and overhanging trees hid Him at once from view. Though they often lost sight of Him, they yet followed Him by the print of His sandals in the wet sand of the shore; and at length came in view of Him, as He was leaving the river bank, and going toward the desert, between two hills, which hid Him from their eyes. But one of the young men said to the other, while both were burning with wonder and love:

"Let us not fail to overtake Him, and follow Him, whithersoever He goeth; for with Him must be the well of life, as He is the highly favored of God."

So they went on; but though they moved on rapidly, they next saw Him far distant, crossing the arid plain that stretches south toward Jericho and the desert. They ran very swiftly, and at length overtook Him, calling "Master, good master, stay for us, for we would follow and learn of thee!"

He stopped, and turned upon them a look so pale, and marred with sadness and anguish, that they both stood still and gazed on Him with amazement at such a change. The glory of his beauty had passed away, and the beaming splendor which shone from his countenance was wholly gone. The expression of unutterable sorrow that remained, pierced them to the heart. Lazarus, who had been so long his bosom friend, wept aloud. "Weep not, thou shalt see me another day, my friends," he said. "I go now to the wilderness in obedience to the Spirit which guideth me thither. Thou shalt, after a time, behold me again. It is expedient that I go whither I go."

"Nay, but we will go with thee," said Lazarus, earnestly, "if thou art to endure evil, we will be with thee."

"There must be none to help. There must be none to uphold," He said firmly, but sadly. "I must tread the wine-press of temptation alone!"

He then left them, waving his hand for them to go back, which they did sorrowfully, wondering what his words meant, and wherefore it was needful for Him to go into the desert, where certain mysterious trials seemed to wait for Him; and they wondered most of all at the change in his countenance, which from being lustrous with celestial light, was now, said Lazarus, "marred more than the sons of men." From time to time the two young men looked backward to watch the receding figure of the Christ, till they no longer distinguished Him in the distance of the desert, toward which He steadfastly kept his face.

The two friends then came to the house of Rabbi Amos, at Gilgal, the same night, and there Lazarus made known to us what I had just related. It affected us all deeply; and we sat together late at night upon the porch under the fig trees, talking of Jesus, and the things that had transpired concerning Him that day; and though we all rejoiced that He was on earth, we wept to think that He was driven by some destiny, unknown and unfathomable by us, to dwell alone in the wilderness.

Now, my dear father, how wonderful is all this! That a great Prophet is among us cannot be denied. The sun of John the Baptizer's fame dwindles into a star before this Son of God! That He will draw all men unto Him, even into the wilderness, if He takes up His abode there, cannot be questioned. But all is mystery, awe, curiosity, wonder, and excitement just now. No one has settled upon any opinion as to what will be the end of these things. Rabbi Amos advises all persons to wait patiently the issue, for if God has sent a Prophet, He must have a mission which in due time He will come forth from the wilderness to deliver. In my next I may be able to write you something further touching the development of that which remains so much enveloped in mystery. May the God of our father's house come forth indeed from the Heavens, for the salvation of His People.

Your devoted and loving
ADINA.

LETTER XI.

My Dear Father: In my last letter to you, I spoke of our return from Jordan to Gilgal, to the country house in the wheat fields of Peniel, where Rabbi Amos sojourns during the two weeks of harvest. At the house were assembled, not only John, the cousin of Mary, and the noble Lazarus, but also Gamaliel, and Saul, his disciple, of whom I have before spoken, who were invited to partake of my uncle's hospitality for the night; besides, the court of the dwelling was thronged with strangers, and the common people, who, being far from their homes, and without food, had freely been invited to lodgings and food by the hospitable priest.

As we sat up late, conversing upon the remarkable events of the day, an observation made by John, when speaking of the change in the face of Jesus, that "His visage was marred more than the sons of men," led the venerable Gamaliel to say to us:

"Those are the words of Esaias, and are truly spoken of Messias, when He shall come."

"Let us consult Esaias, then, and see what further he hath said," cried Rabbi Amos. "Mary, bring hither the roll of the Prophets."

My cousin Mary returned, and placed it on a small stand before him, for, as I said in my last, we were all seated in the porch, where the evening breeze was cool. A lamp then being brought, I held it above the roll of parchment, while my uncle found the part of the Prophet to which the words belonged.

"Read aloud, worthy Rabbi," said the philosopher Gamaliel, "we will all listen for though I do not believe this young man who was today baptized is Messias and Christ, who is to restore all things to us, yet I am prepared to reverence Him as a Prophet."

"And," answered Rabbi Amos, "if we find the prophecies do meet in him which we look for to meet in Messias when He cometh, wilt thou believe, venerable father?"

"I will believe and reverently adore," answered the sage, bowing his head till his flowing white beard touched his knees.

"Read, Adina, for thy eyes are young," said my uncle and obedient, though embarrassed before such an audience, I read as follows:

"Behold, my servant shall deal prudently, he shall be exalted and extolled, and be very high. As many were astonished at thee, His visage was so marred more than any man, and His form more than the sons of men."

"How completely," said John, "these words described his appearance on the verge of the desert."

"But," said Saul, Gamaliel's disciple, "if this be prophesied of the Christ, then we are to have a Christ of dishonor, and not one of honor and glory. Read one part that you have omitted, and you will see that there are words that import a higher condition than that of this unknown person, whom John the Baptizer himself confessed he did not know, nor ever beheld before."

I read on, as follows: "Behold my servant shall be exalted and extolled, and be very high. He shall sprinkle many nations; the kings shall shut their mouths at Him. He shall lift up his hand to the Gentiles, and set up his standard to the people. Kings shall bow down to Him with their faces to the earth, and lick up the dust of his feet!"

"There! such is our Messias," exclaimed Saul.

"Yes, it is a Christ of power and dominion who is to redeem Israel," added Gamaliel "not an unknown young man, scarcely thirty years of age, who came from whence no one knoweth, and hath gone as he came. As for the Christ, we shall know whence He cometh!"

At hearing this great and good man thus discourse, dear father, my heart sank within me; for I could not but confess that these prophecies of honor could not apply to the humble person John had baptized; for Lazarus had already told us that his friend Jesus was of humble birth, a carpenter's son, and his mother a widow; that he had known him from boyhood, but known him only to love him. I now looked toward him, but I took courage when I saw that the words of Gamaliel did not in the least dim the light of his faith and confidence, which sparkled in his eyes, that his friend Jesus was truly Messias of God. But my eye fell on what follows, and as I read it I gained more confidence: "He hath no form nor comeliness: and when we shall see him there is no beauty that we should desire him."

"If the first part of this prophecy," said Lazarus, his fine eyes lighting up, as he looked at Saul, "be of the Christ, as you have confessed, then is this last of him; and the fact that you reject him is but the fulfillment of this part of the prophecy."

Hereupon arose a very warm discussion between Gamaliel and Saul on one side, and Rabbi Amos, John, and Lazarus, on the other, the former contending that the prophecies referred to two distinct Christs, one of whom was to be lonely and a sufferer, and the other honorable and a conqueror; while the latter maintained, that the seemingly opposite predictions referred to but one Christ in two different periods and circumstances of his life.

"But let this be as it may," said John, after the arguments on both sides had been exhausted, "how will you, O Gamaliel, and you, Saul, get over the extraordinary voice and fiery appearance which distinguished the baptism?"

"That must have been a phenomenon of nature, or done by the art of a Babylonish sorcerer, whom I saw in the multitude," answered the philosopher.

"Did you not hear the words?" asked Rabbi Amos.

"Yes, Rabbi nevertheless, they may have been thrown into the air from the lungs of the sorcerer; for they do marvelous things."

"Would you suppose that a sorcerer would be disposed to apply the sacred words of the Lord?" asked John earnestly.

"By no means," he answered reverently.

"If Rabbi Amos will allow me, I will show you the very words in King David's prophecies of Messias."

All looked with interest on John, as he took from his mantle a roll of the Psalms. He read as follows, looking at Gamaliel:

"Why do the rulers take counsel together against the Lord, and against his anointed? I will declare the decree. The Lord hath said unto me, Thou art my son; this day have I begotten thee."

Upon hearing this read, Gamaliel was thoughtful. Rabbi Amos said: "Of a truth, we Jews believe these words were to be spoken to our Christ by the Lord Jehovah. Have we not heard this prophecy fulfilled this very day in our ears?"

"It is extraordinary," answered Gamaliel. "I will search the Scriptures when I reach Jerusalem, to see if these things be so."

"And the light in the form of a dove! Dost thou find an explanation for that?" asked Rabbi Amos.

"No," answered he; "and I will withhold all further opinion for the present."

"It becomes you, O Gamaliel," said Rabbi Amos, "who art a father and teacher in Israel, to know whether these things be so, that thou mayest teach thy disciples."

"But," said Saul, with some vehemence, "listen while I read some prophecies also." And he unrolled a book of the Prophets and read these words:

"Thou Bethlehem Ephratah, though thou be little among the thousands of Judah, yet out of thee shall he come forth unto me that is to be the Ruler in Israel, whose goings forth have been ever of old, from everlasting." "Now, you will confess, Rabbi Amos," he added, with a look of triumph, "that this refers to our expected Messias."

"Without doubt," answered my uncle -- "but --"

"Wait," said Saul, "until I read you another prophecy: I have made a covenant with David, Thy seed will I establish forever, and build up thy throne to all generations. His seed shall endure forever and his throne as the sun before me. Behold, the days come, saith the Lord, that I will raise unto David a righteous branch. Now you will all admit, brethren, that these prophecies refer to Messias. He is, therefore, come of the lineage of David, and he is to be born in Bethlehem. Show me that this Jesus the Nazarene, fulfills both conditions in his own person, and I will prepare to believe in him."

This was said haughtily, and with the air of one who cannot be answered.

But immediately Lazarus rose to his feet and said: "Although I did not before know of this prophecy, that Christ was to be born in Bethlehem, yet I am overjoyed to find the fact respecting Jesus fulfills it. He was born in Bethlehem of Judah. This I have known some years; and ---"

Here, while my heart was bounding with joy, Gamaliel said sternly, "I thought this man was born in Nazareth?"

"He has lived," answered Lazarus, "in Nazareth from childhood only. During the days when Caesar Augustus issued a decree that all the world should be taxed, his mother, and Joseph, her husband, went up to the city of David to be taxed, which is Bethlehem, and there Jesus was born, as I have often heard from her lips. But it is on the records in the proper office of the Temple, and can be referred to there."

"Admitting, then, that he was born in Bethlehem," said Saul, who appeared to be much given to argument, "you have to prove his lineage from David's line."

"Wherefore did his parents go to Bethlehem, David's city,

96

unless they were of the royal line?" asked Rabbi Amos "for none went to any other city to be taxed than that of their own family. The fact that they went there is strong evidence that they were of David's house."

"Everyone born in the city of David," remarked Gamaliel, "is not of necessity of David's house; but it is surprising if this Jesus was born in Bethlehem."

"But may not his lineage be ascertained without a doubt from the records of the tribes, and of their families, kept by the command of the law in the Temple?" I asked of my uncle.

"Without question. These books of the generations of our people are to be relied on," he answered.

"In fact," said Gamaliel, "they are kept with the greatest accuracy, and so ordained by God, for the very reason that when Messias cometh we may know whether he who claims to be such be of the house of David or no. I will examine the book of the Generations, and see if his mother and father come of the stock and seed of David."

"And if you find that they do," asked John, with emotion, "can you doubt any longer whether Jesus be the Christ. Will not the fact of his being born in Bethlehem, and of the lineage of David, not to speak of the witness of God's own audible voice, heard by our ears this day -- will not these facts lead you to believe that he is the Christ?"

"They will prevent me from actually rejecting him," answered the cold philosopher. "But every child born in Bethlehem, and of the house of David, and there are many in Judah, fulfills, so far, the conditions of these two prophecies; they are not, therefore, Messias."

"What more can you ask for?" asked Mary, with feeling, for she as strongly believed that Jesus was the Christ as I did, and she was pained by so many doubts, and such subtlety of objection from those who were so learned in the Prophets. But men reason and reason, while women simply believe.

"Miracles?" answered the disciple of Gamaliel, and glancing at the face of his master inquiringly.

"Yes, miracles," answered the sage. "The Messiah is to heal the sick by a word, restore sight to the blind, cast out devils, and raise even the dead." And here he desired Saul to read the particular prophecy giving the power of miracles to the Christ.

"If he restore the blind and raise the dead, I will doubt no longer," answered Saul.

There was, at this moment, an interruption caused by a noisy dispute in the court among some of John the Baptist's disciples, some of whom were disposed to acknowledge fully the superiority of Jesus; while others, still indulging the full fervor of their first conversion, stoutly contended for the transcendent greatness of him whom they regarded as their own Prophet. Rabbi Amos, as host, went out to put an end to these disputings, when Gamaliel retired to his chamber, and the conversation was not renewed.

Thus you see, my dear father, that even on the very day of these events by eye-witnesses themselves, there is much difference of opinion concerning who Jesus is; I do not expect you, who are so remote from the scene, and who know them only by report, to believe all at once, as I myself do. Will you write me, and tell me what view you take of all this subject, and what can be brought from the Scriptures to prove that Messias has not yet come?

The next morning, early, the people departed from the court where they had lodged; and when the sun was about an hour high, we also took saddle and rode to Jericho, where we passed the day with Miriam, the daughter of Joel, who was cousin to my mother. We found them in very great affliction, and they could not be comforted by any consolations which we could administer. It seems that her daughter Marah, or Mary, as they call her, had been so unfortunate, from her extraordinary beauty, as to attract the notice of Aemilius Lepidus, the Prefect of the Legion, who did honorably, though a Roman, and one of our conquerors, ask her in marriage of her parents. But they, being Hebrews, could not consent to such a union with a Gentile, and kept her with great strictness, so that he might never behold her again. But Marah, being very much devoted to the love of the noble Roman, and he being so attached to her, they met by stratagem, and she fled with him to the town of Magdala where he has a villa. She is, therefore, lost forever, to the faith of her fathers, by this simple flight with a Gentile lover, who, though he marry her according to Roman laws, doth not make her an honorable wife according to our own. This event was the cause of our finding the house of Miriam a house of mourning. It has produced great indignation among the Jews against the Romans. Mary was, I am told, the most beautiful maiden of the tribe of Benjamin, with golden brown hair that flowed to her very feet, and she was beloved by all who knew her. Thus I am disappointed in seeing her, as I hoped to have done; and the pearl armlet which you wished me to bestow upon her I still retain in my possession, a sorrowful memorial of the loved and lost.

Lazarus has returned to Bethany, where his occupation demands his attendance; but his friend, John remained with us, having agreed, with Lazarus, that he would go into the desert and not give up his search for the Divine Prophet, Jesus, until he had found him; for both young men feel as sad as if the had lost a beloved and honored brother. Your daughter,

ADINA.

LETTER XII.

My Dear Father: How shall I thank you for your forbearance with me, and your kind answers to all my letters, filled, as they are, with so many inquiries and opinions, which must surprise, and perhaps, displease you. You say that you have read all that I have written with impartiality, and that you do not marvel that "one whom you are pleased to call so imaginative and full of sensibility as myself, should be affected by what has passed under my observation in Judea." You nevertheless refuse, on your part, my dear father, to listen with the least approximation to belief to the extraordinary recital I have given you. You are pleased to question the reality of the voice at Jordan, and the presence of the dove of fire, and to refer it, as many others try to do who actually witnessed it, to an illusion of the senses. You are willing to admit that Jesus may be born at Bethlehem, for many whom you know "who are not prophets, neither sons of prophets, were born there." You are willing to admit that he "may be of the lineage of David, for David's descendants are as numerous as they are poor and obscure, yet they are not Messias, nor pretend to be Christs. You are content with doubting the accuracy of the memory of the mother of Lazarus, as to the scene in the Temple, though acknowledging you have often seen both Simeon and Anna in the Temple, and about the time stated by her. But your main objection to receiving John's evidence that this is the Christ, is, "that he is poor, of humble station, destitute of influence, received baptism of a man, when the Messiah was to be the baptized of God." "Who," you ask, "of the wise and the venerated, and the learned, and the aged, with years and experience; who of the doctors, and lawyers, and priests; who of the Scribes, and who of the Pharisees, and of the great men of Israel, are to unite in acknowledging as Him of whom Moses and the Prophets did write, as the central sun, around which all the dazzling prophecies of Esaias revolve; as the end and crown of the law; as the Lion of the tribe of Judah; as the Shiloh of the nations; as the Wonderful, the Counsellor, the mighty God and the Prince of Peace; as the glory of Israel, and the Joy of the whole Earth -- an obscure young man of thirty, unlearned in letters, the son of a carpenter, a citizen of Nazareth, a city proverbially mean, without name, character, power, rank, wealth, influence, or talents, and the last that was heard of whom was, that he had fled into the desert." You add, dear father, that this mere enumeration of what the true Christ ought to be, with the enumeration of what is wanting in this man, should be sufficient to convince me that I have given my sympathies and faith to one who has no claim to them. You say, further, "that you do not call my Messias an impostor, because, so far as you can learn, he has professed nothing, declared nothing, respecting himself. In silence he appeared, and in silence disappeared, none knowing whence or whither;" and you close your review of my history by saying, "that you shall wait for further development before you can give the subject your serious consideration."

In your next letter, where you again allude to the theme, you say, that if this prophet reappears, and from his own lips declares himself sent from God, and by an appeal to undisputed miracles, gives proof of his divine mission, declaring himself to be the Christ, you will then believe in Him, provided the whole of the prophecies can be shown to meet in his person.

On this ground, I am willing that the issue should be met, dearest father; and you add, with your usual candor, "that you will not hesitate to acknowledge as the Christ a man who fulfills all prophecy in his own person, though he come in a state and condition contrary to your preconceived notions of the character of the Messias; for that it would be safer for you to question the correctness of your own interpretation of the Messias prophecies hitherto, than the identity of one, in whom, without question, do meet all the golden threads of the predictions relating to the Christ." Here I am content, my dear father, to let it remain, being fully persuaded that though this humble young man, Jesus, hath come lowly and obscure, yet He will prove himself to the world that He is the true Messias, Christ of God.

Now, my dear father, let me resume the interesting subject, of which my letters have been so full; and, moreover, as you have desired me still to keep you informed of all that transpires touching Jesus of Nazareth, and as no theme upon which I can write is so pleasing to me, I will narrate all that I have heard since I last wrote to you.

It is now eight weeks since our return from Gilgal. For five weeks after we reached Jerusalem, we heard nothing of Jesus until John reappeared. He and Lazarus came into the city together, and to the house of Rabbi Amos. Our first inquiry was:

"Have you seen him? Have you heard anything from him?"

"John has seen him," answered Lazarus, seriously; "ask him and he will tell you all."

We looked at John, who sat sad and pensive, as if he were dwelling in his mind upon some painful, yet tender sorrow. The eyes of my cousin Mary, which always caught their luster from his, were shaded with an inquiring look of sympathy and solicitude.

"You are not well, I fear," she said, placing her fair hand upon his white brow, and putting back the hair from his temples. "You have been long away, and are weary and ill."

"Weary, Mary? I shall never complain of weariness again, after what I have beheld."

"What have you seen?" I asked.

"Jesus in the desert; and when I remember him there, I shall forget to smile more."

"You found him, then?" I eagerly asked.

"Yes, after days of painful search. I found him in the very center of the desert of Ashes, where foot of man had never trod before. I saw him upon his knees, and heard his voice in prayer. I laid down the sack of bread and fishes, and the skin of water I had brought with me to succor him, and with awe drew near where he stood."

"How did you find him there?" I asked, with that painful interest which exacts all details.

"By his footsteps in the sand and ashes. I saw where He sat down to rest, and where two nights he reposed upon the ground. I expected to find him perished, but each day I discovered his progressing footsteps, and followed them. As I now drew near him, I heard him groan in spirit, and He seemed to be borne down to the earth by some mortal agony. He seemed to be talking to some invisible evil beings who assailed him."

"Master, good master," I said, "I have brought thee food and water. Pardon me if I have intruded upon thy awful loneliness, which is sacred to some deep grief; but I weep with thee for thy woes, and in all thy afflictions I am afflicted. Eat, that thou mayest have strength to endure thy mysterious sufferings."

"He turned his pale countenance full upon me, and extended toward me his emaciated hands, while he smiled faintly, and blessed me and said:

"Son, thou art very dear to me. Thou shalt one day be afflicted for me, but not now, and understand wherefore I am now a sufferer in the desert."

"Let me remain with thee, Divine Messias, I said."

"Thou believest, then, that I am He?" he answered, regarding me with love.

"I replied by casting myself at his desert-parched feet, and bathing them with my tears. He raised me, and said, "Go thy way presently. When the time of my fasting and temptation is past, I will see thee again."

"Nay, I will not leave thee," I asserted.

"If thou lovest me, John, thou wilt obey me," he answered, with a tone of gentle reproof.

"But thou wilt first eat of the bread I have brought, and drink of the water," I entreated.

"Thou knowest not what temptation thou art offering to me," he replied sadly. "Thou hast not enough for thine own needs. Go, and leave me to gain the victory over Satan, for which I was led by the Spirit hither!"

"I once more cast myself at his feet, and He lifted me up, kissed me, and sent me away. You would not have known him. Worn to a skeleton by long abstinence, weak through suffering, He looked but the shadow of himself. He could not have lived if there had not been a divine power within to sustain him. His existence so long, for He had been at the desert five weeks without food, when I found him, was a miracle, proving the power of God to be in him!"

"For what mighty work among men is God preparing him?" said Rabbi Amos, with emotion. "Surely he is a Prophet come from God."

"Think you He is still alive?" I asked, with anxious fears.

"Yes," answered John, "I am come to tell you he was sustained through all, and after forty days He came forth from the wilderness, and suddenly presented himself on the banks of Jordan, among John's disciples. I was standing near John, discoursing of the Christ, and marveling when his exile to the desert would terminate, when the Prophet, lifting up his eyes, cried with a loud voice full of joy:"

"Behold the Lamb of God, upon whom the Spirit descended! He hath come forth from the furnace, like gold seven times tried in the fire! He it is who taketh away the sins of the world."

"I turned, and beheld Jesus advancing. He was pale, and wore an expression of gentle, uncomplaining suffering, on his benign countenance. His calm, chastened, dignified aspect, the serene composure and peace of his looks, awed me, while they caused me to love him. I hastened to meet him, and was kneeling in joy at his feet, when He embraced me as a brother, and said, "Faithful, and full of love, wilt thou follow me?"

"Whithersoever thou goest," I answered. "Where dwellest thou, Divine Master?" then asked one of John's disciples, Andrew by name, who was with me.

"Come and see," he answered and we went after him with joy unutterable, that we had at length found him.

"What passed between him and the Baptizer," asked Rabbi Amos, "at the river side, on this meeting?"

"Not a word. They met and parted like strangers, John going away across Jordan into the wilderness, as Jesus entered the village of Bethabara; and, approaching the house of a widow, where he abode, He went in, and we followed him, and took up our abode with him. Oh, how shall I be able to make known by words," added John, "the sweet expression of his discourse? In one day, in his presence, I grew wise; his words filled the soul like new wine, and made the heart glad. The next day He wished to go into Galilee, and so to Nazareth, where his mother dwelleth; and, as I had made up my mind to follow him as his disciple henceforth, I have only come hither to make known my purpose to Mary, to arrange my affairs in the city. Tomorrow I have again, to join this, my dear Lord, at Cana of Galilee."

"Oh, happy, and to be envied, friend and brother," said Lazarus. "How gladly would I go also, and be one of his disciples! but the care of my mother and sisters cometh upon me, and I must deny myself the happiness of being ever near this divine man, and listening to the heavenly wisdom that flows from his lips. How blind I have been, not to have discovered, under his gentle and loving character, and unobtrusive wisdom, the Messias. Truly, he was among us, and we knew him not."

"Canst thou divine at all his purpose?" asked Rabbi Amos of John, "whether he intends to found a school of wisdom, to preach like the prophets, to reign like David, or to conquer like his warrior namesake, Joshua!"

"I know not save that he said He came to redeem that which was lost, and to establish a kingdom that shall have no end!"

Upon hearing this, all our hearts bounded with hope and confidence in him, and we altogether burst forth into a voice of thanksgiving, and sang this hymn of praise:

"O sing unto the Lord a new song: for he hath done marvelous things: his right hand and his holy arm hath gotten the victory.

The Lord hath made known his salvation: his righteousness hath He openly shewed in the sight of the heathen.

He hath remembered his mercy and his truth towards the house of Israel: all the ends of the earth have seen the salvation of our God.

Make a joyful noise unto the Lord, all the earth: make a loud noise, and rejoice, and sing his praise.

Sing unto the Lord with the harp: with the harp and the voice of psalm.

With trumpet and sound of cornet make a joyful noise before the Lord, the King."

There was this morning no little excitement produced among the Chief Priests by a formal inquiry sent by Pilate to Caiaphas, the High Priest, asking whether this new prophet was to be acknowledged by them as their Messiah, "for if he is to be, it will be my duty," said the Governor, "to place him under arrest, inasmuch as we understand the Jewish Messiah is to declare himself king!" Upon this, there was a tumultuous assembling together of the Priests in the porch of the Temple, and with many invectives, they agreed to send answer to Pilate that they did not acknowledge Jesus of Nazareth to be the Christ. They were led to this the more urgently, inasmuch as they feared an arrest of Jesus would give the Romans occasion for arresting other Jews, and so bring on the nation great troubles; just as a few years ago, when a certain impostor rose up and called himself the Christ, the Romans were not satisfied with taking and destroying him, but they punished with fines every city in Judah. Therefore, the Priests both denied to the Procurator any knowledge of Jesus, and entreated him not to pay any attention to him, till, indeed, he should find that he openly took the lead of armed men. What Pilate will conclude to do, I know not. Rabbi Amos informed us that the Procurator had got some news by a courier that morning, that Jesus, on his way to Cana, had been followed by full a thousand people, who, having recognized him as having been him baptized of John in Jordan, hailed him as the Christ.

Thus, you see, my dear father, that this divine person is already taking hold of the hearts of the people, and arousing the jealousy of our enemies. Be assured that the day will come when He will lift up his standard to the Gentiles, and draw all men unto Him. The developments of his power are daily taking place; and although He has yet performed no such miracle as would be deemed by you a test of his divine mission, yet I have no doubt that in due time He will give this proof, and all other needful manifestations, that He is the Christ of God.

Your loving   ADINA.

LETTER XIII.

My Dear Father: I have received your last letter by the Cairo merchant, Heber, the son of Malachial, and having read it to Rabbi Amos, he said, after careful reflection thereupon, that he could not agree with you in your opinion touching the undimmed glory of Messiah, viz.: "that he is to come as a King, and Mighty Leader of Hosts, and reign and prosper, and rule the earth, King of the kings of the earth." He desires me to ask you what is meant by "Messias being a man of sorrows and acquainted with grief," as prophesied of him; and how you interpret, dear father, other than as referring to a violent end, the words of the wise Daniel, "And after threescore and two weeks shall Messiah be cut off, but not for himself?" Uncle also desires me to ask you to examine into the time named by Daniel, when Messiah, the Prince, is to come, and take note that we live in the day of the close of the threescore and two weeks, whereof the prophet writeth and saith, "Know, therefore, and understand, that from the going forth of the commandment to restore and to build Jerusalem unto Messiah the Prince, shall be seven weeks and threescore and two weeks." Rabbi Amos says, the time for the appearing of Christ is come, as all must confess who read the Prophets; and the only reason Jesus is not believed to be he, is that he comes in poverty and humility, fasting and suffering. But, my dear father, may it not be ordained that He shall come in lowliness and end in power? Oh, that you could have the faith in Jesus of Nazareth, that He is Messias, that I have, dearest and most honored father! Since I last wrote you, my faith has been confirmed by the testimony, which in one of your letters you demanded. You said, "let me hear that he has done an authentic miracle in attestation of the divinity of his mission, such a miracle as was prophesied Messias shall do, as healing the sick by a word, restoring the blind to sight, and raising the dead, and I will prepare to believe in him."

A miracle he has performed, dear father, and one, the genuineness of which is not disputed by anyone. I can give you the particulars best by extracting from a letter written by John to Mary, a few days after his departure to join Jesus at

107

Nazareth; for John has joined himself to him, and become his disciple.

"Upon reaching Nazareth," says the letter, "I was guided to the humble dwelling occupied by the mother of Jesus, by a large concourse of people gathered about it, of whom inquiring, I learned that it was to see the new Prophet they had assembled. What new prophet? I asked, wishing to know what the multitude thought of Jesus."

"The One John of the wilderness foretold." answered ones.

"They say he is Messias," replied another.

"He is the Christ," boldly asserted the third.

Hereupon, a Levite, standing by, said scornfully, "Does Christ come out of Galilee? You read the prophets to little purpose, if you see therein any Christ prophesied to come out of Nazareth of Galilee." Hereupon, seeing the faith of many staggered, I said, "Brethren, Christ is truly of Bethlehem and verily Jesus, though he dwelleth in this place, was born in Bethlehem." "Thou canst not prove it, man," said the Levite angrily. "The stranger speaketh truly," spoke up both an old man and a gray-haired woman in the crowd; "we know that he was not born here, and that when his parents moved here, when he was an infant, they then said he was born in Bethlehem. We all remember this well."

Hereupon, the Levite, seeing that he had not the people with him, passed on his way, while I went to the door of the house where Jesus dwelt with his mother. There were two doors, one of which led into a workshop, where I noticed the bench and tools of the occupation at which he toiled to support himself and his mother. This sight made me half question whether he who was an humble artisan, whose tools and shop I saw before me, could in truth be the Christ of God, the Prince Messias whom all the patriarchs and prophets looked forward to with the eye of faith, desiring to see his day! and it required the recalling of the wonderful scenes of his baptism, the holy dove and voice of God, and his miraculous preservation in the wilderness, to revive my assurance; but when, as I entered the dwelling, I saw him standing, teaching those who hung on his lips, and listened to his calm voice, and heard the sublime wisdom of his instructions, beheld the dignity of his aspect, and the heavenly benignity of his manner. I forgot the carpenter, I forgot the man, and seemed to behold in Him only Messiah the Prince, the Son of God.

Upon beholding me, he extended his hand, and received me

graciously, and said, pointing to five men who stood near him, regarding him with mingled love and reverence, "These are thy brethren, who have also come out of the world to follow me."

Of these, one was Andrew, who was, as well as myself, John's disciple, and we were talking with him when Jesus came forth out of the wilderness. Another was Andrew's brother, whose name is Simon, who, hearing his brother speak of Jesus as the Christ, had gone with him to see him; and had no sooner beheld him than he joined himself to him; and Jesus, from the firmness and immovable zeal of his character, which He seemed to understand, called him also Peter, or Stone. The fourth disciple was of Bethsaida, the city of Andrew and Peter. His name was Philip, and he followed Jesus from having been prepared by John the Baptist to receive him. He was, however, so overjoyed at finding the Christ, that he ran to the house of his brother Nathaniel, and finding him in his garden, beneath a fig tree, at prayer, exclaimed, "We have found Him of whom Moses in the law and the prophets did write, the Messias of God!" "Where is He, that I may behold Him?" asked his brother, rising. "It is Jesus of Nazareth, the son of Joseph," Philip answered. Upon hearing this answer, the countenance of Nathaniel fell, and he replied, "Can there any good thing come out of Nazareth?" "Come thou, and see for thyself," answered Philip. Nathaniel then went with him where Jesus was. When Jesus saw him approaching, he said to those about him, "Behold an Israelite, indeed, in whom there is no guile!" "Whence thou knowest me?" asked Nathaniel, with surprise, for he had heard the words which were spoken. Jesus answered, and said, "Before Philip called thee, when thou wast under the fig tree, I saw thee." Upon hearing this, Nathaniel, who knew that he was all alone in his garden, and unseen at prayer, when his brother came, regarded the serene face of Jesus steadfastly, and then, as if he beheld therein the expression of divinity, he cried before all the people, "Rabbi, Thou art the Son of God! Thou art the King of Israel!" Jesus looked upon him as if pleased at his confession, and said, "Because I said unto thee, I saw thee under the fig tree, believest thou? Thou shalt see greater things than these. Verily, verily, I say unto you, hereafter ye shall see heaven open, and the angels of God ascending and descending upon the Son of Man."

These four, Andrew and Peter, Philip and Nathaniel, were then present in the house with him and, to my surprise and joy, with them stood my own brother James, whom Jesus had seen on the lake in his boat, and called him, when James left all and followed him. Thus we were six disciples in all, bound to him by ties of confidence and love. The mother of Jesus, a noble and matronly woman, still beautiful, and with a face of the holiest serenity, was present, and gazed with love and tenderness upon her Son, listening to his words, as if she also would learn of him that wisdom which hath descended upon him from above. The next day James and I went to the sea of Tiberias, but two hours' distant, to see our father Zebedee, and transfer our interests to him, and, during the afternoon, Jesus passed near the shore on his way to Cana, when, calling us, we left our ships with our father and joined him. His mother, and many of her kinsfolk were of the company, all going to a marriage of the cousin of the family. Upon our arrival at Cana, we were ushered into the guest-chamber, and Jesus, in particular, was received with marked respect by the Hebrew master of the house, though he was an officer in the service of the Romans. We here met Elizabeth, the mother of John the Baptizer, who is a relative of Mary, the mother of Jesus. The meeting between them was very touching.

"Ah," said the mother of the prophet, as she looked upon Jesus, who was talking with the governor of the feast, "How blessed art thou, O Mary, to have thy son ever with thee! while I am a mother, and yet no mother. The son whom God gave me He hath taken from me to be his prophet, and he is to me as if he were dead! Since his twelfth year he has been in the wilderness, knowing no man, until six months ago he came forth to proclaim the advent of thy holy Son!"

The marriage feast at length commenced. The wine which should have come from Damascus had not arrived, the caravan having been delayed by the insurrection near Cesarea. The guests had, therefore, but little wine, and the chief ruler of the town presiding at the feast, seeing that the wine had given out, bade the servants to place more upon the board. The mother of Jesus, who knew that the wine was out, turning to him, said, "They have no wine!" for it seems that she knew the power that was within him, though he had not yet manifested it openly. I sat next to him, and heard her when she whispered to Jesus. He looked grave, and said with a slight tone of respectful reproof, and applying to her that title, which we in Judea believe most honorable of all others, "Woman," he said, "what have I to do with thy private requests for the exercise of my power? You wish me to perform a miracle before this noble company, that they may behold and believe on me. Mine hour for manifesting my glory to men is not yet come, nevertheless, in obedience to thy wish, my honored mother, I will do what thou desires me to do."

She then thanked him with deep emotion, and turned to the servants and beckoned to them, while her cheek borrowed a rich color from her hidden joy, and her eyes kindled with the feelings of a mother about to see her son display powers such as only come by the gift of God, and which were to seal Him as a prophet, before the eyes of Jew and Gentile. For myself, Mary, not anticipating, or suspecting what was to take place, I regarded the nervous emotions of the joyful mother with marvel. When two or three of the servants approached, she said to them:

"Whatsoever He saith to you, do it."

They then fixed their regards upon him, awaiting his commands, as little suspecting what they would be as I did. The face of Jesus, ever calm and dignified, now seemed to express a certain consciousness of power within, that awed me. Casting his eyes upon several stone vases, which stood by the door, empty, he said to them:

"Fill the water-pots with water."

In the court, in full sight from the table, was a well, to which the servants went with jars, which I saw them fill with water, bear in upon their heads, and pour it out into the water-pots until they had filled them all, six in number. While this was going on, the governor of the feast was relating to the guests, and fixing their attention, as well as his own how Herod and Pontius Pilate had recently become enemies, because the latter, on his way from Cesarea Philippi to Jerusalem, to be present with his forces during the weeks of the Passover, having come to a caravansera at night, which was occupied by Herod and his bodyguard, turned them out to make room for his own, saying that a Roman Procurator was more honorable than a Jewish King of Galilee. "It will be long," added the governor, as the last water-pot was filled, "before this quarrel will be made up between them. But we talk, my friends, and forget our wine."

"Draw out now, and bear unto the governor of the feast," said Jesus to the servants.

They obeyed, and pouring rich, blood-red wine into the jars which I and others had seen filled up with water from the well, the amazed servants bore it to the chief of the feast. He had no sooner filled his goblet and tasted it, than he called to the bride-groom, who sat in the middle of the table, and said:

"Every man, at the beginning, doth set forth good wine, and when men have well drunk, then that which is worse, but thou hast kept the good wine until now."

"Who hath brought this wine?" asked the bride-groom, drinking of the water that was made wine. "Whence it came, sir, I know not."

Then the servants and others told that they had filled the six water-pots with water to the brim, at the command of Jesus, and that when they drew out, behold, it flowed forth wine instead of water. Upon this there was a general exclamation of surprise; and the governor of the feast crying out, "A Prophet hath been among us, and we knew it not," rose to approach and do honor to Jesus; but he had already conveyed himself away, rising, and passing out through the door, and sought the solitude of the garden. Thither I followed him, and worshiping him, sat at his feet and listened to him, while he unfolded to me wonderful things concerning himself, showing that he is truly the Son of God, and the very Christ. But these things I cannot speak to thee of now, for I do not clearly understand all that he is to be, save that I know he is destined to suffer, and to be exalted. "Doubt not," concludes the letter to Mary, "doubt not that Jesus is the Christ. His miracle at Cana, of turning water into wine, is a public display of his divine power. All men at the feast have believed on Him, and his fame is spreading abroad throughout Galilee and Samaria. He has told me privately that he must soon visit Jerusalem and he will there openly proclaim his mission as the Christ of God."

In this manner, my dear father, writes the betrothed husband of my cousin Mary; and I have given you the extract from this letter, in order that you may see that Jesus is already attracting great attention, that he has disciples, and that he is by no means poor, who has the power to convert wells of water into wine. From this letter, you must perceive that Jesus is, at least, a Prophet, equal to Elijah, who kept full the cruse of the widow of Zarephath. If, therefore, you acknowledge this much, you must confess that he is a good man. Now, a good man will not lie. Yet, Jesus hath said to John that He is the Christ! How, then, dear father, can anyone deny, who believes him to be a prophet, that he is more than a prophet, even

Messias? Pardon your daughter for thus presuming to reason with you, but I am so earnest that you should believe, that I sometimes forget the daughter in the disciple of Jesus. As for my uncle, the good and learned Rabbi Amos, he is more than half his disciple and I have no doubt that when Jesus shall present himself in Jerusalem, and he can see him, and hear his divine teachings, he will cast off all prejudice and become his follower.

The rumor of the miracle at Cana has reached Jerusalem since I began this letter, and I hear that it has produced no little excitement in the market-places and courts of the Temple. Rabbi Amos, on his return from sacrifice, a few minutes ago, said that he saw more than thirty priests, with rolls of the Prophets in their hands, engaged in looking up the prophecies of Christ. So, my dear father, you see that the young man "who came," as you remarked, "no one knew whence, and went no one knew whither," is already taking hold of the attention of Israel, and stirring up the minds of all men to investigate his claim to be the Christ.

Your affectionate daughter,

ADINA.

LETTER XIV.

MY DEAR FATHER: You will not require the testimony of my letters to enable you to appreciate the fame of the wonderful young man of Nazareth, Jesus, who is daily proving himself a Prophet, indeed, and mighty before God, showing all the people that God is with Him. Not a stranger cometh into Jerusalem who does not bring report of some new miracle which He hath done, some wonderful manifestation of his power. He still delays coming to Jerusalem, but is engaged in preaching the coming of the kingdom of David and of God on earth, teaching in the synagogues, and showing from the Prophets that He is truly the Messias. And his fame for wisdom, for knowledge of the Scriptures, for power to teach, and for miracles, has gone abroad through all Syria, so that they bring to him sick persons, both rich and poor, even from Damascus, to be healed of him; and he heals all who are brought unto him, whether possessed of devils, lunatic, or having the palsy. His footsteps are attended by thousands, wheresoever he goes, and even the Governor of Philippi, in his chariot, hath mingled in the throng, and kneeling at his feet, asked the health of his son, who was palsied; and his son was healed by him, by a word, though many leagues distant. While I now write, a company is passing by the open window, bearing upon beds two wealthy men of Jerusalem, who have been given over by their physicians, who are going to him to be cured; for all Jerusalem talks of nothing else than the wonderful miracles of Christ. There was a man who wove baskets, who has occupied a stall opposite our house for many years. He had lost entirely the use of his legs, for twelve years, and had to be carried to and fro. Hearing of the fame of Jesus, he was seized with a strong desire to have him perform a miracle upon him. For this purpose he begged money from the priests, as they went by to the Temple, but though some gave, all laughed, saying that he could not be cured, inasmuch as one of his limbs was withered. But the man had faith, and having begged money enough for his journey from the benevolent, hired two men to convey him five days' journeying into Galilee. At the end of three weeks he returned, walking upright, and well in body and limbs! All the city flocked to behold him and he related that how when he had reached Capernaum, where Jesus was, the crowd was so great that his bearers could not for some time get near him. At length, Jesus moved on, healing the files of sick as he passed through them, at a word. "Seeing me," said the man, "he fixed his eyes upon me, and said, calling me by name:

"Great is thy faith. As thou hast believed, be it done unto thee."

"Immediately my legs and ankle bones received strength; I leaped from the litter to the ground, and found that I was whole, without pain or illness. I would have fallen at his feet in ecstasy of joy, but the crowds which pressed him separated me from the sight of him. But I filled the air with shouts and hallelujahs to the Son of David!"

This man, my dear father, I now see daily, moving about, sound in limb and health; but this one instance is but one of a thousand. John, who follows Jesus everywhere he goes, and is a witness of all that he does and teaches, writes to Mary, that "the sick and afflicted from all parts of the land of Galilee, from Decapolis, from Jerusalem, from beyond Jordan, even from Lesser Asia, come to him. When my beloved master," he writes, "comes forth from a synagogue, where he has been reading the Prophets to the people, who hear him gladly, I have beheld two hundred persons, the lame, the palsied, the withered, the blind, the possessed of devils, and persons afflicted with all manners of diseases, laid in rows before the gate of the synagogue, awaiting his coming forth. Those who bore them were standing eager, expectant groups near them. It was a painful, yet sublime spectacle, to behold the hollow eyes of those wretched sufferers, turned toward the door as the people came running forth, shouting, "He comes! He comes!" The writhing torments of the possessed with devils ceased for the moment, and groans gave way to expecting silence. Jesus at length appears, and upon seeing his face, that ever expresses holy benignity and innate power, they set up touching cries of the most thrilling appeal for his aid, and such appeals are never uttered in vain. Going through the rows of beds and litters, He lays his hand upon some, speaks a word to others, touches the eyes of the blind and the ears of the deaf, lays his hand gently upon the head of the lunatic, and commands in tones of authority, the devils to leave the bodies of the possessed. And what is extraordinary," continues John, "the devils always conduct themselves with more terrific violence as he draws near, and while they leave the man with curses, they confess loudly that Jesus is the Son of David -- the Son of God! and implore him, in the most abject manner, not utterly to destroy them!

"So great is the multitude which everywhere follows him, that he is often compelled to withdraw from them by stealth, to get to some by-place of quiet, where he can refresh his wearied strength for a few days. At such times we, who are his immediate followers, have the benefit of his teaching and private instructions. But he cannot remain long away from the people. They soon penetrate his retirement, and he never can refuse their appeals to his miraculous powers to do them good. How wonderful is he who thus holds in his hand divine power! The power of kings is nothing before that which he possesses in his voice yet; he is serene, humble, oh, how humble! to our shame, and always calm and gentle. He spends much time in private prayer to God, whom he always addresses as his Father."

"Never was such a man on earth. We, who know him most intimately, stand most in awe of him; yet, with our deep reverence for his holy character is combined the purest affection. In one and the same breath, I feel that I adore him as my Lord, and love him, even as my brother. So we all feel toward him. His engaging manners, his patience with our ignorance, his forbearance with our grossness, his ready excuses for us when we are in fault, ere we have time to exculpate ourselves, all have bound us to him with ties that can never be sundered. When I next write to you," continues John, "I will relate to you, so far as they are understood by me and my fellow-disciples, the things which he reveals respecting himself and the object of his mission on earth. Some things, however, are not comprehended by us, but he promises that we shall by and by understand what now appears obscure to us."

Such, my dear father, is the tenor of the letters which my cousin Mary receives from John, the disciple of Jesus. They are all filled with accounts of his miracles, of his teachings, and of his journeying. When we shall see Jesus at Jerusalem, I shall be able, from personal observation, to write to you more particularly concerning his doctrines and miracles. That He is the Christ, thousands now believe; for they ask, very naturally, how could he do these things unless God were with him? What is also of importance, it has been proven by the results of the examination made by some of the scribes of the Temple, that he was truly born in Bethlehem, and that both his mother, Mary, and Joseph, her husband, are lineally descended of the house of David. Moreover, Phineas, the venerable priest, whom you know, hath borne testimony to the fact, that when Jesus was an infant, during the reign of the elder Herod, there arrived in Jerusalem three eminent princes, men of wisdom and learning. One of these came from Persia; one from the Grecian province of Media and one from Arabia; and brought with them gifts of gold and spices, and were attended by retinues. These three princes reached Jerusalem the same day by three different ways, and entered by three different gates, each unknowing the other's presence or object, till they met in the city before Herod's palace. One represented himself descended from Shem, another from Japhet, the third from Ham. The king hearing that these three strangers had arrived in Jerusalem, he sent to know wherefore they had honored his kingdom with a visit. "They answered," says Phineas, as he yesterday related the narrative in the presence of Caiaphas, and many of the rulers and Pharisees, "that they came to do homage to the young Prince, who was born King of the Jews." And when Herod asked what prince they spoke of, they answered, "We have seen his star in the East, and are come to worship him!"

"How know you the star you have seen indicates the birth of a Prince of Judea?" demanded King Herod, greatly troubled at what he heard.

"It had a motion toward this city," they answered, "and we have been led by a heavenly impulse to follow it, and lo, it has led us to Jerusalem, over which, were it now night, you would see it suspended, burning with the glory of a planet; and it hath been revealed to us that it is the star of the birth of one who is to reign King of Judah! Tell us, therefore, oh, king, where this august Prince is now to be found, that we may worship him!"

"Hereupon," says Phineas, "the King issued an edict for all the chief priests and scribes of the people to assemble in the councils chamber of high palace. He then addressed them:

"Ye, to whom is given the care of the Books of the Law and of the Prophets, whose study they are, and in whom lies the skill to interpret the prophecies, search therein, and tell me truly where the Christ is to be born. Behold here present these august and wise men, who have come from afar to do Him homage; nay, more, as they aver, to worship Him as God.

Let us have the courtesy to give them the answer that they seek, and let us not be found more ignorant of these things than those who dwell in other lands!"

Several of the Chief Priests then rose and said, "It is known, oh, king, to all who are Jews, and who read the Prophets, that Messiah cometh to the house of David, of the town of Bethlehem for thus it is written by the prophet: And thou, Bethlehem, in the land of Judah, art not least among the Princes of Judah, for out of thee shall come a Governor that shall rule my people, Israel!"

"This question being thus decided," continued Phineas, "Herod dismissed the council, and, retiring to his own private room, sent to the three princes of the East to inquire of them what time the star appeared. And when they had named the very day and hour on which they had first seen it, he was thereby enabled to arrive at the probable age of the infant. He then said to them:

"You have my permission, noble strangers, to go to Bethlehem, and search for the young child; and when ye have found him, bring me word again, that I may come and worship him also; for it is but meet that we should pay all possible honors to a Prince of our realm, whose birth is heralded in so unusual a manner, and to worship whom even the East sends forth her wise men." They then left the presence of Herod, and, it being dark when they left the palace, they were overjoyed to behold the star which they saw in the East, going before them. They followed it until it left Jerusalem by the Bethlehem gate, and it led them on to the town of Bethlehem, and stopped above a humble dwelling therein. When they were come into the house, they saw a ray of the star resting upon the head of an infant in the arms of its mother, Mary, the wife of Joseph. They at once acknowledged and hailed him as Prince and King of Israel, and falling down, worshiped him; and opening their treasures they presented unto him gold, frankincense, and myrrh, gifts that are offered on the altar to God alone!"

When Phineas was asked by Caiaphas how he knew this fact, he answered, that he, himself, prompted by curiosity to see the Prince they had come to worship, had followed them out of the palace of Herod, out of the gate, and even into Bethlehem, and witnessed their prostrations and offerings to the infant child of Mary. "And," he added, "if this be doubted, there are many Jews now living in Jerusalem, and a certain slaughter, by Herod's command, of the infants of Bethlehem; for this captain Jeremias led on the soldiers."

"And wherefore this slaughter? asked Caiaphas, "It is not on record."

"Kings do not record their deeds of violence," answered Phineas. "Herod kept it hushed up when he found that he gained nothing by it but hatred. He slew them, in order that the infant Jesus might be destroyed among them, for the three wise men, instead of returning through Jerusalem to their own country, and informing him where they had found the child, departed by another way; and when Herod found that they were gone, he became so enraged, that he sent out a party of troops, under Jeremias, their captain, who now liveth to testify, ordering them to slay every child under two years of age in Bethlehem, hoping, as I have said, to kill the infant Jesus among the number. But the child escaped, doubtless, by God's powerful protection; and his fame in his manhood this day fills the ears of all Israel. The adoration of these three men, who were sons of Shem, Ham, and Japhet, represents the homage of the whole race of mankind that shall yet be paid to Him!"

"Dost thou believe in him, also?" asked Caiaphas, with angry surprise, looking sternly on Phineas.

"I will first see, and hear him speak; and if he appear to me to be Messias, I will gladly worship Him."

"Hereupon," said Rabbi Amos, who gave me the details of the foregoing interview between Caiaphas and Phineas, "there arose a great uproar, some crying that Jesus was the Christ, and others, that Phineas should be stoned to death."

Thus, you see, my dear father, how the evidence increases in value and importance, proving Jesus to be the Messiah. His very cradle bears testimony to his divine character; and, surely, do his miracles now confirm the pledge given by the remarkable circumstances attending his childhood. The captain Jeremias, now a gray-headed old soldier, having been called upon, testifies that he obeyed such an order of Herod, and that it was given within three days after the three Princes of the East quitted Jerusalem for Bethlehem. Now, my dear father, let me sum up the evidences that Jesus is the Messiah. First, his presentation in the Temple, when holy Simeon and Anna worshiped and prophesied of him. Secondly, the star which led the wise men to Bethlehem. Thirdly, their adoration of him in his cradle. Fourthly, the testimony of John the Baptist. Fifthly, the voice of God at his baptism. Sixthly, the descent of the Holy Ghost upon him in the form of a dove. Seventhly, his miracle at Cana of Galilee. And, lastly, the glittering coronet of miracles that now encircles his brow, shedding a light and glory upon his path that blinds and dazzles the eye steadfastly to behold. Tell me, dear father, is not this the Christ?

Your affectionate and loving

ADINA.

LETTER XV.

My Dear Father: The inquiry you made in your last letter, "What hath become of John of Jordan, since the fame of Jesus hath so far eclipsed his own?" I can answer, but with sadness. Your inquiry seems to infer that he would feel envious of the power and the miracles that distinguish his Successor. But, on the contrary, John always plainly declared in his preaching, that "he was not worthy to unloose the shoe latchet of Him who was to come after him;" and he distinctly said many times to all, that "He to whom I bear witness must increase, but I must decrease!" The mission on which John came terminated when Jesus came. Soon afterward he left the wilderness, and entered Jericho, where Herod was then dwelling. Here he preached in the public places, and in the market, and on the very steps of the palace, that God's judgments were coming upon the earth, and that men must, by repentance, appease his wrath and that Christ would be the Judge of men! Now, while he was thus speaking to the people, and the officers and soldiers of the Tetrarch's guard, Herod himself came forth upon the balcony to listen, for he had heard much of John, and had long a desire to hear him. The prophet no sooner beheld him, than he boldly addressed him, and sternly reproved him for the sin of having married the widow of his brother Philip, contrary to the law. Now, Herod, it is said, did not show resentment at this plain dealing, and inviting the prophet into his hall, talked much with him and in parting, offered him gifts, which John refused to touch. The next day he sent for him again, to ask him some questions touching the Messias whom he preached. Now, Herodia, when it was reported to her how that the prophet had publicly spoken against her marriage with Herod, became every angry; and when she found that John was still favored by her husband, she sent for Herod, and said, "that if he would please, her he must throw the prophet of Jordan into prison." Herod would have excused him, asserting that he was a man of God; but Herodia only the more vehemently insisted that he should be cast into prison. At length Herod yielded, against his own will, and gave orders for the arrest of the prophet, who the same night was thrown into the ward of the castle. When this intelligence reached the followers of John, it created great sorrow; and many went to see him and talk with him. But he told them they must think of him no longer that his short stay was drawing to its close; but that they must turn their eyes toward the Christ the Sun of Righteousness, whose rising was unto an everlasting day. "Said I not unto ye," he asked of them, "He must increase and I must decrease?" For some weeks this holy man, whose only offense was that he had courage to reprove sin in high places, remained in prison, while Herod each day sought to find some excuse for releasing him without displeasing Herodia, of whose anger he stood in great fear, he being an abject slave to his love for her. At length the birthday of Herod arrived, and he conveyed word to John that in honor of the day he would send and fetch him out of prison, so soon as he should obtain the consent of his wife, which he believed she would accord to him on such an anniversary.

Now, after the feast, Philippa, the daughter of Herodia and of her former husband Philip, came in and danced before Herod; and being beautiful in person and full of grace in every motion, she so pleased her stepfather that he made oath, having drunk much wine with his guests, that he would give her whatever she would ask, were it the half of his kingdom. Her mother then called to her, and whispered to her imperatively:

"Give me," said the maiden, turning toward Herod, asking what her mother had commanded, "the head now of John Baptist in a charger."

The king no sooner heard this request than he turned pale, and said fiercely:

"Thy mother hath been tampering with thine ears, girl." Herodia, however, betrayed no confusion, but sat unconcerned. Herod, it is said by those who were present, hesitated a long time, and at length said: "Ask half of my kingdom and I will give it thee but let me not shed blood on my birthday."

"Wilt thou falsify thine oath?" asked his wife scornfully

"For mine oath's sake, and for these who have heard it, I will grant thy desire," he at length answered, with a sigh of regret and self-reproach. He then turned to the captain of the guard, and commended him to slay John Baptist in prison, and bring presently there his head upon a charger.

At the end of a quarter of an hour, which was passed by Herod in great excitement, walking up and down the floor, and by his guests in silent expectation, the door opened, and the captain of the guard entered, followed by the executioner, who carried a brazen platter upon which lay the gory head of the eloquent forerunner of Christ. "Give it to her!" cried Herod sternly, waving him toward the beautiful, but cruel and heartless maiden, who stood near the inner door. The executioner placed the charger in her hands and, without turning pale, but with a smile of triumph, she bore it to her mother, who had retired to an inner chamber. It is said, that no sooner did she behold it, than she spat in the face, and setting it up before her, reviled it. His disciples, when they heard of his death, came to Herod and asked the body of John, and taking it away, buried it; but when they would have asked the head also of Herodia, she answered, "that she had given it to her dogs to devour!" So terrible can be the revenge of a woman who fears not God!

All the disciples of the murdered prophet then went where Jesus was preaching and healing, and told him what had been done to John. "When Jesus heard of the death of John he was very sorrowful," writes John, his disciple, to Mary, "and went away into a desert place apart, in order to mourn over the fate of his bold and holy forerunner." In the meanwhile the disciples of John Baptist, believing that the murder of their prophet was but the first blow of a general slaughter, fled into the deserts, and sought Jesus to protect and counsel them. At length he found himself surrounded by a great multitude, who had fled from the cities, chiefly of John's disciples, besides many who came to hear him preach, and be healed of him. The place was a desert, and far from any town. Forgetful of all else, save following Jesus, they were without food. "Which," says John, writing to Rabbi Amos, "we who were his disciples seeing, suggested that Jesus should send them away to the village to buy themselves victuals. But Jesus answered us and said quietly:

"They need not go away, give ye them to eat."

And Simon said, "Master, where can we get bread for so many? There is verily here an army to be fed, and we have among us but five loaves and two small fishes." Upon hearing this Jesus said, "It is enough; bring them hither to me."

We collected the bread and fishes, and I, myself, laid them upon a rock before Jesus. He then said to us, "Command the multitude to sit down on the grass." And when they were all seated he took the five loaves, and laying his hands upon them and upon the two fishes, he looked up to heaven and blessed them; and then breaking them into fragments, he gave them to us, his disciples, and bade us distribute to the people. As often as we would return for more, we found the loaves and the fishes undiminished, and I saw with wonder how when he would break off a piece of one of the fishes, or of a loaf, the same part would immediately be seen thereon as if it had not been separated; and in this manner he continued to break and distribute to us for nearly an hour, until all ate as much as they would, and were filled; and when no one demanded more, and he ceased to break, he commanded us to gather up the fragments which lay by his side, which he had piled up about him as rapidly as he broke them off, and there were twelve baskets full, over and above what was needed. The number that were thus miraculously fed was about five thousand men, besides nearly an equal number of women and children. And this mighty prophet, who could thus feed an army, voluntarily suffered forty days and nights the pangs of hunger in the desert! He seems both a man in suffering, and a God in creating!"

This wonderful miracle, my dear father, is one that has too many witnesses to be denied. He who could feed five thousand could feed all men! Must not He then, who could feed all mankind, be divine? Surely, this must be the son of God! If I should mention to you all the miracles which have been done by him, I should fill many letters. Not a day passes that we do not hear of some more extraordinary exhibition of his power than the preceding. Every morning, when men meet in the marketplaces, or in the courts of the Temple, the first inquiry is, "what new wonder has he performed? Have you heard of another miracle of this mighty Prophet?" Indeed, so great is the interest here felt to see Jesus and witness his miracles, that where one went to hear John preach in the wilderness of Jordan, ten go to see Christ in Galilee. The priests alone are offended, and speak evil of him through envy. They say that he draws off people from the sacrifices; that he is preaching another law than that of Moses; that he eats with sinners; that he enters the houses of Samaritans; and that he loveth Galilee rather than Jerusalem, which they contend, is an evidence that he is not the Christ who was "to come to the Temple and send forth his law from Jerusalem."

They have even gone so far as to assert that he performs his miracles by magic and the aid of Beelzebub, the Prince of the devils. "If we suffer him to take men's minds as he doth," said Caiaphas to Rabbi Amos yesterday, when he heard that Jesus had walked on the sea to join his disciples in their ship, and stilled a tempest with a word, "the worship in the Temple will be at an end, and the sacrifice will cease. He draweth all men unto him."

Herod having, as I have said, slain John, and hearing soon after of the fame of Jesus, said to Herodia: "This is John Baptist risen from the dead, and therefore do mighty works show forth themselves in him."

"If he rises from the dead threescore and ten times, I will have his head," answered Herodia; whereon Herod privately sent to Jesus, supposing him to be John Baptist, to keep in the parts of Galilee where he was. The Levites and Scribes of the city contend that he is Elias, who it is prophesied must come and restore all things before Messias. Others believe that he is Isaiah, or Jeremiah, raised from the dead; and some say one thing, and others another thing. They are willing to believe Jesus to be everything but that which he is, viz., the true Christ, Son of the Highest.

You have asked, dear father, in your letter, "Where is Elias who is to precede Messias, according to the Prophet Malachi?" This question Jesus himself has answered, says John, when some Rabbis put it to him. He answered them thus:

"Elias has come already, and ye have done unto him whatsoever ye listed.'

"Dost thou speak of John the Baptist?" asked those about him when they heard this.

"John came in the spirit and power of Elias, and therefore was he thus called by the prophet," was the answer of Jesus.

I have written you mainly of the miracles of Jesus, dear father, as being evidence conclusive of his divine power and authority to teach and restore Israel. I have said little of his teaching, as I have not yet heard him but I have heard those who have listened to him repeat much that he has taught them. Such words of wisdom, such pureness of teaching, such holy precepts, and divine instruction, never fell from lips of man. Oh, when shall I be so blessed as to hear his voice, and hang on the eloquence of his lips! I envy all who have heard him speak.

I did not tell you that besides the six disciples whom I have named, he has chosen six others, which twelve he keeps near his person as his more favored followers, and whom he daily instructs in the doctrines he came down from heaven to teach. Of the thousands who never weary going from place to place in his train, he has selected seventy men, whom he dispatched by twos into every city and village of Judea, commanding them to proclaim the kingdom of God as at hand, and that the time when men everywhere should repent and turn to God, had come.

Thus you see, my dear father, that the solitary and unknown young man, who was baptized not a year since in Jordan, is now wielding more influence in the land than the Roman Procurator Pilate or Herod. Nay, not many days since, after he had fed another multitude by a miracle, the people would have made him a king by force; but he withdrew from the press, and retired into a mountain alone, to escape this honor. Therefore, dear father, he is no ambitious leader. His kingdom, if he is to be a king, is not to be received as the gift of men. Yet that he will be a king is as certain as that he is the Christ for the prophecy says that Messias "shall sit upon the throne of his father David." Who can look into the future and behold the limit of his glory? Already by faith I see him crowned by the same mighty God who proclaimed from heaven that he was his beloved Son, crowned King of kings and Lord of lords; with his throne upon Mount Zion, and the nations of the earth tributary to his scepter of righteousness, and illimitable dominion. He is the stone cut out of a rock without hands, that shall fill the whole earth.

You may charge me with being enthusiastic, my dear father; but if Jesus be the Christ, earth has no language that can express the splendor of his reign.

It is now commonly reported that he will be here at the Passover. I shall then behold him, and like the wise men, I shall worship him with mingled awe and love. I will again write you, dear father, after I see and hear him. Till then, believe me your affectionate daughter.

ADINA.

LETTER XVI.

My Dear Father: While I write, the city is agitated like a tumultuous sea. The loud murmurs of the multitudes in the streets, and even in the distant market place, renew my startled ears. A cohort of Roman cavalry has just thundered past toward the Temple, where the uproar is greatest; for a rumor of an insurrection begun among the people, has come to Pilate the Procurator. But this is no insurrection against the Roman authority, dear father; alas, our people, who were once God's people and the masters of the East, are now too servile and submissive to their pagan masters, the Romans, to lift up a finger to remove their degrading yoke! Would that it were a movement for the liberties of Judea! The occasion of the tumult, which seems to increase each moment, is an extraordinary act of power on the part of the new prophet, Jesus, that name become, by means of my pen, so familiar to you, -- a name at which, I can say without enthusiasm, every knee will yet bow, both of Jew and Gentile! I will relate to you the circumstances; for this act of power from him is another proof of his divine mission.

In my last letter, dear father, I stated that it was commonly reported that this wonderful man would be up to the Passover, and that all men were talking of the approaching event, and really thinking more of his presence here, than of the Passover itself. Nay, it was said that many who would not otherwise be in Jerusalem, would come hither in order to see him, and to witness some new miracle; and today Rabbi Amos says the number of strangers in the city is hitherto unprecedented.

Yesterday my cousin John came unexpectedly into the hall of the fountain, in the rear of the house, where we were all seated in the cool of the vines, with which Mary's taste has covered a wall of trellis-work. Uncle Amos was in the act of reading to us from the Prophet Jeremiah, a prophecy relating to the Messias that is to come (nay, that is come, dear father), when John appeared. Mary's blushes welcomed him, and showed how dear he was to her. Uncle Amos embraced and kissed him and seated him by us, and called for a slave to bathe his feet, for he was dusty and travel-worn. From him we learned that his beloved master, Jesus, had reached Bethany, and was reposing from his fatigues at the hospitable though humble house of Lazarus, Mary and Martha. When we heard this, we were all very glad; and uncle Amos particularly seemed to experience the deepest satisfaction.

"If he comes into Jerusalem," said he warmly, "he shall be my guest. Bid him to my roof, O John, that my household may be blessed in having a Prophet of God step across its threshold."

"Oh, by all means do not forget to ask him to remain through the Passover with us," exclaimed Mary, earnestly looking up into the young disciple's face, and laying her hands confidingly upon his wrist.

"I will tell my beloved Master thy wish, Rabbi Amos," answered John. "Doubtless, as he has no home, nor friends in the city, he will remain under your roof."

"Say not no friends!" I exclaimed. "We are all his friends here, and fain would be his disciples."

"What! Rabbi Amos also?" cried John, with a glance of pleasurable surprise at the venerable Priest of God.

"Yes, I am ready after all that I have heard and seen, I am ready to confess him a Prophet sent from God."

"Yes, he is more than a prophet, O Rabbi Amos!" answered John. "Never prophet does the works Jesus does. It seems that all power is at his command. If you witnessed what I witness daily, as he traverses Judea, you would say that he was Jehovah descended to earth in human form!"

"Nay, do not blaspheme, young man," said Rabbi Amos, with some severity of reproof.

John bowed his head in reverence to the rebuke of the Rabbi, but nevertheless answered respectfully and firmly, "Never man did like him. If he be not God in the flesh, he is an angel in flesh invested with divine power."

"If he be the Messias," I said, "he cannot be an angel: for are not the prophecies clear that Messias shall be a man of sorrows? Is he not to be the seed of the woman? a man and not an angel?"

"Yes," answered John, "you remember well the prophecies. I firmly believe Jesus to be the Messiah, the Son of God. Yet,

130

what he is more than man, what he is less than God, is incomprehensible to me and to my fellow-disciples. We wonder, love, and adore! At one moment we feel like embracing him into our arms as a brother dearly beloved; at another, we are ready to fall at his feet and worship him! I have seen him weep at beholding the miseries of the diseased wretches which were dragged into his presence, and then with a touch -- with a word, heal them; and they would stand before him in the purity and beauty of health and strong manhood! I have seen him with a voice of command, as never man spake, expel devils from those who were possessed by them; and I have heard the devils submissively beg not to be sent to their own place, but to be permitted by him to remain roaming still in the air and on the earth, until the hour of their final sentence shall proceed from the lips of God. Even the devils are thus subject unto him, so mighty is his power and all diseases disappear before his eye, like the foul air of the fens before the beams of the morning sun!"

"And yet," said Nicodemus, a rich Pharisee, who listened without interrupting, for it is his wont to come in and out as he will, being a friend of my uncle, "and yet, young man, I heard you say that Jesus, of whom you and all men relate such mighty deeds, has remained at Bethany to recover from his fatigue. How can a man, who holds all sickness in his power be subject to mere weariness of body? I would say unto him, Physician, heal thyself."

This was spoken with a tone of incredulity by this learned ruler of the Jews and stroking his snowy beard, he waited of John a reply; for like many of the chief men, nay, most of them, he was hard to believe all he heard of Jesus; for as yet he had not seen him; nor would he be likely to visit him were he to come into the city, in order to see for himself, lest his popularity among the Jews be diminished; for he is a man of remarkable ambition, and aims one day to be the chief governor of the people; therefore though he should really be convinced that Jesus is the Messias, I fear he would not have candor enough, for fear of the Jews, to confess it. Such is my opinion of my uncle's friend, the rich and powerful Pharisee. But John answered him and said:

"So far as I can learn the character and power of Jesus, his power over diseases is not for his own good, but for the benefit of the multitude. He uses his power to work miracles to do good to others from love and compassion, and to show forth the divine power in him. His miracles are used only as the proofs of his Messiahship. Being a man with this divine power dwelling in him, for us, he is subject to infirmities as a man; he hungers, thirsts, wearies, suffers, as a man. I have seen him heal a nobleman's son and restore him to strength and activity by a word, and the next moment seat himself, supporting his aching head upon his hand, looking pale and languid, and without strength; for his labors love are vast, and he is often overcome by them, those who follow him to be healed not giving him time to repose at night. Once, Simon Peter, seeing him ready to sink with very weariness, after healing all day, asked him and said: "Master, thou givest strength to others, why suffer thyself when all health and strength are in thee, as in a living well, to be weary!"

"It is not mine to escape human infirmities by any power my Father hath bestowed upon me for the good of men. It behooves me to suffer all things. Through suffering only can I draw all men after me."

John said this so sadly, as if he were repeating the very tones in which Jesus had spoken it, that we all remained silent for a few moments. I felt tears fill my eyes, and I was glad to see the proud Pharisee, Nicodemus, looked moved. After a full minute's serious pause, he said:

"This man is doubtless no common prophet. When he comes into the city I shall be glad to hear from his own mouth his doctrines, and to witness some potent miracle."

"Surely," said Amos, "if he be in truth a prophet, we ought not to reject him. We ought to examine fairly his claims to be sent from God to our people."

"Certainly," answered Nicodemus, "we Pharisees are ready to give him a fair hearing. It would seem that by coming to Jerusalem from the provinces, where hitherto he has been preaching and doing miracles, he means to challenge the whole people to acknowledge him as a prophet."

"Prophet he is, without doubt," answered Amos. "It is not the question now whether he be a prophet or not, for the hundreds he has healed are living witnesses that he has the spirit and power of the old prophets, and is truly a prophet. The question that remains is, whether he be the Messiah, or not?"

Nicodemus slowly and negatively shook his head, and then answered:

"Messias cometh not out of Galilee."

"He will prove himself to be Messias with power," answered my cousin John, with zeal. "When you hear him speak, Rabbi Nicodemus, the grace of his lips, and the depths of his wisdom, will charm you into belief and without miracles you will acknowledge that he is the Christ."

At this moment, a sudden, wild, joyful cry from Mary, thrilled our nerves, and, looking toward the door, we saw her folded in the arms of a young man whom I had never seen before. My surprise had not time to form itself into any definite opinion of what I saw, when I beheld the young man, who was exceedingly handsome, and the picture of health, after kissing the clinging Mary upon her cheeks, leave her to throw himself into the arms of Rabbi Amos, crying:

"My father, my dear father!"

My uncle, who had stood amazed, and wonderingly gazing on him, as if he could not believe what his eyes beheld, now burst into profound expressions of grateful joy, and as he clasped the young stranger to his heart, fell upon his neck, and wept, with scarcely power to articulate the words:

"My son! my son! Lost, but found again! This is the Lord's doing, and is marvelous in our eyes."

John also embraced the newcomer, while the Ruler stood silent with wonder. Who the young man was whose arrival was producing such emotion, and why he should be hailed as a son by my uncle Amos, I had no idea and while I was looking bewildered upon the scene, Mary ran and said to me, with tears of gladness shining in her dark eyes:

"It is Benjamin, my lost brother, beloved Adina!"

"I did not know you had a brother," I answered in surprise.

"We have long regarded him as dead." she replied, with mingled emotions. "Seven years ago he became lunatic, and fled to the tombs without the city, where he has long dwelt with many others who were possessed with devils. For years he has been a mad-man, and has neither spoken to nor known us, and we have tried to forget that he lived, since to remember it made us miserable, without hope of his restoration. But oh, now behold him! It seems a vision! See how manly, noble, like himself, he is, with the same sweet smile and smiling eyes."

She then flew to take him by the hand and lead him toward

133

me, all eyes being fixed upon him, as if he had been a spirit.

When he saw their wondering gaze, he said:

"It is I, both son and brother to those dearest to me. I am in my right mind, and well."

"Who has effected this change, so extraordinary, oh, my son?" inquired Rabbi Amos, with trembling lips, and keeping his hand on Benjamin's shoulder, as if he feared he would vanish away.

"It was Jesus, the Prophet of the Highest," answered he, with solemn gratitude.

"Jesus!" we all exclaimed in one voice.

"I could have said so," answered cousin John calmly. "I needed not to ask who had effected this great work upon him. Nicodemus, thou knowest this young man well! thou hast known him in childhood, and beheld him in the madness of his lunacy, among the tombs. Dost thou doubt now, whether Jesus be the very Christ?"

Nicodemus made no reply; but I saw from the expression of his face that he believed.

"How was this thing done to thee, young man?" he asked, with a deep interest and visible emotion.

"I was wandering near Bethany this morning," answered the lost and restored one, with modesty and feeling, "when I beheld a crowd which I madly followed. As I drew near, I beheld in their midst a man, whom I had no sooner cast my eyes upon, than I felt seize me an ungovernable propensity to destroy him. The same fury possessed seven others, my comrades in madness, and together, with one mind and will, we rushed upon him, with great stones and knives in our hands. The crowd gave way and fell back aghast, and called him to save himself. But he moved not, but, left alone in a wide space, stood calmly awaiting us. We were within a few feet of him, and I was nearest, ready to strike him to the earth, when he quietly lifted one finger, and said "Peace!" We stood immovable, without power to stir a foot, while our rage and hatred increased with our inability to harm him. We howled and foamed at the mouth before him, for we then knew that He was the Son of God, come to destroy us.

"Come out of the men, and depart quickly!" he said, in a tone of command, as if to us, but really to the demons within us. At his word I fell at his feet in a dreadful convulsion, and my whole body writhed, as if it had been wrestling with an invisible demon. Jesus then stooped and laid his hand upon my brow, and said, "Son, arise! Thou art made whole!"

At these words a black cloud seemed to be lifted from my mind, and to disappear; the glory of a new existence appeared to dawn upon my soul, while his voice melted my heart within me. Bursting into tears, the first I have shed for seven years, I fell at his feet and kissed them, and embraced them, wholly overcome with a new sense of peace, and of inward happiness unspeakable.

"Go thy way, and fear God, that thou fall not a second time into this captivity to Satan!" he said, raising me to my feet. I then followed him, rejoicing and blessing God, until he entered the house of a Centurion, near Bethany, when I hastened hither, to gladden your hearts with the sight of me restored to my right mind."

When Benjamin had done speaking, we all gave glory to God, who had given him back to us, and who had sent so great a prophet among men. As Nicodemus took his leave, I overheard him, congratulating the happy father, say, that he should embrace the first opportunity to have an interview with Jesus; and when my uncle told him that he hoped to entertain the mighty prophet as his guest, the Ruler desired permission to visit him here upon his arrival "but secretly," I heard him add, in Rabbi Amos' ear, as he took his leave.

I commenced this letter, dearest father, by an allusion to a great commotion, which is agitating the whole city, and which was sensed by an act of power on the part of the Prophet Jesus, who, this morning, two hours ago, entered the city, and proceeded at once to the Temple, followed through the streets by an innumerable multitude, such as was never known in Jerusalem before. But as I have taken up so much of this letter in relating what passed yesterday in the hall of the Fountain, I will leave the account of the tumult, the voices of which are still to be heard, for my next letter, which I shall write this evening; for now, that all events are so interesting connected with the great Prophet Christ, I shall write to you almost daily, that I may keep you advised of all things that come to pass, even as you desired me to do. This request, dear father, filled me with joy. It was an assurance to me that you have begun to take an interest in these wonderful things concerning Messias, and it leads me secretly to hope that you may yet believe in Him, and accept Him as the Anointed One of God, which, without doubt, he is, as both his words and his mighty works do testify.

When I get a package of letters made up, I shall send them

by Israel Ben Judah, with the caravan that leaves eight days after the Passover.

May the God of our Fathers be with you, and bless you, and all the holy people of the Promise.

Your loving daughter,

ADINA.

LETTER XVII.

My Dear Father: The last letter which I sent to you, was written during an extraordinary tumult which prevailed in the city, an account of which I promised to give you in the present one. I will do so now. When, on the morning of the Passover, it was noised abroad that the Prophet of Galilee was entering the city by the gate of Jericho, the whole city was stirred, and from the houses and shops poured forth crowds, which turned their steps in that direction. Mary and I went upon the housetop, hoping to see something; but far and near was visible only a sea of heads, from which a deep murmuring arose, like the ceaseless voice of the ocean chafing upon a rocky shore. The top of the gateway was visible from the place where we stood; but it was black with the people who had crowded upon it to look down. There was heard, at length, an immense shout, as of one voice, which was followed by a swaying and onward pressure of the crowds.

"The prophet must have entered the gate," said my cousin Mary breathlessly. "How they do him honor! It is the reception of a king!"

We were in hopes he would pass by our house, as we were on one of the chief thoroughfares; but were disappointed, as he took the way round the foot of Mount Zion, and ascended the hill of Moriah to the Temple. A part of the ascent to the house of the Lord is visible from our roof, and we had the satisfaction of seeing the Prophet at a distance. We knew him, only because he was in advance, and the people, while they walked near him, yet left him a little space. The nighest one to him, Mary said, was her cousin John, though at the distance I could not have recognized him; but the eyes of maidenly affection, though mild as the dove's, are piercing as the eagle's. The head of the multitude disappeared beneath the arch of the Temple, and thousands upon thousands followed after; and, in the rear, rode the young Roman Centurion, whom I have before spoken of, at the head of four hundred horse, to keep order in the vast mass. Mary could not recognize him, saying it was too far to tell who he was; but I knew him, not only by his air and bearing, but by his scarlet pennon, that fluttered from his iron lance, and which I had bestowed upon him for he told me he had lost one his fair Roman sister, Tullia, had given him, and, as he so much regretted its loss, I supplied its place by another, worked by my own hands. As this was an act of kindness only to a stranger, dear father, I know you will not disapprove of it though being done for an idolater may not please you. But I am full of hope, dear father, that this noble and excellent youth may yet become a Jew for he loves to listen to my teachings from the Prophets, and last week he told me that he could never weary hearing me read to him from the books of Moses, and from the sublime Psalms of King David which, he says, surpass any poems, either in his own tongue, or the Greek. Thus, by attention and forbearance, I assuredly believe that he may be led to renounce his idolatrous faith, and become a worshiper of the God of Hosts.

The multitude, as many as could gain admission, having entered the great gate of the Temple, for a few minutes there was a profound stillness. Mary said:

"He is worshiping, or sacrificing, now."

"Perhaps," I said, "he is addressing the people, and they listen to his words."

While I was speaking, there arose from the bosom of the Temple, a loud, irregular, strange outcry, of a thousand voices, pitched to high excitement. The people without the gate responded by a universal shout, and then we beheld those nighest the walls retreat down the hillside in terrified confusion, while to increase the tumult, the Roman horse charged up the hill, seeking to penetrate through the masses, to reach the gate out of which the people poured like a living and tempest-tossed river, before which the head of the cohort recoiled, or was overwhelmed and down-trodden! I held my breath in dreadful suspense, not knowing the cause of the fearful scene we beheld, nor to what it might lead. Mary, who knew both her father, and her cousin and betrothed were exposed to whatsoever danger was threatening those who had gone into the Temple, became overcome by her apprehensions of evil to them, and, burying her face in her hands, she sunk down almost insensible by my side. My attention was then drawn to her, away from the scene on Mount Moriah, and, leading her down into the apartments of the house, I saw no more of what followed. But a quarter of an hour had not passed, when Samuel Ben Azel, who had, the day before, come up from Nain, to the Passover, with his mother, who is a distant relative of Rabbi Amos, entered, and explained to us the cause of the scene I had witnessed, assuring Mary, at the same time, of the safety, both of her cousin and her father. His account was thus:

The Prophet Jesus having entered into the Temple, with the multitudes following him to see what he would do, found all the courts filled with merchants, changers of money, and sellers of cattle to the sacrificers. Portions of the sacred place were divided off by fences, in which thousands of sheep and cattle were stalled and between almost every two columns of the vast portico, sat at their tables, men, whose business it was to change the foreign money brought by the Jews from Greece, Egypt, Elam, Parthia, and Africa, who had come up to the Passover, for Jerusalem and Roman coin, which only the sellers of the cattle and sheep will receive for what they sell. On his way to the inner Temple, the Prophet found his path so obstructed by the stalls and the tables of the brokers, that he had to go round them, and often turn back and take a less hedged-up avenue. At length, finding upon the very lintel of the Court of the Priests, a priest himself engaged at a table as a money-changer, and near him a Levite, keeping a stall for selling doves and sparrows to the worshipers, he stopped upon the step, and, turning round, cast his calm, terrible eye (for it was terrible then, mild as it was before), over the scene of noisy commerce and bartering. Every face was turned toward him in expectation. The half-completed bargain was suspended, and buyer and seller directed their gaze, as by a sort of fascination, not unmingled with a strange awe and fear, upon him. Those who had crowded about him, drew back farther and farther, slowly, but irresistibly widening the space between them and him, they knew not by what impulse, till he stood alone, save nearest him was John, his disciple. The uproar of buying and selling suddenly subsided, and even the loud lowing of the cattle, and the bleating of the sheep, stopped, as if a supernatural awe had seized even the brute creation at his presence; and only the soft cooing of doves stirred the vast, death-like stillness of the place, but a moment before a scene of oaths, cries, shouts, running to and fro, buying and selling, the ringing of money, and the buzz often thousand voices. It was as if a hurricane, sweeping with deafening uproar of the elements over the lashed ocean, had been suddenly arrested, and followed by a great calm. The silence was dreadful. It stopped the very beating of my heart. Every eye of the vast multitude seemed to fasten itself on the Prophet, in expectation of some dread event. I thought of the world hereafter to be assembled before the tribunal of Jehovah, awaiting their sentence. The step of the Temple upon which he stood seemed to be a throne, and the people before him expecting judgment. Suddenly, the silence, which had become oppressive, was broken by a young man near me, who gave vent to his feelings by a piercing shriek, and fell insensible upon the marble floor. There was a general thrill of horror, yet the same awful stillness succeeded this startling interruption. That one intense shriek had spoken for us all, given expression and outlet to what we all felt. Suddenly, the voice of the Prophet was heard, clear, authoritative, and ringing like the trumpet that shook Sinai when the Law was given, and made all the people to quake:

"It is written, my Father's house shall be called a House of Prayer! but ye have made it a den of thieves!"

He then picked up from the pavement at his feet a small cord, which someone had thrown down, and, doubling it in the form of a scourge, he advanced. Before him fled the changers of money, priest, and Levite, sellers of oxen, sellers of sheep, and sellers of doves, escaping in such haste from the terrible displeasure of his countenance, that they left their property to its fate, seeking only their personal safety.

"Take these things hence," he cried, "make not my Father's house a house of merchandise!"

Such a scene of confusion and flight was never witnessed as now followed! The whole mass was in retrograde motion. I was borne along with the current. Money-tables were overturned on all sides; but not the most avaricious thought, at that moment, of stopping to gather any of the gold and silver which the rushing thousands trampled beneath their feet. It was not the whip of small cords before which we fled, for he touched no man therewith but it was from his presence! We were driven like chaff before him. To the eyes of all, the little whip seemed to blaze and flash above their heads, as if it were the fiery sword of the destroying angel. Nothing but terror, flight, escape, was thought of.

In a few moments, the Priests' Court of the Temple was cleared of every soul, and we were driven across the Court of Israel, and the broader Court of the Gentiles, toward the south gate. On looking back, I saw that the prophet no longer pursued, but stood alone, Master and Lord of the Temple. The whip was no longer in his hand and his whole attitude and expression of face was changed from that of their late terrible power, to an air of the profoundest compassion, as he looked after us, still flying from his presence.

"But I had no time to marvel at this extraordinary change, for the multitude still sought to escape, and bore me onward, and I lost sight of him. At the gate we were met by a cohort of Pilate's cavalry, and pressed backward into the Temple. The scene now became appalling. What, with the Roman spears in front, and the Prophet behind, the multitude fearing to go either way, trode one upon another, trampled the weak under foot, and filled the air with curses, shrieks, and horrible outcries, of mingled pain, rage and terror. How I escaped, I know not," added Samuel, as he completed his narration, "but, on finding myself outside of the gate, I at once, with hundreds, sought shelter in the city, and happy am I to have reached this place of security for the Romans are scouring the streets, driving all the people into their houses."

When Samuel had ended, and we were wondering at this new exhibition of the mighty power of the Prophet Jesus, the street in front of our dwelling was filled with persons seeking their homes. Some cried, "the terrible Prophet!" others, "the Romans!" and some, by their outcries, seemed to fly from equal fear of both. In the midst of this tumult, dear father, I sat down to write you my last letter, while the events were fresh, and lest other events should come in and crowd these from my mind.

Ah, my dear father, Jesus of Nazareth must be, indeed, invested with powers divine! He, who, with a word and a look, for the whip in his hand could not, says Rabbi Amos, have hurt a child, can thus impel thousands of men before him, could make the whole world fly from the terrible majesty of his presence! My uncle, Rabbi Amos, who, on his return from the Temple, corroborated what Samuel had stated, added, that as Jesus stood alone, possessor of the gold-strewn floors of the Courts of the Temple, the High Priest advanced toward him, and with awe, not unmixed with anger, demanded of him by what authority he did these things, seeing that he took upon himself to purify the Temple.

His answer was, "My Father's House must not be made a house of merchandise. Zeal for the glory of His Temple hath caused me to do these things."

"Art thou the Christ?" asked the High Priest, still standing some distance off from him.

"If I tell thee that I am, ye will not believe."

"When Christ shall come, he will restore all things," answered the High Priest.

"And I have begun this restoration by expelling from the Temple those who defile it, and restoring it to be a House of Prayer, according as my father hath ordained."

"And who is thy father?" asked Caiaphas.

"God is my Father; and to do His will am I sent into the world. I came not of myself, but my Father sent me. It is written of me, He shall suddenly come to His Temple, and be as a purifier and refiner of silver."

"What sign showest thou that thou art sent, and hast authority to do what thou does here today within the Temple?"

"Hast thou not had proof of my power from heaven?" answered Jesus, stretching forth his hand toward the still terror-stricken multitude. "Destroy this temple, and in three days I will raise it up! Be this to you, and all Judea, the sign that I am sent by my Father, who is in heaven. As He hath given me commandment, so I do!"

At this there was a great murmuring, said Rabbi Amos, for many of the priests, with Annas also, had got boldness, and drew near to hear.

"He cannot be a just man," said Annas, "nor doth he honor God, if he would have us destroy the Temple!"

"Yet, if he be not sent of God, whence hath he thus power over men?" answered another.

"He doeth this by Beelzebub, whose prophet he doubtless is," said Annas, in a loud tone, "for a true prophet would not seek the destruction of God's holy House!"

Thereupon, there was a multitude of voices, some crying one thing, and some another; but the most part asserting their belief that Jesus was a just man and divine prophet. Caiaphas at length obtained silence, and said to him:

"Tell us plainly -- Art thou the Christ, the Son of the Blessed, that we may believe in Thee?"

"I am!" calmly and firmly answered the Prophet and, raising his eyes to heaven, he added impressively, "I am come down from God!"

When, adds, my uncle, Annas heard this, he lifted up his voice an exclamation of horror, and, rending his clothes, he cried out: "Hear ye this blasphemer! Let us cast him forth from the Temple, which he pollutes!"

But no man dareth approach the Prophet, whose mighty power had so recently been expressed in the expulsion of the merchants and buyers from that sacred place.

"Bear witness," then said he sorrowfully, rather than in anger, "that I have come unto my own, and ye have received me not! This Temple of my Father, from which you would drive me forth, shall no longer be the dwelling-place and altar of Jehovah. The day cometh when your priesthood shall be taken away and given to others, and among the Gentiles shall arise to my Father's name, on every hill, and in every valley of the earth, holy temples, wherein he shall delight to dwell and men shall no longer need to worship God in Zion, but in all places shall prayer and praise be offered to the Most High. This Temple, which ye have polluted, shall be thrown down, till not one stone remaineth standing upon another and ye shall be scattered, because ye knew not the time of your visitation!"

Thus speaking, the Prophet quitted the Temple, leaving the High Priest, and priests, and Levites, standing gazing after him, without power to utter a word. Rabbi Amos, who saw and heard all this, says that nothing could have been more striking than the contrast presented between the two men, the High Priest and Jesus (if it be lawful to call him a man, dear father), as they talked with each other; the one clothed in magnificent garments, with a glittering tiara upon his brows, his port lofty and proud, his hair and beard white as snow, and his whole appearance majestic and splendid with outward richness! the other, youthful, clad in coarse garments, with a gray Galilean mantle folded about him, sandals much worn upon his feet, and his whole garb mean and covered with the dust of his journey on foot from Bethany; while the severe sadness of his face, which seemed beautifully, and touchingly chastened by prayer and suffering, contrasted strongly with the stern, harsh face of Caiaphas, flushed with anger and envious hostility.

He passed out of the Temple with an even pace, neither looking back at his enemies, nor followed by them. I beheld John join him, and hastened to ask him to invite him to my house, to sojourn and eat the Passover with me, but he disappeared, and I lost sight of him. But, at the gate, I encountered a man, leaping and singing, whom the Prophet had healed by a touch, as he passed out, though the man had been paralytic for thirty-one years. Thus does this mighty person never cease to do good.

Such, my dear father, is the account given by Rabbi Amos of what passed in the Temple. That Jesus is the Christ, is now beyond question; for he has openly acknowledged it to the High Priest.

Adieu, dearest father. The servants are bringing in boughs for the booths, and I must close this letter, with prayers to our father's God for your peace and welfare.

ADINA.

LETTER XVIII.

My Dear Father: The last letter, which I received by the hands of the Roman courier, filled me with gratitude, at learning from it your recovery. When I heard from Ben Israel of your ill health, I felt like flying with the wings of a dove to reach your pillow, and administer to the comfort of the venerated and loved author of my being. The God of our fathers be praised in raising you up; and that He may preserve you long to me, shall be my daily prayer.

You say in your letter, dear father, that you have read with interest all my letters, and more especially those which relate to Jesus of Galilee, the mighty Prophet now vouchsafed to Israel. You say that you are ready to acknowledge him as a prophet sent from God, "for evidently no man could do such great works, except God be with him." "But," you add, "while I am ready, my child, to recognize him as a prophet of the Lord, I am far from seeing in him the Messias promised to our people! Aside from the lowliness of his parentage, and his humility of condition, traveling on foot, and without retinue (while Messias is to be a Prince and King), he can have no claim to be the Christ, because he comes out from Galilee. Doth Messias come out of Galilee? Let Rabbi Amos, who seems ready, I perceive, to acknowledge him as the Christ, let him examine the writings of the Prophets, and see! Hath not the Scripture said that Christ cometh of the seed of David, and out of the town of Bethlehem, where David was born? Search and look, for no prophet, much less Messias, cometh out of Galilee."

To this objection, dear father, also made, I believe, in a previous letter, Rabbi Amos desires me to say, that he has investigated the records of births kept in the Temple, and finds, as I have before named to you, that Jesus was born in Bethlehem. He afterward removed, with his parents, to Egypt, and thence returning to Judea, settled in Galilee, where he was brought up. Of these facts in his history, not only Rabbi Amos is satisfied, but Nicodemus also, whose learning you will not gainsay, and the latter, very much to our surprise, and my own delight, added, yesterday, when we were talking over the subject at supper, "there is a prophecy, O, Rabbi Amos, which strengthens this mighty Prophet's claim to be the Messiah."

"What is it? Let me hear all that can strengthen!" I asked earnestly not, dear father, that my confidence in him needs confirmation, but I wish others to believe.

"You will find it in the Prophet Hoseas," answered Nicodemus, "and thus it readeth: I have called my son out of Egypt. These words refer to Messias, without question, as say all the doctors of the law."

"It is a new argument for Jesus, then," answered Rabbi Amos.

My heart bounded with joy, dear father, at hearing this prophecy named: but judge my emotions when Nicodemus, taking the roll of the Prophet Isaiah in his hand, read the words that follow, and applied them to Jesus, "Beyond Jordan, in Galilee of the Gentiles, the people which sat in darkness have seen a great light!" This changes the objections to his coming from Egypt and from Galilee, into additional proofs of his claims to be the Messiah.

I hear you now ask, dear father, with many of the rich and influential citizens of Jerusalem, "Have the rulers begun to believe in him?" Yes, Nicodemus does begin to believe that He is the Christ, being more and more assured of it the more he examines the divine Scriptures. O, my dear father, that you could see Jesus, and hear him discourse, as I have done! All your doubts would then be dissipated, and you would be willing to sit at his feet, and learn of him the words of life. How shall I describe him -- how shall I cause you to hear and see him, as I have heard and seen?

In my last letter, I informed you that Rabbi Amos had invited him to sojourn with us during the Passover. John, the cousin of Mary, conveyed to him the invitation of my uncle, and he graciously accepted it, and came hither yesterday, after he had quitted the Temple, from which he had with such commanding power driven forth the merchants and money-changers.

Hearing the rumor flying along the streets, "The Prophet comes! The Prophet comes!" uttered by hundreds of voices of men and children, I hastened to the house-top, which commanded a view of the street, to the foot of the Temple. The whole way was a sea of heads. The multitude came rolling onward, like a mighty river; as I have seen the dark Nile when pouring its freshening floods along its confined banks.

Mary stood by my side. We tried to single out, amid the advancing throng, the central person around whom undulated the sea of heads, and whose progress gave occasion to so mighty a commotion. But all was so wildly confused with the waving of palm branches that we could distinguish nothing clearly. While I was straining my gaze to make out the form of the Prophet, Mary touched me, and bade me look in the opposite direction. As I did so, I beheld Aemilius Tullius, the young Roman Centurion, of whom I have before spoken, now Prefect of Pilate's Legion, advancing at the head of two hundred horses, at full spur, in order to meet and turn back the advancing column of people.

As he came opposite the house, he looked up, and seeing us upon the parapet, he gracefully waved his gleaming sword, saluting us, and was dashing past, when Mary cried out:

"Noble sir, there is no insurrection, as some of the people have doubtless told thee, but this vast crowd moving hitherward is only an escort to the Prophet of Nazareth, who cometh to be my father's guest."

"I have orders from Pilate to arrest him, lady, as a disturber of the peace of the capital."

"Shall a prophet suffer because his mighty deed draw crowds after his footsteps, noble Roman if thy troops advance, there will be collision with the people. If thou wilt withdraw them a little, thou wilt see that when the Prophet crosses my father's threshold, they will go away in peace."

The Prefect said nothing, but seemed to look at me for some words, which seeing, I earnestly entreated him to do the Prophet no violence.

"For thy wishes' sake, lady, I will here draw up my troop especially, as I see that the people are unarmed."

The Centurion gave orders to his horsemen to draw up in a line opposite the house. The multitude now drew near but many of those in advance, seeing the Roman horse, stopped or fell back, so that I now beheld Jesus appear in front, walking at an even, calm pace, John at his side, and also Rabbi Amos was with him. As he came nigher, the people, for fear of the long Roman spears, fell back, and he advanced, almost alone. I saw John point out to him the house. The Prophet raised his face and gazed upon it an instant. I saw his features full. His countenance was not that of a young man, but of a person past the middle age of life, though he is but thirty. His dark, brown hair was mingled with gray, and in his finely-shaped, oval face were carved, evidently by care and sorrow, deep lines. His beard "was black, mingled with gray, and fell upon his breast. His large, hazel eyes, appeared to be fixed on us both for an instant, with benignity and peace. Deep sadness, gentle, not stern, seemed to be the characteristic expression of his noble and princely visage. There was an air of manly dignity in his carriage and mien; and as he walked amid his followers, he was truly kingly, yet simplicity and humility qualified this native majesty of port. He seemed to unite both awe and love, in those who saw him, to command our homage and sympathy.

As he drew near where the Roman Prefect sat upon his horse, the Prophet inclined his body slightly, but with a courtesy indescribable, to the young chief, who bent low to his saddle-bow in acknowledgment, as if to a monarch. We were both surprised, as well as gratified, dear father, at this act of homage from the Roman knight to our Prophet, and I thought more kindly than ever of Aemilius.

Passing the horsemen, John and Rabbi Amos conducted Jesus to our door; but before they reached it, there was a loud cry from several harsh voices to the Roman, to arrest him. On looking from whence these shouts came, I saw that they proceeded from several of the priests, headed by Annas, who were pressing forward through the crowd.

"We call upon you, O Prefect, to arrest this man! Shame on thee, Rabbi Amos! Hast thou also believed in the impostor? We charge this Galilean, O Roman, with having made sedition. He has taken possession of the Temple, and, unless you see to it, he will have the citadel out of your hands. If you arrest him not, we will not answer for the consequences that may befall the city and the people."

"I see nothing to fear from this man, O ye Jews," answered Aemilius. "He is unarmed, and without troops. Stand back keep ye to your Temple. It is from your outcries comes all the confusion! Back to your altars! If commotions arise in the city, Pilate will make you accountable. All the rest of the people are peaceable, save only yourselves."

"We will take our complaint before the Procurator," cried Annas, who was the chief speaker and, followed by a large company of angry priests and Levites, with staves in their hands, he took his way toward the palace of the Roman governor.

I looked my gratitude to Aemilius, for taking part with the Prophet.

The multitude now began to retire, as the Roman horse slowly moved up the street, and Jesus being received into the house by Mary, who descended to open the door, quiet was soon in a measure restored; though at one time a large concourse of persons, whose money-tables had been cast down, came to complain of their losses, and would have attacked the house but for Rabbi Amos, who went forth and civilly addressed them showing them that if they had sold and bought in the Temple, contrary to law, and that if Jesus had driven them forth alone, he must be a prophet, for only a prophet could make a thousand men flee before him; "and if he be a prophet, my friends, he has acted by command of God and take heed, lest in avenging yourselves against him, you be found fighting against God."

With such words he caused them to retire, though many sick, lame, halt, and blind, and infirm, as well as a group of lepers, stood a long time without, calling upon the prophet to come forth, and touch them and heal them.

In the meanwhile, Jesus was taken into the inner hall, and water being brought, Rabbi Amos himself removed his sandals, and washed his feet while Mary, to do him all honor, dried them with a rich veil, which she had just worked in anticipation of her coming bridal with her cousin John. It was at this moment I entered the hall. Desirous as I had been to behold and speak with the Prophet, now that I could behold him face to face, I shrunk with awe. He raised his eyes, and beholding me, said:

"Daughter, come thou also, and bid me welcome with these dear friends; for I know thou believest in me, and wouldst that thy father also should believe. Be patient, and hope; for thou shall yet behold him whom thou lovest, my disciple!"

As thus he spake, he extended to me his hand, upon which I let fall a rain of tears of joy. I knew that he knew my heart and thoughts, and that his words would prove true. Yes, dear father, you also will believe, as we all believe. You also are to acknowledge Him as the Christ.

There were in the room, not only Amos, and John, and Mary, but the Priest Elias, cousin to Caiaphas, who, desirous of hearing from the lips of the Prophet his sublime teachings, had

come in with him. There were also present five men whom I
never saw before but who, as John said, were his disciples.
One of them was a short, compactly-made man, with high,
energetic features, a bold brow and an eagle eye, with an air of
singular determination, like a soldier. His name was Simon
Peter. Another was a tall, intellectual person, with a calm,
thoughtful air, who seemed to hang on every word his master
uttered, as if he were listening to the very oracles of God. His
name was Andrew, and he is a brother to Simon. But I had no
eye or ear for anyone but Jesus. I saw that he seemed weary
and pale, and for the first time I noticed a wound oozing blood
upon his temple, from which he seemed to suffer, as from time
to time he raised his hand to it. Desirous of serving so holy a
person, I hastened to prepare liniment, with which, bringing it
into the hall, I was about to bind up his wound, which John
said had been caused by a stone thrown by some wicked hand.
But the Priest Elias put me rudely back, and said, "Nay, maiden,
let us witness a miracle!" He then turned to the Prophet and
said, "Master, we have heard much of thy power to do
miracles, but have seen none done by thee! If thou wilt
presently show me a miracle, I will believe, I and all my house!
Thou hast a wound gaping in the temple heal it with a touch,
and I will acknowledge thee the Christ, the Son of the
blessed!"

Jesus turned his eyes upon him and said, "Elias, thou readest
the Prophets, and should know whether he who speaketh
unto thee be the Christ or no! Search the Scriptures, that thou
mayest know the time of his visitation is come and that I am
He! One prophecy fulfilled is of more value than many
miracles. But I do no miracles to relieve my own sufferings. I
came into this world to suffer. Isaiah wrote of me as a man of
sorrows, and acquainted with grief! Blessed are they who not
seeing, shall believe. Ye believe that I am a prophet, and come
out from God. It is well. Shall a prophet, then, deceive? If I
am a prophet (and ye doubt it not), and I say that I am the
Christ, why will ye not believe me? If I am a true prophet,
come out from God, I cannot lie. Yet ye believe me when I say
I am a prophet, and ye are displeased if I say I am the Christ. If
ye believe me at all, then believe what I say unto you, that I am
the Christ."

"But, master," said the aged Levite, Asher, "we know whence
thou art -- even from Galilee. But when Christ cometh, no
man knoweth whence he is!"

"It is true, O man of Israel, ye both know me and whence I am. Yet ye know not Him who sent me. Ye do not understand the Scriptures, or ye would indeed know me, whence I am, and who hath sent me. But ye know neither me nor Him that sent me, for I am come out from God. If ye had known Him, ye would know me also. The time cometh when ye shall know whence I am and believe in me; but now your hearts are darkened through ignorance and unbelieving. I have told you plainly I am the Christ."

When he had thus spoken with great dignity and power, there were many present who were offended, and some voices murmured against him. Then Rabbi Amos led him forth to the apartment he had prepared for him; but the people remained warmly discussing the subject, and were greatly divided about him, some saying that he was Christ, and others denying it; while others cried aloud that he did his miracles by Beelzebub, Prince of the devils.

"And so," said my cousin John bitterly, "and so it is wherever my beloved master goes. Detraction and envy, malice and unbelief, follow his footsteps, and daily his life is menaced, and no place is a place of shelter for his aching head."

In going to his apartment, the Prophet had to cross the court, and as I was watching his retiring footsteps, I saw four men who had climbed to the housetop from the street, the doors being shut, let down a fifth in a blanket at the very feet of Jesus. It was a man afflicted with the palsy, and grievously tormented, and their own father. Jesus, seeing their filial love, stopped and said, kindly:

"Young men, what would you have me to do?"

"Heal our aged father, holy Rabbi."

"Believe ye that I can do this?" he asked, fixing his gaze earnestly on them.

"Yes, Lord! We believe that thou art the Christ, the son of the living God! All things are possible unto thee."

Jesus looked benignantly upon them, and then taking the venerable man by the hand, he said to him in a loud voice, so that all who were looking on heard him:

"Aged father, I say unto thee, arise and walk!" The palsied man instantly arose to his feet, whole and strong, and after casting a glance around upon himself, he threw himself at the Prophet's feet, and bathed them in tears. The four sons did the same, while all the people who witnessed the miracle shouted, "Glory to God, who hath given such power unto men!"

Jesus then withdrew himself from the grateful group, who, embracing their father, wept upon his neck, and then the whole four escorted him, two on each side, with their arms about him, and about each other, into the street, where they were received by the multitude with loud cries of gratulation for the old man had been well known in the city by all men, as palsied and unable to walk for thirty years.

Such, my dear father, are the increasing testimonies Jesus bears, by miracles, as well as by words, to his being Messiah.

The God of our fathers keep you in health.

Your loving daughter,

ADINA.

LETTER XIX.

Dear Father: The visit of the Prophet Jesus to the city has produced results of the most amazing character. His numerous miracles, performed in the open day by a word, or a look, or a touch, or a command; the power of his preaching, the excellency of his doctrines, which are evidently divine, his clear assertions that he is the very Christ, have all contributed to bring the first men of Israel, rulers as well as people, to believe in him! During the four days he remained at the house of my uncle Amos, the chief men of the city came to hear him, and, if possible, to see some miracle performed by him. The priesthood is divided. Caiaphas has publicly recognized him as a prophet, while Annas has publicly declared that he is an impostor and thus two parties are formed in the city, headed by the two priests, and all men have taken sides with one or the other. But the majority of the common people are in favor of Jesus, believing him to be the Christ. The Pharisees most oppose him, because he boldly reproves their sins and hypocrisies; and though they fear him, they hate and would destroy him, for he preaches so plainly against their wickedness, that the people have ceased to respect them. Even Nicodemus, who at first was inclined to accept Jesus as a Prophet, finding the Pharisees against him, and being unwilling to lose his popularity with them, kept away from the house where Jesus was by day; but his curiosity to learn more of him, led him to visit the holy Prophet secretly by night. This he did twice, coming alone in the darkness, and being let in by his friend, Rabbi Amos. What the result of these interviews was, I can only tell you from Mary's account. She overheard their conversation, her window opening upon the corridor, where Jesus had been seated after supper, alone in the moonlight for full an hour, gazing meditatively heavenward. His pale and chiseled features in the white moonlight seemed radiant as marble, and as cold, when Rabbi Amos came and announced the ruler Nicodemus, as desirous to speak with him.

"Bid him come in and see me, if he has aught to say to me," answered the Prophet, turning toward him.

"Nicodemus," added my cousin Mary, "then came to the corridor, carefully wrapped in his mantle; and looking about to see if he were unobserved, he dropped it from his face, and, bowing reverently, said to the Prophet:

"Pardon me, O Rabbi, that I come to thee by night but by day thy time is taken up with healing and with teaching. I am glad to find thee alone, great Prophet, for I would ask thee many things."

"Speak, Nicodemus, and I will listen to thy words," answered the Prophet.

"Rabbi," said the ruler of the Pharisees, "I know thou art a teacher, come from God; for no man can do these things that thou does except God be with him. That thou art a mighty Prophet, I believe, as do all men: but art thou the Messias? Tell us plainly!"

"If I tell thee, Nicodemus, thou wilt not believe," answered Jesus mildly. "I will ask you one question. Whence cometh Christ?"

"He is the son of David, and cometh out of Bethlehem."

"Thou hast well answered. Rabbi Amos, here, will tell thee that he has examined the records. Ask him whose son he is who speaketh unto thee."

"The son of Joseph and Mary, of the lineage of David's house," answered Rabbi Amos. "The record of his birth I have seen, O Nicodemus, and so also have Caiaphas and many others. Thou canst examine for thyself, if thou wilt come to the Temple with me tomorrow."

"Thy word suffices, O Rabbi Amos, for who ever knew thy lips to utter falsehood?"

"The same record shows that the great Prophet, now here among us, was born in Bethlehem, in the days of the taxation," answered Rabbi Amos.

"Then whence is it, O Prophet, that thou cometh out of Nazareth of Galilee?" asked Nicodemus doubtingly.

"I will tell thee, Nicodemus," answered Jesus. "My parents dwelt in Nazareth, and as they sojourned at Bethlehem, to be registered in their own family town, David's town, I was born! Thus am I of the line of David, of the town of Bethlehem, and also as it was prophesied of me, a Nazarene. Dost thou ask more? Dost thou believe?"

"Yea, Lord; but how read the Prophets that Messias is to be a king, and to rule the whole earth?"

"My kingdom, O ruler of the Pharisees, is not of this world! I am indeed, a king, but of a spiritual kingdom. My kingdom, unlike all earthly kingdoms, has no end and those who become its subjects must be born again, or they cannot see it!"

"Born again?" answered Nicodemus, with surprise, "How can a man be a second time born after he is grown to manhood? O Rabbi, thou speakest in parables."

"Art thou a wise man of the Pharisees, and a master in Israel, and knowest not what I say?" answered the Prophet. "Verily, verily I say unto thee, except a man be born of water and of the Spirit he cannot enter my kingdom. He who is born of Adam is of the flesh, and of Satan's kingdom, of which Adam was; but he that is born again is born a spiritual man, and is of my kingdom; for I come to build up a kingdom on the ruins of Satan's seat. Marvel not, then, that I say that the sons of Adam must be born again to be sons of God. If ye would enter into my kingdom and live forever, ye must be born again, even of water and of the Spirit."

"How can these things be? Pray, master, explain, that I may know what this mystery meaneth. How can a man be born when he is old?"

"What! Dost thou stumble at the very threshold of the doctrine of my kingdom, O Pharisee? If ye cannot believe earthly things, how shall ye understand the heavenly things, which ye seek to know? He that would be my disciple must be born again! Your first birth is under Satan's power, which rules the world as it now is in bondage; your second birth is into His kingdom, who has come to destroy Satan's and build up His own. This birth is spiritual."

Upon this Nicodemus rose and said, with a shake of the head: "I will hear thee again, O Rabbi, of this matter touching the new birth, of which thou speakest."

When Nicodemus left him, Rabbi Amos said, "Is it indeed true, O master, that thou art to establish a kingdom?"

"Yes, Rabbi Amos, a kingdom in which dwelleth righteousness," answered the Prophet.

"And shall all nations pay us tribute?"

"Thou knowest not what thou sayest, O Rabbi. But the veil shall be removed from thine eyes when thou sees the Son of man lifted up on his throne, as Moses lifted up the serpent in the wilderness."

"Where will be thy throne, O Messias? Wilt thou expel the Romans from the city of David, and reign there?"

"Thou shalt yet behold me on my throne, O Amos, raised above the earth, and drawing all men unto me."

"Wilt thou have thy throne in the clouds of Heaven, O Master, that thou shalt be raised above the earth upon it?" asked Rabbi Amos.

"My throne shall be set on Mount Calvary, and the ends of the earth shall look unto me, and acknowledge my empire. But thou knowest not these things now; but hereafter thou shalt remember that I told thee of them."

Jesus then rose, and bidding his host good-night, retired to the apartment which was assigned him, and Mary remained wondering at his sayings.

Thus, dear father, it is made certain from his own words, that Jesus is the Christ; that he is to establish a kingdom; that he will stand on "a throne high and lifted up," as saith the Prophet, and all the earth shall acknowledge him. But why his throne should be on Calvary instead of Mount Zion, Rabbi Amos wonders greatly, in conversing with us today; for Calvary is a place of skulls, and of public executions, and is covered with Roman crosses, where every week some malefactor is crucified for his crimes! And yet it is more mysterious still, his saying that we must be born again. But John remarked that there are many things which he says to him and his disciples, which Jesus plainly tells them they cannot yet understand, but will by and by remember; and that he tells them now that then, when they see these things fulfilled, they may remember that he told them of them and believe in him and have confidence that other sayings and prophecies of his, yet further in the future, will come to pass.

Jesus, in all that he says, in all that he does, proves that he is omniscient and omnipotent! Whatever he wills to do, he doeth. Never man had power such as dwells in him. This morning, as he was going forth from the house to depart into the country, a man lame from his youth, seated upon the threshold, caught him by his robe, saying, "Master, heal me!"

"Son, thy sins be forgiven thee," answered Jesus, and then passed on; but the Scribes and Pharisees who stood about, when they heard this, cried, "This man, be he prophet or no, blasphemeth for God alone can forgive sins!"

Jesus stopped, and turning to them, said:

"Which is easier, to say to this man, who hath not walked for

twelve years, and whose legs and arms are withered, as you see,
Thy sins be forgiven thee, or to say, Rise and walk? If I can bid
him rise and walk as aforetime, and he does so before your
eyes, is it not proof to you that I have power to forgive his sins
also? For who could make him to rise and walk but the power
of God alone, who also forgiveth men's sins? But that ye may
know that the Son of God hath power on earth to forgive sins,
Behold!"

The Prophet then said in a loud voice to the lame man,
"Arise, take up thy bed, and go to thine house!"

Immediately the man rose to his feet, leaping and praising
God, and taking up the mattress upon which they had brought
him to the door, he ran swiftly away to show himself to his
kinsfolk, while all the people shouted and praised God!

Thus did Jesus publicly show men that he could forgive sins,
if he could heal, as the power to do both came equally from
God. Does not this prove that he is the Son of God?

You should have seen him, dear father, as he left our house,
to go away into Galilee. Mary and I fell at his feet and bathed
them with our tears, Rabbi Amos, and even Nicodemus,
kneeled before him, with many others, asking his blessing;
mothers came with their infants, that he might lay his hands
on them; and the sick and impotent were placed by their
friends in his path, that his shadow in passing by might heal
them. Hundreds brought handkerchiefs, amulets, and sprigs of
cypress torn from the booths, in order that they might bring
them in contact with his garments. The street was lined with
all the afflicted of Jerusalem; and as he moved on between the
rows of wretched sufferers, whose hollow eyes and shriveled
arms were turned imploringly toward him, he healed by words
addressed to them, as he moved on, so that where he found
disease before him, stretched on beds, he left behind him
health and empty couches. We all wept at his departure, and
followed him to the Damascus gate. Here there were
assembled a large company of Levites and priests, among
whom were mingled some of the most desperate characters in
Jerusalem. Knowledge of this fact reached Rabbi Amos, who
at once sent a message to Aemilius, our Roman friend,
informing him that he apprehended that there would be an
attempt made to assassinate Jesus at the going out of the gate,
and asking his aid.

Aemilius placed himself at the head of fifty horses, and
reaching the gate, pressed the crowd back and took possession

of it. When Jesus passed through the armed guard beneath the arch the young Roman courteously offered him an escort to the next village.

Jesus, graciously looking on him, said:

"Young man, I need not thy help. My hour is not yet come. They cannot harm me till my hour arrives. I am not yet given by my father into their hands! Take my blessing, and one day thou shalt know to whom thou hast offered the aid of thy troops!"

The Levites and their hired murderers now pressed forward, and broke through the cohort to reach Jesus, uttering wild and fearful cries; but Aemilius charging them, routed them, and put several to the sword. He then rode to the side of the Prophet, offering him the best horse in his company. This accommodation Jesus refused, but walked by the Roman soldier, who insisted on escorting him, affably conversing with him, and teaching him wonderful things touching the kingdom of God.

Aemilius, who informed me of these things, conducted him as far as Ephraim, and then was about to leave him to return to the city, when four lepers came from the cemetery of the tombs, near the village, and crying out afar off, said:

"Thou blessed Christ, have mercy on us!"

Jesus stopped, though his disciple Peter would have bidden the lepers to hold their peace, as it was late, and his Master was weary; but Jesus, who never wearies doing good, called the lepers to approach. As they did so the whole company of people, as well as the Roman soldiers, drew back to a distance, in horror at the sight of these dead-living men. They came timidly within twenty paces of Jesus, and stood still tremblingly!

"Fear not," said he, "I will make you whole!" He then advanced toward them, and laying his hand upon each of them, they all, at the touch, were instantly changed to well men, with the buoyant form, clear eye, and rich bloom of health!

When Aemilius saw this miracle, he dismounted from his horse, and falling at Jesus' feet, cried, worshiping him. "Thou art Mercury or Jupiter, O mighty God! Give me wisdom and power from the skies!"

"Rise, young man," answered Jesus, sadly looking upon him "thou shalt have wisdom and grace, but not from thy gods, there is but one God, even the Father; worship him, and he will reward thee!"

Aemilius said to me that his heart thrilled at these words, with others he had spoken in the way, and he promised me that he would henceforth "cast aside his gods and believe in the God of Israel, and in Jesus, his holy Prophet."

Is not this blessed news? "Lo!' he proclaims, "so saith the prophet, liberty to the Gentiles."

Now, my dear father, I have thus far faithfully written all that I have heard and witnessed respecting Jesus, as you desired. You must see that he is more than a Prophet, and is the very Christ, the son of the Blessed. Withhold, oh, withhold not, your belief longer. Thousands believe in him, love and reverence him, as Messiah. Daily his power over the hearts and minds of men is increasing. The common people worship the very dust of his sandals. The priests believe and tremble, but, like Herod, when he was an infant in Bethlehem, would destroy him, lest he should supplant them. They say the daily sacrifice will cease, the Temple fall to ruins, and the faith of Israel depart, if Jesus be suffered to live and preach, and do these mighty signs and wonders among the people. But all this establishes his claims! Did not David prophesy of Messiah, that when he should come, "The kings of the earth would set themselves, and the rulers take council together against the Lord and against his anointed? But he that sitteth in the heavens shall laugh: the Lord shall have them in derision." Thus, dear father, all things more and more go to prove Jesus of Nazareth to be the Christ of God.

Your affectionate and loving daughter,

ADINA.

LETTER XX.

My Dear Father: It is many months since you have received a letter from me, written with my own hand; and I rejoice that I am so far restored to health as to resume my correspondence with you. I cannot speak to you too warmly in praise of my uncle Amos and cousin Mary, during my illness. By their care and nursing, under the blessing of God, I am now nearly well. The pure air of the mountains of Galilee being recommended to me, they journeyed with me thither, and, at the foot of Mount Tabor, in the lovely village of Nain, I have passed many weeks, reviving each day.

We are now at the humble abode of a widow, whose husband has been lost, on the Great Sea, which he was a seaman, in one of the merchant ships of Cesarea. The cottage of the widow stands in a garden, from which is a sublime view of Tabor; in all the majesty of his mountain grandeur. One day, while I was in the garden walking, two men, dusty and travel-worn, stopped at the half-open gate, and, saluting us, said:

"Peace be to this house, maiden, and all who dwell here."

"Enter," said the widow, overhearing them, "enter, and ye shall have water for your feet, and bread for your hunger."

The two men then entered and seated themselves and having been refreshed by the poor, but hospitable widow, one of them rose and said:

"This day is salvation come to this house. We are ambassadors of Jesus of Nazareth, and go from city to city, proclaiming the day of the Lord at hand, for Messias is come!"

At hearing these words, Mary and I both exclaimed with joy that we had both seen and heard Jesus at Jerusalem, and believed on him. Upon this they looked greatly pleased; and answered our inquiries respecting the Prophet; that he was in Samaria, preaching and working miracles, and proclaiming his kingdom. When we heard this we rejoiced exceedingly, for we had not heard of him for a long time. From them we learned that he had chosen twelve apostles, who always went with him, and were daily taught of him, and also, more recently, seventy others, whom he sent, two and two, into every city, to herald his approach.

161

"Will he, then, come to Nain?" said the widow, with emotion. "I should be willing to die, so that I could lay my eyes once upon, so great and holy a man!"

"Yes, he will come hither," answered the men "and when we shall report to him your hospitality to us, he will visit your house for he never forgets a cup of water given to one of his disciples."

The men then departed, calling the peace of God upon our abode. They had not been gone many minutes, before we heard a great commotion in the market-place, near by. Upon going to the housetop, we beheld these two men standing upon an elevation, and preaching the kingdom of Christ at hand, calling upon all who heard them to repent of their evil deeds, and lead a godly life; for Jesus would one day judge them according to the deeds done in the body. Upon this, some cried out against Jesus, and others threw stones at the two men; and when we reached the housetop, we saw one of them remove his sandals and shake the dust from them, saying, in a loud voice:

"As ye reject the words of life, your sins remain upon you, as I return to you again the dust of your city."

They then departed, followed by Levites, and men of the baser sort, who fairly drove them from the town. This hostility, we found, was caused by an order from the Great Sanhedrim, to all the synagogues and priests in the land, that they should denounce all who preach Jesus of Nazareth as the Christ.

While we were grieving at this enmity against a Prophet sent from God, whose life was a series of good deeds, there entered hastily a fair young maid, whose name was Ruth. She held an open letter in her hand, and her beautiful face glowed rosily with some secret joy, which contrasted strangely with the present sadness of our own. We knew Ruth well, and loved her as if she had been a sister. She was an orphan, and dwelt with her uncle, Elihaz, the Levite, a man of influence in the town. She was artless, unsuspecting, and very interesting in all her ways.

"What good news, dear Ruth?" asked Mary, smiling at her bright smiles. "A letter from whom?"

"Poor Sarah," answered the pretty maid, blushing so timidly and consciously, that we half suspected the truth.

"But, that is not telling us from whom," persevered Mary, with a little playfulness.

"You can guess," she answered, glancing over her white shoulder, as she bounded away from us into the house.

We were soon after her, and heard her as she cried, putting the letter into the dear widow's hand:

"From Samuel!"

"God be blessed," cried the widow, "my son liveth, and is well."

"Read, dear Sarah," cried the maiden. "He was at Alexandria when he wrote this, and will soon be at home. Oh, happy, happy days" added the over-joyed girl, quite forgetful of our presence. But we had long known the story of her pure love for the widow's son, and she had made us confidants of all her hopes and fears, and read to us all the letters that came from him on the seas, for he went down to trade in the sea in ships, like his father before him. We knew, too, that the youthful wanderer loved her with as much devotion as she loved him, and our hearts sympathized with her in her true affection.

"Nay," said the widow, "my eyes are filled with tears of gladness; I cannot see to read. Do thou read it aloud. Let Adina and Mary also know what he writeth. Is the letter to me, or thee, child?"

"To -- to me, dear Sarah," answered the maiden, with a momentary embarrassment.

"Likely -- likely it is most natural that thou shouldst get the best part of the epistles. But so I hear and know he is well, it is the same, writeth he to me or thee!"

Ruth then cast a bright look upon us, and thus read aloud from the letter from over the sea:

"Dearest Ruth: I fear you have been impatient at my long silence but I love you not less, though you do not often hear from me. Now that I am safe, I will write to you, which I would not do in a state of uncertainty. Know, that after our ship left Cesarea for Crete, we were caught by a north wind, and, in striving to make the east end of the island, we lost way, and were driven upon Africa, where we were wrecked, losing all our cargo, and the lives of many who sailed with us. With others, I was taken by the barbarians, and carried inland to a country of rocky mountains, and there became a bondman to one of the chief men of the nation wherein I was captivated. At length, inspired by a consciousness of the anguish you and my beloved mother must suffer, should you never more hear tidings from me, I resolved to effect my escape. After great perils, I reached the seaside, and, at the expiration of many days, by following the coast, I was taken on board by a small ship of Cyprus, and conveyed to Alexandria. The vessel was owned by a rich merchant of my own people, Manasseh Benjamin Ben Israel, who, finding me sick and destitute of all things, just as I escaped, took me home to his hospitable house, and treated me as a son, till I recovered my health and strength saying that he had a daughter far away in Judea, and he hoped that if she ever needed the aid of strangers, God would repay him by making them kind to her."

Here Mary and I looked at each other with agitation and pleased surprise.

"It was my father," I exclaimed, with emotion; "I rejoice that his house became thy son's home, O lady. Blessed be my father!"

When Sarah heard that it was at your house, dear father, her son had been so hospitably entertained, she embraced me again and again, and entreated me to convey to you her heartfelt gratitude; which I do herewith. And it is, dearest father, because you know and love this young man, so providentially thrown upon your care, that I shall be so particular in recounting what I am about to do concerning him.

Ruth ended the reading of the letter, which told that he should return in the first ship bound to Sidon, or Cesarea, when he hoped to behold her and his mother face to face, and to receive as his bride, the maiden he had so long loved and cherished in his heart.

Sarah seemed now to be drawn closer to me in affection, and so also did Ruth, since they have learned that I am the daughter of the noble Jew who did so much for Samuel in a strange land. At length as the day drew near for me to leave, to return to Jerusalem, my health being quite invigorated, we were all taken with delighted surprise at the appearance of the long absent son and lover in the midst of our happy circle.

Mary and I had once seen him, and we were now impressed with his manly and sun-browned beauty, his bold air, and frank, ingenuous manner. We could not but agree that the pretty Ruth had shown fine taste. He gave to me the package which you desired him to forward to Jerusalem, and thus, we all round had reason to rejoice at his coming. But alas! my dear father, our joy was short-lived! Little did we anticipate how speedily our rejoicings were to end in mourning! The very night of his return, he was seized with a malignant fever, which he had brought from Africa with him and we were all overwhelmed with grief.

It would be impossible to paint to you the anguish of the mother; the heart-rending distress of his betrothed, as they bent over his couch, and saw the fierce plague burning him, as if he were in a furnace.

Unconscious of their presence, he raved wildly; and sometimes fancied himself suffering thirst on the burning sands of Africa and now, battling with the barbarians for his life. All that physicians could do, and his friends could do -- for he was greatly beloved as well for his own sake as for his mother's and Ruth's -- all was of no avail. This morning, the third day after his return, he expired, amid the most distressing agonies. Poor Ruth! the She cast herself, in perfect abandonment of grief, upon his lifeless and disfigured corpse and, now that they have removed her from the chamber of death, her shrieks fill the house. His mother sits by him, the image of despair, holding his cold hand in hers, and uttering wails of woe sad enough to rend a Roman's heart:

"My son! my son! lost and found, to be torn from me forever! Oh, that I had died for thee! Thou and Ruth would then be happy. Would to God I had died for thee, oh, my son, Samuel, my son!" It is like David bewailing Absalom.

I write this sad news to you, dear father, knowing how deeply you will mourn his death; for your letters show me that you have formed for him almost a paternal attachment, carried so far as a promise to provide him with a ship to trade in Egypt, after his marriage with Ruth shall have taken place. Alas! instead of a bridal, behold a funeral. Already the bearers are at the door, and in a few minutes he will be borne forth upon the dead-bier to the burial place without the city.

"Oh," sighs Mary near me, as I write, "oh, that Jesus the mighty Prophet, had been here; he could have healed him!" John had sent to her a message, saying that he is traveling this way, on his message of healing and teaching, and may be here this evening. But what will it avail, dear father? Even Jesus cannot return the dead to life! It was never known that the dead rose again. Oh, if he could have been here yesterday, his power over diseases would have enabled him to save his precious life! But regrets are useless. The noble young man is dead, and will live again only in the resurrection of the just.

I hear the heavy tread of the dead-bearers in the court below. The shrieks and wails of the mourning women thrill my soul with awe. But above all, pierces the wild cry of anguish of the bereaved mother! Ruth's voice is hushed. She has been, for the last hour, inanimate as marble, sitting, with a glazed eye and rigid features, gazing on vacancy! Only by her pulse can it be said she lives. Poor maiden! The blow is too terrible for her to bear.

My cousin Mary has, this moment, received a small roll of parchment, which, from the flush in her cheek, I know to be from her betrothed. She smiles sadly, and with tears in her eyes, hands it to me.

I have read it, dear father. It reads as follows, if I have time to transcribe it before the call to follow the dead forth to burial is given:

"Gadara, beyond Jordan."
"The bearer, beloved, is one of the disciples of Jesus. His name is Bartimeus. He was blind and poor, and subsisted by begging; and, as you see, his sight is restored, and he insists now on going from town to town, where he has been known as a blindman, to proclaim what Jesus has done for him. He takes this to you. I write to say that I wish thou mayest prosper in all things, and find the health for which thou and thy cousin sought the air of Mount Tabor. I have no greater joy than to hear of your welfare. This letter cometh, beseeching thee, lady, that as we love one another unfeignedly, so may we soon be united in that holy union which God hath blessed and commanded. I would have thee bear in remembrance that thou gavest thy promise here to, when last we met at Nazareth. But, having much to say, here upon, I will not commit it to paper and ink; but, by tomorrow, or the day after, I trust, to come to you, and speak with you, dearly beloved, face to face, those things which now come to my lips. Farewell, lady, and peace be with you, and all in your house. Greet thy friends in my name, letting them know that we shall shortly be with you, with Amos, your father, now our dear brother in the Lord. There are many things which I have seen and heard, touching my holy Master, Jesus, and his holy mission to the world, which I will declare unto you when we meet, that you also may have fellowship with us in those things which we know and believe concerning him. My Master saluteth thee, and all in your house; Amos, also, greeteth thee with a kiss. This is the second epistle I have written unto you from this place."

"Oh, that the mighty Prophet had come one day sooner!"

cried Mary. "What woe and anguish would have been spared poor Ruth and his mother! But the will of Jehovah be done."

We hear now, dear father, the voice of the governor of the funeral, bidding us come down to bury the dead.

Farewell, dearest father. I know you will shed a tear to the memory of the noble youth, whose death has this day filled all Nain with mourning. As I look from the lattice, I see the concourse of people to be immense, filling all the street. Now, may the God of our father Abraham preserve and keep you, and suffer us once more to meet face to face in joy and peace.

Your dutiful and sorrowful daughter,

ADINA

LETTER XXI.

Dearest Father: I seize my pen, which I laid down an hour ago, in order to follow to his burial, the son of our hostess, to recount to you one of the most extraordinary things which ever happened, and which fills us all with such joy and wonder, that I fear my trembling fingers will scarcely express legibly what I have to tell you.

As I told you in my letter just finished, I was called away to accompany the weeping mother to the burial place outside of the gates. But when I reached the courtyard, where the body of her son lay upon a bier, which the bearers had already raised upon their shoulders, the deep grief of poor Ruth overcame her wholly, and I led her to her room, where she sank insensible upon her couch. I could not leave her in her situation, and the procession went forth from the house without me; Mary, as she walked, supporting upon her arm the bereaved mother, clad in her mourning weeds.

As the funeral train passed the lattice, it seemed endless, so vast a number of people accompanied the body, to do honor to a widow in Israel. At length it passed by, and I was left alone with the motionless Ruth. She seemed to sleep, though every few moments she would murmur the name of the dead. I sat by her, reflecting upon the mysterious ways of God in bringing this widow's son safely home from the thousand dangers to which he had been exposed, from shipwreck and bondage, to gladden her soul with his presence for a few hours, and then to die in her arms! As I gazed on the marble countenance of the bereaved maiden, I could not but pray that she might not recover from her swoon, to revive to the bitter realization of her loss, and to the renewal of her grief.

Suddenly, I heard a very great shout. I started and hastened to the lattice. It was repeated louder, and with a glad tone, that showed me it was a shout of joy. It seemed to come from beyond the city walls, and from a hundred voices raised in unison. I knew that the housetop overlooked the walls, and seeing that Ruth moved not, I ascended rapidly to the parapet, the shouts and glad cries still increasing as I went up, and exciting my wonder and curiosity. Upon reaching the flat roof, and stepping upon the parapet, I saw coming along the street, toward the house, with the speed of the antelope, Elec, our Gibeonite slave. He was waving his hands wildly, and crying out something which I could not distinctly hear. Behind him I saw two youths running also, appearing to be the bearers of some great tidings.

I knew something wonderful must have occurred, but could not divine what it could be. On looking toward the gate, from which direction the shouts, at intervals, continued to approach, I discovered, on the hillside of the cemetery, many people crowded together, and evidently surrounding some person in their midst; for the whole order of the procession was broken up. The bier, I could not discern, nor could I comprehend how the solemnity of the march of the funeral train was so suddenly changed to a confused multitude, rending the sky with loud acclamations. The whole body of people was pressing back toward the city.

The persons whom I had first seen running along the street, now made themselves audible as they drew nigher.

"He is alive! He is alive!" shouted Elec.

"He has been raised from the dead!" cried the young man next behind him.

"He lives, and is walking back to the city!" called the third, to those who, like me, had run to their house-tops to know the meaning of the uproar we heard.

"Who -- who is alive?" I eagerly demanded of Elec, as he passed beneath the parapet. "What is this shouting, O Elec?"

He looked up to me with a face expressive of the keenest delight, mixed with awe, and said:

"Young Rabbi Samuel is come to life! He is no longer dead. You will soon see him, for they are escorting him back to the city and everybody is mad with joy. Where is Ruth, the maiden? I am come to tell her the glorious news."

With emotion that I cannot describe, hardly believing what I heard, I hastened to Ruth, in order to prevent the effects of too sudden joy. Upon reaching the apartment, I found that the voice of Elec, who had shouted the news, of which he was the bearer, in her ears, had roused her from her stupor of grief. She was looking at him wildly and incomprehensibly. I ran to her, and folding her in my arms, said:

"Dear Ruth, there is news -- good news! It must be true. Hear the shouts of gladness in all the town!"

"Lives!" she repeated, shaking her head "no,no, no! Yes, there." she said, raising her beautiful, glittering eyes to heaven, and pointing upward.

"But on earth also," cries Elec, with positiveness. "I saw him sit up, and heard him speak, as well as ever he was!"

"How was it? Let me know," I cried.

"How? Who could have done such a miracle but the mighty Prophet we saw at Jerusalem?" he answered.

"Jesus? " I exclaimed with joy.

"Who else could it be? Yes; he met the bier just outside -- But here they come!"

Elec was interrupted in his narrative by the increased noise of voices in the streets, and the tramp of hundreds of feet. The next moment the room was filled with a crowd of the most excited persons, some weeping, some laughing, as if beside themselves. In their midst I beheld Samuel walking, alive and well, his mother clinging to him, like a vine about an oak.

"Where is Ruth?" he cried. "Oh! where is she? Let me make her happy with my presence."

I gazed upon him with awe, at if I had seen a spirit.

Ruth no sooner heard his voice than she uttered a shriek of joy. "He lives -- he indeed lives!" and springing forward, she was saved from falling to the ground by being clasped to his manly breast.

"Let us kneel and thank God!" he said.

For a few moments the scene was solemn and touching, beyond any spectacle ever exhibited on earth. The newly risen from the dead knelt in the midst of the floor, with his mother on his right, leaning her head upon his shoulder, and Ruth clasped in his left arm, and fast embracing him as if he were an angel, who would else spread his wings and ascend, leaving her behind. Mary and I knelt by her side, while all the people bowed their heads in worship, as he lifted up his voice in grateful acknowledgments to the Giver of life and health, for restoring both to him. When he had performed this first sacred duty, he rose to his feet, and received all our embraces. Hundreds came in to see his face, and every tongue was eloquent in praise of the power at Jesus.

"And where is this holy Prophet?" I asked of Mary. "Shall he be forgotten amid all our joy?"

"We thanked him there with all our hearts, and bathed his hands with tears of gratitude," she answered "but when they would have brought him into the city in triumph, he conveyed himself away in the confusion, and no one could see aught of him. But John, who was with him, told me he would come into the city as the quiet was restored, by and by, and he would bring him to our abode."

"Oh! I shall then behold him, and thank him also," I cried. "Make known to me, Mary, the particulars of this wonderful miracle," I asked of her; for though I saw Samuel now seated, and eating in the room, served by his glad mother and the happy Ruth, while all looked on, to see if he really ate, and though I believed in the power of Jesus to do all things, yet I could hardly realize that he whom I had seen carried out a dead man on his bier, I beheld now seated at table, partaking of food, alive and well.

"I will tell thee all," answered Mary, whose face shone with a holy light, radiating from her intense happiness and, leading me apart, she said:

"As we went weeping forth, slowly following the bier and had passed the gate, we saw, coming along the path through the valley leading to Tabor, a party of twelve or thirteen men on foot. They were followed by a crowd of men, women and children from the country, and were so moving that they would meet us at the crossing of the stone bridge. Hearing someone say, "It is the Prophet of Nazareth, with his disciples," I looked earnestly forward, and joyfully recognized Jesus at their head, with John walking by his side.

"Oh, that Jesus had been in Nain, when thy son was sick!" I said to the widow, pointing him out to her, as the Prophet and his company stopped at the entrance to the bridge, and drew to one side, for the way was too narrow for both parties to cross at the same time. Upon looking up and seeing him, and marking his benign countenance, and how sorrowfully he gazed upon her, and recollecting how he might have prevented her son's dying, had he been in Nain, the poor lady could no longer command her grief, which broke forth afresh; and covering her face with her veil, she wept so violently that all eyes were piteously fastened upon her. I observed that the holy Prophet's rested upon her with compassion and, as the widow came opposite where he stood, he advanced a step toward us, and said in a voice of thrilling sympathy:

"Weep not, mother. Thy son shall live again!"

"I know it, O Rabboni, at the last day," she answered. "He was so noble -- so young -- he was all to me, and had been so long absent in far lands, only to come home to die. I know that thou art a Prophet come from God, and that all good works follow thee. Oh, if thou hadst been here, my son need not have died. Thy word would have healed him. But now he is dead! deal! dead!"

"The bereaved mother then poured forth her tears afresh.

"Daughter, weep not. I will restore thy son!"

"What saith he?" cried some Pharisees who were in the funeral, "that he will raise a dead man? This is going too far." And they smiled and scoffed.

"But Jesus laid his hand upon the pall over the body, and said to those who bare the bier:

"Rest the bier upon the ground."

"They instantly stood still and obeyed him. He then advanced amid a hushed silence, and, uncovering the marble visage, touched the hand of the dead man, and said, is a loud and commanding voice:

"Young man, I say unto thee, Arise!"

"There was a moment's painful stillness through the vast multitude. Every eye was fixed upon the bier. His voice was heard by the spirit of the dead, and it came back to his body. There was visible a living trembling emotion of the hitherto motionless corpse! color flushed the livid cheek; the eye lids opened, and he fixed his eyes on Jesus; he raised his hand, his lips moved; he sat up on the bier, and then spake aloud in his natural voice, saying:

" Lo! here I am."

"Jesus then took him by the hand, and, assisting him to alight upon his feet, he led him to his mother, and delivered him to her, saying: "Woman, behold thy son!"

"Upon seeing this miracle, the people shouted with joy and wonder, and there came a great fear on us all and, lifting up their voices, they who so lately mourned and bewailed the dead, glorified God, saying, "God has indeed visited his people Israel. A great Prophet is risen up among us. The Messias is come, and Jesus is very Christ, with the keys of death and hell."

"With such words and exclamations, and great shouts of rejoicing, the multitude surrounded the restored young man, and proceeded to escort him back to the city; the great mass of the people being attracted more by the raised to life than by the august person by whose act it had seen done. I sought out Jesus, to cast myself at his feet, but he shrunk from the homage and gratitude which his mercy to us had awakened. Thus, humility is an element of all power."

Such, my dear father, is the narrative of the restoration to life again of Samuel, the son of Sarah, of Nain. I give it to you in its simple outlines. It will not fail to command your belief. The miracle was performed in open day, in the presence of thousands. The opposers of Jesus, the hostile Scribes and Pharisees, do not deny the miracle, for they were convinced of the reality of the death of the young man; for he died, as I have before said, of the plague, and his corpse was a loathsome sight to those who beheld it; yet, wonderful to relate, when he was restored to life by the power of Jesus, he sat up free from all external signs of the putrid disease, his skin fair and smooth, and his whole aspect that of ruddy health and manly beauty. No man could doubt, therefore, that a miracle had been performed, and of the most extraordinary kind; for never was it heard before that the dead were restored to life. This miracle of restoration from the dead, of Samuel, the widow's son, has caused hundreds this day to confess his name, and to believe in him as the anointed Shiloh of Israel.

Since writing the above, I have conversed with Samuel upon the consciousness which he had of being dead. He replies, that it seemed to him that he had been in a dream, the chain of which was now broken, and could not be recollected again. "Fragments," said he, "of a delightful condition of splendor; of glory and bliss; of music ineffable, and scenes indescribable, passed before my mind for a few moments after standing upon my feet; but they presently melted away; and I can now only recollect that there were such! When I found myself upon the bier, I felt no surprise; for, the fact that I was being taken to my burial seemed instinctively to present itself to my reanimated consciousness." Many of the doctors have been to see him through the day, and have put profound questions to him, touching the state of the soul out of the body; but he could give them no satisfaction, all appearing to him like shining fragments of a gorgeous vision.

Jesus came into the town during the evening, and abode with us. You should have witnessed how the gratitude of the happy mother, and of the no less happy Ruth, exhibited itself. They anticipated his every wish, and seemed to desire that he had a thousand wants, that they might administer to them. But his life is simple -- his wants few. He thinks little of comforts; and so that he can speak of the kingdom of God to those about him, he forgets to partake of the food before him. We also forget all things else when he speaks, and stand or sit around him, drinking in the rich eloquence of his wise lips. The more I see of him, dear father, the more I stand in awe of him, and love him.

Mary is tomorrow to become the bride of John, and Jesus will be present at the wedding, for, while he severely rebukes sin and folly, he sanctifies, by his presence, the holy rite of marriage, which God ordained. Next month, the seventh day of the month, the happy Ruth consents to give her hand to the noble youth whom she has so wonderingly received alive from the dead.

On the eve of the seventh day I shall depart hence, with John and Mary, for Jerusalem, whence I will write you again.

Your loving daughter,

ADINA.

LETTER XXII.

Once more, my dear father, I address a letter to you from this holy city. This morning, when I awoke at the sound of the silver trumpets of the priests, ringing melodiously from the top of Mount Moriah, I experienced anew that profound devotion which the children of Abraham must always feel in the city of God, and in the presence of His very Temple. As I ascended the roof of the house to prayer, the gorgeous pile of the Temple towered heavenward from the summit of Moriah, in all the magnificence of its celestial beauty. The azure wreaths of incense were already curling upward into the still skies, while the murky cloud sent up by the burnt sacrifice rolled darkly above the pinnacle, casting an awful shade over all the Temple. As it sailed slowly onward, and hung above the valley of Kedron, the sun rose and gilded its massive edges as if they had been turned out with gold. Louder and clearer rang the trumpets, and every house-top soon had its group of worshipers, while along the streets rolled the tide of people, some leading lambs, others driving goats before them, others carrying doves in their bosoms, to be offered to the Lord by the priests.

It was a joyous morning to see, dear father, for Aemilius, the noble Roman Prefect, was this day voluntarily to present himself at the Temple, to be made a proselyte to the holy faith of Israel. I will not now detain you by recording the arguments by which he was led to renounce idolatry and become a Jew! Pilate, the Procurator, favored, instead of opposing it, believing that it would conciliate the Jews in favor of the Romans; he resolved, therefore, to grace the rite with his presence. I could see him proudly rolling onward toward the Temple in his gilded chariot, escorted by a score of guards, blazing in their Grecian cuirasses. I sought in vain the form of Aemilius; but he reached the Temple by another street. The morning was, therefore, additionally lovely to me. I thought I had never seen the olive groves, on the hill side, beyond the king's gardens, so green, nor the harvest so yellow, as they undulated in the soft breeze of the opening morn. The lofty palms everywhere appeared to bend and wave their verdant fans with joyous motion. The birds in the palace gardens sang sweeter and louder; and Jerusalem itself seemed more beautiful than ever. While I was gazing upon the scene, and adoring God, and thanking him for the conversion of Aemilius, Rabbi Amos came, and said that he would take us to the Temple, for he was at leisure on that morning. We were soon on our way, climbing the paved pathway to Moriah. Oh, how sublimely towered the divine Temple above our heads, seemingly lost in the blue of the far heavens! The great gates opening North and South, to the East and West, were thronged with the multitude pressing through; while, from the galleries above each gate pealed forth the clear-voiced trumpets of God in ceaseless reverberation. My uncle pointed out to me the massive doors, all overlaid with sheets of beaten gold, and the floor of green marble, on which we trode. He bade me notice the costly entablature of colored stones, exquisitely worked with the Grecian's chisel; and especially the roof of fretted silver, set with precious stones, the onyx, beryl, sapphire, carbuncle, and jasper. I was dazzled by the magnificence, and awed by the vast extent of the space of splendor surrounding me; while ten thousands of people were to be seen moving toward the altar of sacrifice. From that superb court, I was led into a hall nearly a hundred cubits in length, its ceiling of pure gold, sustained by a thousand and one columns of porphyry and white marble, ranged alternately. Such richness I had never conceived of, or thought possible on earth. But when Rabbi Amos explained that they all were made after patterns of heavenly things, I ceased to marvel, and only wished I might one day dwell in those celestial abodes, where, the holy Jesus teaches us, are mansions not made with hands, of endless duration, reserved for all the good and virtuous.

I was not permitted to approach the sacred chamber, where stood the four thousand vessels of gold of Ophir, used in the sacrifices on great days; and this being a high day, I saw no less than six hundred priests standing about the altar, each with a golden censer in his hand. Beyond was the holy ark of the covenant, over which the cherubim hovered, their wings meeting, and between them is the mercy-seat! As this was the Holy of Holies, I was not permitted to see it; but its position was pointed out to me within the veil, which conceals from all eyes but that of the High Priest once a year, the seat of God's throne on earth, alas, now left vacant since the glory of the Shechinah departed from the Holy of Holies!

The air of the vast Temple was delicious with the fragrance of burning frankincense. As the victims bled, and the smoke ascended, the people fell on their faces and worshiped God. It was an impressive scene, and made my heart stand still. I seemed to expect to hear the voice of Jehovah breaking the stillness that followed. But, after a few moments' silence, a sudden trumpet note thrilled every soul in the countless multitude. It was followed by a peal of music that shook the air, from a choir of two thousand singers, male and female, of the sons and daughters of Levi, who served in the Temple. Entering from the southern court, they advanced in long procession, singing sacred chants, and playing on sacbut and harp, psalter and nebble, chinna and tympana. As they ascended to the choir, their voices, mingling with the instruments, filled all the Temple. I never heard before such sublime harmony; especially when, on reaching the elevated choir, a thousand Levites, with manly voices, joined them, and the whole company chanted one of the sublimest of the Psalms of David. I was overcome - my senses dissolved in a sea of seraphic sounds my heart swelled as if it would break, and I found relief only in a flood of tears.

When the chant was concluded, the whole multitude responded, "Amen, and Amen," like the deep voice of an earthquake suddenly shaking the foundations of the Temple.

At length I beheld a train of priests following the High Priest as he marched thrice around the altar. In the procession I discovered a company of proselytes, escorted by twelve aged priests with long snowy beards, and in vestments of the purest white. Among the proselytes, which numbered full a score of men, from almost every nation, I detected the tall and noble figure of the Roman Aemilius. He was robed in a black garment from head to foot. But upon approaching the baptismal basin, two young priests removed this sable dress, and robed him in white. I then saw him baptized into the family of Abraham, and a new name given him, that of Eleazer. I heard the silver trumpets proclaim the conversion, and the multitudes shouting their joy!

Of the rest of the ceremony I have no recollection, as after the baptism of Aemilius, I was too happy to see or think of anyone else. There stands now, dear father, no further bar to our union. Aemilius is become a Jew, and henceforth will worship the God of our fathers! I know you said in your last letter to me that you feared the noble young Roman was led by his attachment to me to renounce his religion, and not from honest conviction of its truth or of its falsehood. But I am assured, dear father, that he acts from conviction. The conversations he has had with me, and with Rabbi Amos, and other of the learned doctors of our nation, whom he has met at our house, with the careful reading of the Scriptures of the Prophets, have not only convinced him that the Lord God of Israel is the only God of the whole earth, but that the worshipers of idols are the worshipers of Satan, who hath set up that religion in opposition to that of the true God.

While I was lifting up my heart in gratitude for the happy conversion of Aemilius, and while the Jews were crowding about him to extend to him the hand of fellowship, rejoicing that so noted a person should embrace our faith, Uncle Amos drew my attention by exclaiming with gladness:

"Behold! there is Jesus!"

"Where?" I cried, trying to discover the divine Prophet among the multitude.

"Standing by yonder pillar of porphyry. John is on one side of him and Peter on the other. He is pointing to the altar, and explaining or teaching them something. Let us try and approach him!"

We at once made our way, but with difficulty, toward the spot where we had discovered him. The rumor that the Christ was in the Temple rapidly spread, and the whole multitude pressed toward the same point. At length, we attained our object so as to get within a few feet of him. Here a tall, richly attired Greek addressed Rabbi Amos, saying:

"Sir, tell me who that youthful Jew is, whose countenance is stamped with firmness and benevolence so finely combined in its expression; whose air possesses such dignity and wisdom; whose noble eye seems filled with a holy sadness; and whose glance is full of innocence and sweetness. He seems born to love men and to command them. All seek to approach him. Pray, sir, who is he?"

"That, O stranger is Jesus of Nazareth, the Jewish Prophet," said Uncle Amos, delighted to point him out to a foreigner.

"Then am I well rewarded for my journey in turning aside to Jerusalem," answered the Grecian. "I have ever heard of His fame in Macedonia, and am rejoiced to behold him. Think you he will do some great miracle?"

"He performs miracles not to gratify curiosity, but to bear testimony to the truths he teaches, that they are delivered to him of God. Hark! He speaks," cried my uncle.

Every voice was hushed, as that of Jesus rose clear and sweet, and thrilling, like a celestial clarion speaking. And he preached, dear father, a sermon so full of wisdom, of love to man, of love to God, of knowledge of our hearts, of divine and convincing power, that thousands wept, thousands were chained to the spot with awe and delight, and all were moved as if an angel had addressed them. They cried, "Never man spake like this man!" and certainly never human lips dispensed such wisdom.

When he had ended, the priests, seeing that he had carried the hearts of all the people, were greatly enraged, and not being able to vent their hatred and fear in any other way, they hired a vile person by the name of Gazeel, a robber, to take one of the blood-stained sacrificing knives from the altar, and creep toward him behind the column and assassinate him. The robber drew near, and taking a favorable position to execute the deed, raised his hand to strike the Prophet from behind, when Jesus turning his head, arrested the hand of the assassin midair, by a look! Unable to move a muscle, Gazeel stood betrayed to all eyes in this murderous attitude, like a statue of stone.

When Jesus had exhibited him to all the vast concourse in this manner for a few minutes, he said to him:

"Return to those who hired thee. My hour is not yet come, nor can they have any power over me until my Father's will be fulfilled concerning me."

The assassin bowed his head with deep humility; the knife dropped from his hand and rang upon the marble floor; and he sank at Jesus' feet, imploring forgiveness. The people would have torn Gazeel in pieces, but Jesus said:

"Let him depart in peace. The day shall come when he will be willing to lay down his life to save mine. Ye, priests, go about to kill me," he added, fixing his clear gaze upon the group which had sent Gazeel. "For what do ye seek my life? Because I bear testimony to the wickedness of your own. Ye lay heavy burdens on the people, and will not lift them with one of your fingers. I have come to my own, and to my Temple, and ye receive me not. The day cometh when this

Temple shall be thrown down, and not one stone left upon another; and some who hear me shall behold and mourn in that day. Oh, Jerusalem, thou that killest the prophets, and stonest them that are sent unto thee, how oft would I have gathered thy children together, as a hen gathered her chickens under wings and ye would not. Thou shalt be left desolate and cast out from among the cities, because thou knewest not the day of thy visitation. But ye, who would escape these troubles, seek to enter my kingdom, which shall have no end; fly to the Jerusalem which is above, and which is above all, whose foundation is eternal, and whose Temple is the Lord God Almighty, who is also the light and glory thereof."

Upon hearing these words, there arose a great cry from ten thousand voices:

"Hail to Jesus, the king of Israel and Judah! Hosanna to the Prince of David! We will have no king but Jesus."

At this shout, which was caught and repeated beyond the four gates of the Temple, the priests cried aloud that the people were in insurrection.

Pilate, who was, with his guard, just leaving the Court of the Gentiles, hearing it, turned to ask what it meant. One of the priests, desirous of having Jesus slain, quickly answered, "That the people had proclaimed Jesus, the Nazarene, king," and that he was already placing himself at the head of the people.

Hearing this, Pilate sent off messengers to the Castle of David for soldiers, and with his bodyguard turned back to the Temple gate, charging the people, sword in hand.

The tumult was now fearful, and the bloodshed would have been great, but Jesus suddenly appeared before him -- none saw how he had reached the place -- and said:

"There is no insurrection, O Roman! I am Jesus. I seek no kingdom but such as my Father hath given me. Neither thy power, nor thy master's, is in peril. My kingdom is not of this world."

Pilate was seen to bend his proud head with low obeisance before the Prophet, and said graciously:

"I have no wish to arrest thee. Thy word, O Prophet, is sufficient for me. Of thee I have hitherto heard much. Wilt thou come with me to my palace, and let me hear thee, and see some miracle?"

"Thou shalt see me in thy palace, but not today; and thou shalt behold a miracle, but not now."

When Jesus had thus said, he withdrew himself from Pilate's

presence; and those who would have sought him to make him a king could no where discover him.

The result of this attempt of the people to make the Prophet their king, and under his direction to overthrow the Roman power, has been, that the Roman authorities, instigated by Annas and the priests, begin to look upon Jesus with eyes of jealousy; and Pilate this morning told a deputation of priests, who waited on him to petition him to arrest and imprison the Prophet, that on the first proof they could bring him of his hostility to Caesar, he would send soldiers to take him. Today Jesus was refreshing himself in our house, when several Scribes and Pharisees came in. I saw by their dark looks they meditated evil; and secretly sent Elec with a message to Aemilius (now Eleazer), asking him to be at hand to protect Jesus; for Aemilius is devoted to him as we are, and Jesus takes delight in teaching him the things of the kingdom of God.

Jesus, knowing the hearts of these bad men, said to them, after they had seated themselves, and remained some minutes in silence:

"Wherefore are ye come?"

"Master," said Jehoram, one of the chief Scribes, "we know that thou art a Teacher come from God, and fearest no man. nor regardest the person of any man."

"Yes," added Zadoc, a Levite of great fame among the people, "we have heard how boldly thou speakest at all times and that thou shrinkest from no man's power -- not even Pilate, nor Herod, nay, nor Caesar, could make thee refrain from what thou willest to utter. Is it lawful to us Jews, the peculiar nation of God, to pay tribute to Caesar, who is an idolater? Is it lawful for us to obey the laws of Pilate, rather than of Moses? We ask this as Jews, to a Jew. Tell us frankly; for thou fearest not the face of any man."

"Let the question rest simply upon the tribute to the Romans," answered Jehoram. "Master, ought we, the holy nation, to give tribute to the Emperor Caesar?"

Jesus looked fixedly upon them, as if he read their wicked designs and said:

"Show me the tribute money."

Zadoc handed him a penny, the Roman coin sent into Judea by Caesar, as our currency, and which we return to Rome again in tribute. When Jesus had taken the money, he looked on the head of Augustus stamped upon one side, and then turning to them, as they waited breathlessly for his answer, said sternly:

"Whose image and whose name is here impressed?"

"Caesar's," eagerly answered the whole party.

"Then render unto the Caesar the things that be Caesar's, and unto God the things that be God's," was his calm and wonderful answer.

I breathed again; for I feared he would answer openly that tribute ought not to be paid, which they hoped he would do, when they would immediately have accused him to Pilate as teaching that we ought not to pay tribute to Rome, and so a fomenter of rebellion.

But the divine wisdom of his answer relieved all our minds while the Scribes and Levites, his enemies, looked upon him with amazement, interchanged glances of conscious defeat, and left the house.

Such, dear father, is his wisdom, that his enemies cannot triumph over him. Oh, that you could see him and hear him. It is worth a visit from Egypt to Jerusalem to see and listen to him, and behold his miracles, of which he every day performs one or more, till disease, deformity, leprosy and sickness, seem to have disappeared from Jerusalem and all Judea.

When Aemilius arrived, and found Jesus alone with our family, unharmed, he spoke freely his satisfaction.

"Aemilius," said Jesus to him, "thou art now become a Jew. One step more, and thou shalt enter the kingdom of Heaven."

"What step, dear master?" he asked earnestly.

"Thou must be baptized with the Holy Ghost, and thou shalt be partaker of eternal life."

"Rabboni," said Aemilius, "I verily thought that to be baptized a proselyte of thy people was to be Moses' disciple, and to have the seal to life eternal. Have I still more to do?"

"To be my disciple, Aemilius. I am the end of the Law of Moses. He that believeth in me, though he were dead, yet shall he live. I give eternal life to as many as believe in me. But thou knowest not now what I say; thou shalt know hereafter."

Aemilius would have questioned him further, but Jesus left him, and went forth into the garden, where he remained late at night in meditation and prayer.

I am rejoiced, dear father, that you permit me to accompany my Uncle Amos to Cesarea. We leave after the new moon. Believing, my dearest father, that all I have written you touching Jesus has not been in vain, and that you are, with me and thousands in Israel, ready to believe him that he is the Christ, the Deliverer of Jacob,

I remain, your affectionate daughter.
ADINA.

LETTER XXIII.

My Dear Father: I have received with joy your letter, in which you say you shall leave Egypt with the next Passover caravan, in order to visit Jerusalem. Already you must be on the way, and are by this time near Gaza, where my Uncle Amos says the caravan will halt tomorrow night. My heart bounds to embrace you, and my eyes fill with bright tears at the thought that I shall once more gaze upon your noble countenance, and hear the loved tones of your paternal voice. My happiness is augmented to know that you will be here while Jesus is in the city; for it is said, and John, Mary's cousin, asserts it, that he will certainly be at the Passover. I wish, dear father, oh, wish you to see him, because I feel that you would be unable to resist the conviction that he is the very Messias of God, of whom Moses and the Prophets wrote. But if his words, that divine eloquence and wisdom which flow from his sacred lips, do not convince you, the miracles he will do in proof of his mission will be resistless. These miracles are daily becoming more and more mighty and amazing. For himself, for his own aggrandizement, and personal safety (for often has his life been put in peril by big foes), he never resorts to this divine power; but to give attestation to his words of truth that he came from God, to heal the suffering, to relieve the distressed, he daily performs them. If man never spake like him, man never worked wonders such as he works. He has converted water into wine; healed by a word the dying son of the nobleman, Chuza, Herod's first officer of his household, though many leagues from him at the time; he stilled a fearful tempest on the sea of Tiberias, by speaking to it and commanding peace. In the country of the Gadarenes he cast out unclean spirits from many demoniacs, who, in coming out of the bodies of those they had possessed, acknowledged his power, and confessed him, as if against their will, to be the Christ, the son of David. Of the raising of the daughter of the ruler, Jairus, and

185

of the son of the widow at Nain, I have already written you. Besides these miracles of healing and raising from the dead, he has been seen walking upon the sea a league from the shore, as firmly at if he trode upon a floor of porphyry; which many of the fishermen seeing, they were filled with terror, and made all sail to flee to the land, where they spread it abroad. He has restored sight to the blind, whose eyes were wholly gone; and created new limbs where legs and arms had been lost for years. Last week, Eli, a paralytic, whom you knew, a scribe of the Levites, whose hand has been withered nine years, so that he had been dependent on the alms of the worshipers in the Temple for his bread, hearing of the power of Jesus, sought him at the house of Uncle Amos, where he was abiding; for it was our blessed privilege to have him our guest, for John, his beloved disciple, being betrothed to the fair daughter of Uncle Amos, my gentle cousin Mary, always led the Prophet to our house.

Jesus was reclining with our family at the evening meal, at the close of the day on which the uproar had taken place in the Temple, as described in my last letter but one, when Eli came and stood within the door. Humble and doubting, his knees trembled, and he timidly and wistfully looked toward Jesus, but did not speak. I knew at once what the afflicted man came for, and approached him, saying, "Fear not, Eli ask him, and he will make thee whole!"

"Ah, lady, I fear it is too much happiness for me to expect. It is more than I dare dream of. But I have come to him, hoping." His voice trembled, and tears dropped from his eyes, as he thought of his family in poverty, and of his own helplessness. "How shall I speak to the great Prophet, daughter --- I, a beggar at the gate of the Temple? Speak for me, and the Lord shall bless thee, child. My tongue cleaves to the roof of my mouth!"

Jesus did not see the poor man, his face being turned toward Rabbi Amos, to whom he was explaining the meaning of the sacrifice of Abel. But leaving this conversation, he said, in a gentle voice, without turning round:

"Come to me, Eli, and ask what is in thy heart, and fear not for if thou believest, thou shalt receive all thy wish!"

At this Eli ran forward, and casting himself at Jesus' feet, kissed them and said: "Rabbi, I am a poor, sinful man; I believe that thou art the Christ, the Son of the Blessed!"

"Dost thou believe, Eli, that I have power to make thee whole?" asked Jesus, looking steadily upon him.

"I believe, my Lord," answered Eli, bowing his face to the ground.

"Thy sins, then, be forgiven thee. Rise and go to thy house, and sin no more, lest a worse thing come upon thee."

"This man! forgiveth he sins also? " cried the venerable priest, Manasses, who was at the table. "He is a blasphemer! for God alone forgiveth sins. Will he call himself God?" And he rose quickly up and rent his robe, and spat upon the floor in detestation.

"Manasses." said Jesus mildly, "tell me whether is it an easier thing to do: to say to this man kneeling here, "Thy sins be forgiven thee" or to say, "Stretch forth thine hand whole as the other?"

"It would be more difficult to do the latter," answered Manasses, surprised at the question.

"Who alone can do the latter, oh, priest?"

"God alone, who first made him," answered Manasses, gazing upon the withered arm, which shriveled to the bone, hung useless at his side.

"If, then, God alone heals, and God alone forgiveth sins, both acts, Manasses, would be of God! Therefore," said Jesus to the paralytic, "I say unto thee, Eli, stretch forth thy hand whole!"

The man, looking upon Jesus' face, and seeming to derive confidence from its expression of power, made a convulsive movement with his arm, which, his mantle falling off, was bared to the shoulder, exhibiting all its hideous deformity, and stretched it forth at full length. Immediately the arm was rounded with flesh and muscles; the pulse filled and leaped with the warm life-blood, and it became whole as the other. The change was so instantaneous that it was done before we could see how it was done. The amazed and wonderingly delighted Eli bent his elbow, expanded and contracted the fingers, felt the flesh and pressed it with his other hand, before he could realize that he was healed. And he then lifted up his voice in praise to Jehovah, and casting himself at the feet of the Prophet, cried:

"My Lord, and my God:"

"Thou art now healed, Eli," said Jesus impressively "go, and sin no more!"

"Master, thou knowest all things! Lo! my sin even was not hid from thee, though I believed no eye beheld it. Men and brethren," he continued addressing those who were assembled, "well did this holy Prophet of God say unto me, at the first, "my sins were forgiven,' instead of bidding me stretch forth my hand; for it was a sin that brought on my paralysis, as a punishment for it. I had copied a parchment for the Levite, Phineas, the tax-gatherer for the Temple service, and wickedly altered a figure in an amount, by which I should be a gainer of four shekels of silver. Instantly upon writing the last figure I felt a stroke of palsy, and my arm fell dead at my side. It was God's punishment. This was eight years ago. No eye knew the deed, but God's and my own; but I have repeated it in deep humiliation. Therefore, as my withered arm was for the punishment of sin, well did my Lord, the mighty Prophet, say unto me, "my sin was forgiven" for then would my punishment have been removed; for I felt already at this word the blood coursing through my parched veins!"

Upon this frank acknowledgment, Manasses cried in amazement, "Truly, God is good to Israel. The hour of his promise is come. Verily, oh, Jesus of Nazareth, thou art the Son of the Highest! Forgive a worm of the dust, and my sins also!" And the proud priest fell at Jesus's feet, and bowed his snow-white locks upon them in adoration and reverence.

If then, dear father, the secret sins of men are know to Jesus; if he forgives sins as well as heals; if he removes the temporal penalties which God inflicts upon men for their iniquities, what name, what power, what excellence shall we give to him? Shall we not, with Esaias, call him, "the Wonderful, the Counselor, the Mighty God, the Prince of Peace, who shall sit upon the throne of David to establish it with justice and judgment henceforth, even for ever?" "Who," I repeat, with Manasses, "who forgiveth sins but God alone?"

How shall I be able to remember and repeat all the other mighty works which Jesus has done in proof of his divine power? You must have heard how he fed from a small basket of bread (the frugal provision which a lad had brought into the desert for his mother and his brothers,) no less than five thousand men, not naming the women and children. The vast multitude had followed him far from the cities to listen to his teaching; people of all classes and tongues, including not a few Roman captains. When the mighty host was an hungered, he caused them to sit down on the grass, and from the basket he took forth bread, inexhaustibly increasing unto his hand as he distributed; so that when all had eaten, there were gathered twelve times as much in fragments as the little basket originally held. Who, dear father, but Messias could do this miracle? He who could thus create bread at his will, is He not the Lord of the harvests of the earth? My mind is overwhelmed, my dear father -- I am filled with astonishment and awe, when I reflect upon the might, power, and majesty of Jesus, and I fear to ask myself, -- who more than man is he? Is he verily the awful and terrible Jehovah of Sinai, visible in the human form? Oh, wondrous and incomprehensible mystery! a man with Almighty power, and manifesting the attributes of Jehovah, the Lord of hosts, walking the earth, conversing with men, dwelling in our habitations, eating and drinking with us, and sleeping with the peaceful helplessness of an infant beneath our roofs. I dare not trust my thoughts to penetrate the mystery in which he walks among us in the veiled Godhead of his power. His beloved disciple, John, says that Jesus has promised the day is not far off when this veil will be removed, and we shall then know him, who he is, and wherefore he has come into the world, and the infinite results of his mission.

The Passover is nigh at hand, when we shall again behold the majesty of his presence. I have just heard that Lazarus, the amiable brother of our cousins Mary and Martha, is taken suddenly ill, and I close this letter in order to accompany my cousin Mary and her father to Bethany, from whence they have sent us an earnest message of entreaty. May God preserve his life!

Your devoted daughter,

ADINA.

LETTER XXIV.

My Dear Father: As I was closing my last letter to you, intelligence reached my Uncle Amos, that Lazarus, the amiable brother of Martha and Mary, was very ill. The message was brought by Melec, the old Gibeonite slave, who, with tears in his eyes, communicated to us the sad news. My cousin Mary and I at once set out to go to Bethany with him, Uncle Amos kindly offering his two mules for us to ride upon, promising himself to come out also after the evening service in the Temple, if Lazarus should be no better.

We were soon beyond the city walls, on the road to Bethany, guided by an aged servant, who, every few minutes, would urge us to ride faster; and then, lifting his hands and eyes, he would lament the danger of the young man, and the destitution of his sisters, should he be removed from them, he being, dear father, their only support, as I once wrote you his occupation being that of copying out rolls of the Prophets, for the uses of the various synagogues.

Although we did not expect to be able to do much by hastening to our dear relatives in their affliction yet, we hoped, by our presence and heart felt sympathy, to relieve much of the solicitude of the beloved sisters for their dear brother.

"Knowest thou, Melec, the disease that has suddenly seized my cousin?" asked Mary, as we wound slowly up the path that leads the steepest side of Olivet.

"Ah, dear me, noble lady, I know not," answered Melec, shaking his head. "He has just returned from the city, where he had been staying night and day for a week, laboring industriously to complete a copy of the Five Books of the blessed Moses for the Procurator's chief captain, for which he was to receive a large sum in Roman gold."

"What was the name of this captain who seeks to obtain our holy books?" I asked, hope half answering the question in my heart.

"Aemilius, the brave knight, they say, who was made a proselyte at the last Passover; the same who nearly captured the famous robber, Barabbas, my lady."

I was rejoiced to hear this proof of the steady desire of the princely Roman knight to learn our sacred laws, you may be assured, dearest father. But Melec went on speaking, and said:

"It was his hard work to complete this copy which made him ill for he slept not, nor ceased to toil, until he had completed it; and when he came home, with the silver-bound roll in his hand, and laid it upon the table before his sisters, he fell, at the same moment, fainting to the ground. When they raised him up, he was in a fierce fever, and raved so that he knew no one around him."

"Alas, poor Lazarus!" we both exclaimed, and urged our mules forward at a faster pace, our hearts bleeding for the sorrow of his sisters and for his sad condition. I have already told you in a former letter, in which I described my visit to the house of Mary and Martha, what a noble and good young man their brother was--how he was beloved by all who knew him; and commanded the respect of his superiors by his dignity of bearing, while his manly beauty won the hearts of the maidens who were his sister's friends. I told you how diligently he toiled for the maintenance of those dearly loved sisters and helpless mother, thinking only of their comfort, forgetful of his own. I also related how that his many virtues had won for him the friendship of the equally youthful Prophet Jesus, who loved to make his abode his often abiding place; and lofty must the virtues and excellences of a man be, dear father, to command the holy friendship of this man of God. Nearly of the same age, they walked and discoursed together in sweet companionship, like Jonathan and David in the golden age of our country's glory.

At length, an hour after leaving the gate of the city, we drew near to Bethany, and beheld the roof of the house of Lazarus. Upon it, watching toward Jerusalem for us, we discovered the graceful form of Mary, who no sooner saw us, than she waved her hands in earnest longing. In a few moments we were in her arms, mingling our tears together.

"Does he yet live? " I asked, scarcely daring to ask, as she led us into the house.

"Yes, lives, but fails hourly," answered Mary, with forced composure. "God bless you both for hastening to me."

At this moment, Martha's pale and suffering face, beautiful

even in its pallor, appeared in the door of the inner room. Upon seeing us, she advanced, and, taking both our hands in hers, she said, in a touch in a whisper, "You have come, sweet friends, to see my brother die!"

She then led us into the room, where lay upon a couch the form of the invalid, whose perilous condition had brought a pang to the hearts of so many dear and loving ones around him. Upon entering the apartment, he turned his lustrous eyes upon us, and seemed to recognize us, as he smiled faintly a grateful recognition. Noble and beautiful as his countenance was in health, I thought that its expression, with his brilliant eyes and feverish cheek, was now superhuman.

"He has slept a little," said Martha softly, to me; "but his fever is consuming him. He has closed his eyes again, and seems heavy; but his slumbers are restless, as you see and he seems to think his dear friend, Jesus the Prophet, is by him or he talks of Ruth, as if she were not present."

"And who is Ruth, dear Martha?" I asked, as I was about to follow her out of the room, leaving her brother to his weary repose.

"Alas! it was for Ruth's gentle love's sake he now lies there," she answered "there is the sweet maiden kneeling by the other side of his couch, her tearful face buried in the folds of the curtains of his couch. She leaves him not a moment; nay, though he does not seem to be sensible of her presence, yet, when she has once or twice left the room, he awakes directly and calls for her."

I turned and regarded with tender interest the graceful and half-concealed form of the young girl as she bent over his pillow, her hand clasped by his. At this moment she looked up, and directed her gaze toward me. Her face was inexpressibly lovely, bathed, as it was, in its glittering tear-dew, and her large, glorious eyes seemed like heavens of tenderness and love. Her hair would have been raven black, save that a golden bronze enriched its waving masses at every play of the light upon it. As our eyes met, she seemed to receive me into her soul, and my heart to embrace hers. Lazarus moved and murmured her name, and she dropped her eyes, and bent like an angel over him.

"Who is this marvelously lovely maiden?" I asked of Martha, as we went into the court of the hall.

"The betrothed bride of our beloved brother," answered she; "sit with me here in the shade, beneath this vine, and I will tell thee their sad story. Lazarus, you know, dearest Adina, is a writer in the Temple, and by his labors has lived in humble competence, and surrounded us all with many comforts, nay, luxuries; for all we have, our mother and we owe to his filial and fraternal love. His attachment to us led him to forego the pleasure of all other society; for he said he found in our sweet bond of sisterly love, all that he required to render him happy, He was, therefore, insensible to all the attractions of the maidens who are our acquaintances and friends; and, when, a few months since, our mother was gathered to her fathers, he said he felt more than ever his duty to devote his life to our happiness. We would fain have induced him to seek a companion for life, knowing his noble nature, and how he possessed in an eminent degree those amiable qualities which would render, as his wife, happy and honored, any daughter of Israel. But when urged by us, he would smile, and playfully say, that he had but a very little heart, and that it would hold no more love than mine and Mary's.

A few weeks ago, as he was engaged late and alone in the copying-room of the Temple, upon a roll which the noble Aemilius had ordered, and which he desired to have completed on a certain day, and for which he was to give him a large sum, he was startled by the sudden entrance of a young girl in great terror, who seemed to be flying from pursuit. Upon beholding him, she bounded toward him, and, casting herself at his feet, implored his protection, amazed and interested, he promptly promised it, but had hardly spoken the words, before Annas entered and advanced toward her. His face was flushed with rage and his voice was loud and fierce, as he demanded her at the hand of my brother.

"Nay, my lord Annas," answered Lazarus, boldly "were a dove to seek shelter from a hawk in my bosom, I would protect it, much more a distressed maiden of the daughters of Abraham!" and he placed himself before the fugitive.

"Darest thou protect from me? She is my child, a wicked and disobedient daughter of Belial! Resign her to me, young scrivener, or I will have thee sent to the lowest dungeon of the castle of David."

"Oh, save me! save me!" cried the young girl, as Annas advanced to seize her. "I am not his child! I am the orphan of Rabbi Levi, who left me and my estate to this false priest, as a sacred charge; and, having done, I know not what, with my inheritance, he would sell me in unholy marriage to a Greek captain in the Roman Legion, who offers him large bribes in gold for me. And when but now he would have delivered me up to him, I fled to the altars of my God for the protection which man denied me and, ignorant of the way, and lost in the labyrinth of the Temple, I found myself here. Rather than be given into the hands of this fierce and terrible Grecian, whom I have seen only to dread, I will cast myself down from the height of the Temple!"

And to the surprise and horror of Lazarus, she bounded from the lattice, and stood upon the edge of the rock, which looks sheer three hundred feet down into the valley beneath.

"Thou sees, oh Annas, to what thy cupidity for gold will drive this maiden. Has the land of Israel sunk so low, that its chief priest will sell the daughters of the land for gold to the lust of the Gentiles? Is this the way thou givest protection to orphans? Leave her; and until I find a protector for her, she shall be a sacred guest with my sisters, in their humble abode!"

"Thy life shall pay for this arrogance, young man," answered the priest. "I have power over both, and will exercise it."

"Not to the danger and wrong of this maiden, my lord Annas, whom Jehovah will protect, since she has trustingly sought the sheltering wing of his altars," answered my brother firmly. "If you continue to persecute her, I will appeal to the Procurator, Pontius Pilate, against thee. Thou already knowest, that Roman justice knows how to punish Jewish guilt with terrible severity."

"The result was," continued Martha, "that the wicked priest, alarmed by the threat of appeal to Pilate, relinquished his present purpose, and left them, breathing menaces against my brother. The same day Lazarus conducted the maiden, whom you already guess to be Ruth, to our house; and she has since then been our guest, and has won all our hearts, as well as our dear brother's. Pilate, to whom Lazarus appealed, has placed the shield of his protection between them and Annas. It was to obtain money, to be able soon to wed Ruth, that our brother has at length fallen a victim to his arduous toils, and now lies on the brink of the grave."

"Is there no hope for him?" I asked, after listening to her touching narrative.

"None! The physicians say that he will never rise again."

"There is one hope left," I said eagerly.

"What is that?" demanded Martha.

"Jesus!" I answered; "send to him, oh Martha, and he will yet save him, and raise him up to life and health."

I had no sooner spoken, than Mary, who overheard me, uttered a scream of joy.

"Yes, Jesus has the power to heal him, and Jesus loves him! He will come and save him the moment he hears of his danger."

Immediately, Mary wrote on a slip of parchment, these brief and touching words:

"Lord, behold he whom thou lovest is sick! Hasten to come to us, that he may live; for nothing is impossible with thee."

This message was forthwith dispatched by the hands of a young friend to Bethabara, beyond Jordan, where we learn Jesus at present abides. We have, therefore, no hope for our dear relative, but in the power of the Prophet. I will write as soon as we hear. Dear father.

Your attached daughter,
ADINA.

LETTER XXV.

My Dear and Honored Father: It is with emotions of the deepest grief that I convey to you the sad intelligence of the death of Lazarus. It is amid the low sounds of the plaintive moans of his bereaved sisters over his lifeless form, and with my tears almost blinding my overflowing eyes, that I write to you. The hand of the Lord hath fallen heavily upon this household, and stricken down its prop, smitten the oak, around which clung these vine-like sisters, vine-like in their dependence upon him, and confiding trust in his wisdom and love. Now prostrate in the dust they lie, stunned by the sudden and mysterious stroke of God's providence.

I have spoken to you of the noble character of Lazarus, in a former letter, dear father, how that by writing in the Scribes' room in the Temple, he supported his venerable mother and sisters, while they, in their affection, labored with the needle in embroidery work, wherein they had very delicate skill, in order to lighten his labors. To the young men of Israel, Lazarus was held up by the Elders, as a pattern of filial and brotherly virtue, and honest industry; and to his sisters, Mary and Martha, other maidens were directed to look for examples of maidenly piety and diligent household thrift. Their humble dwelling was the home of hospitality and kindness, and thither the Prophet of God, Jesus, loveth to resort whensoever his great labors will permit him. Nearly of the same age, a holy friendship had sprung up between him and Lazarus, who so loved the Blessed Anointed One of God, that he would readily have laid down his life for him. I have told you, dear father, what a happy household I have seen it when Jesus completed the number; for he stayed so much with them when not preaching, or when wishing to rest a day or two from his weary toil, that they came to regard him as one of their family. Mary would devise ways to do him honor, and show her respect and affection, by working for him silken covers for the Books of the Prophets, which Lazarus would copy and present to his beloved friend while Martha seemed ever to be thinking what and how she should administer to his comfort, by providing every delicacy for her table. But so that Jesus could find listeners to his words of truth and wisdom, like Mary -- who loved to sit at his feet and hear the golden language fall from his sacred lips -- he thought not of meats or drinks.

One day, when I, with Mary and Lazarus, was listening to his heavenly teachings, wrapt in wonder and absorbing interest, Martha, who was preparing the meal, came and desired Mary to come and assist her; but the dear, pious girl, heeded not nor heard her, she was feeding, so forgetful of all else, upon the celestial food that fell from the lips of Jesus, who was talking to us of the kingdom of God and the glories of heaven, and the necessity of holiness to dwell there. At length, Martha, finding that Mary heard not, appealed to Jesus, saying something sharply:

"Lord, dost thou not care that my sister hath left me to serve alone? Bid her, therefore, that she help me."

We turned with surprise to hear her, who was usually so gentle and good, thus forget what was due to the presence of the Prophet and Lazarus, blushing, was about to speak and excuse his sister, who looked as if she were much worried with her domestic troubles; but Jesus said kindly to her:

"Martha, Martha, thou art careful and troubled about many things; thy household takes up too much of thy time and thoughts. In this world, but one care is truly worthy of the regard of men, which is to provide sustenance for the soul for the body perisheth. Mary hath chosen more wisely than thyself. While thou carest much for the wants of the body, she careth for those of the spirit, and thus has that good part which shall not be taken away from her. Think not, beloved Martha, of sumptuous living for me, who have no earthly goods, not even where to lay my head!"

"Say not thus, oh, say not so, dear Lord," cried Martha, suddenly bursting into tears at Jesus' touching words, and casting herself impulsively at his feet; "this house is thy home -- ever beneath its roof, while I have one above me, shalt thou have where to lay thy head: Say not so, my Lord!"

We were all moved at Martha's pathetic earnestness. Jesus raised her up, and said to her gently:

"It is thy love for me, I well know, that maketh thee so

careful and troubled to provide for me at thy bountiful table. But I have meat to eat that ye know not of. Thus, to teach the truths of God, as thou findest me doing to these, is to me meat and drink, for herein I am doing my Father's will, who sent me."

I have been particular in giving you, dear father, these details of the domestic relations existing in the abode of Lazarus, and the sweet friendship that resided in their bosoms toward Jesus, and his familiar, brotherly love for them. You can now understand why, when Lazarus was taken ill, after his laborious vigils to copy the manuscript for the Roman Centurion, a message was at once sent to Jesus, who was in Bethabara beyond Jordan; for a physician of Jerusalem, whom the noble Caiaphas had sent out to Bethany, on hearing of the sudden sickness of the youthful Secretary, to whom he was greatly attached, for all people did love him who knew him -- this physician had at once pronounced him in danger of sudden death from inward bleeding of the lungs.

"Why, then," you may ask, dear father, "should they send for Jesus, when death was certain. Jesus," you add, "was no physician, or if he had been, he could not reverse the fate of the dying young man!"

The fact, dear father, that under these circumstances they did send to Jesus to come and heal him, shows that it was not as a human physician they desired his presence, but as the miracle-working Prophet of God! It proves, and will, I trust, prove to you, dearest father, that they who should best know his power, believe assuredly that he could save their brother. It is testimony irresistible toward sustaining his claim to have come down from God! It is those who are most intimate with others who do know them best. Now, that the sisters of Lazarus sent a message presently to Jesus to interpose between death and his life, shows that they plainly believed he had not only the power of miracles, but had power over death and that they had witnessed instances of his power sufficient to give them faith in his ability to save their brother while they knew that his love for him would certainly prompt him to exert it.

In my last letter I closed with informing you of the departure of the messenger. After he had gone out of sight from the door, and the last echo of his horse's hoofs ceased to be heard by the long listening ears of his sister Martha, I re-entered the room where Lazarus lay. He was as white as marble. His large, black eyes seemed to be twice their usual size and brilliancy. He breathed with difficulty, and every few moments he would be compelled to have his head raised, in order to free his mouth from the welling blood that was constantly bubbling up from the broken fountains of his life. Mary's tender privilege it was to render him this service of love. As she bent over him, looking downward with anxious fondness into his pale, intellectual face, watching every shadow of the change that the sable wing of advancing death cast over it, I thought I had never gazed on a more lovely being! Who, in beholding the seraphim beauty of her face, the brilliant light of her dark eyes, which were now glittering with sisterly grief, the graceful expression of her proud, Rebecca-like head, and the superb outline of her figure, where love and majesty seemed blent to mold a second Eve -- who, in the admiration of her person, could read within and beneath all the secret sorrow of her soul! Who would believe that a dark cloud rested on her spirit, and that her happiness was no longer on earth! As I gazed upon her, I forgot, for the moment, the dying young man, about whose form her snow-white arms were entwined, his head reclining upon her bosom, her raven tresses bronzed with a golden light, all unbound and floating above him, and far over his pillow, like a rich veil interwoven of sable silken gloss and threads of gold. I could not gaze upon that abundant hair without recalling the day not long before, when, at the dwelling of Rabbi Joseph Solomon, she drew near suddenly to Jesus, who was his guest, and bathed his feet with her fast flowing tears, mingling therewith her kisses, and then dried them with her shining hair!

And wherefore did she weep upon the feet of Jesus? you may ask, dear father. They were tears of gratitude and penitence. Her history you know, at least as rumor had it three years ago, with evil additions thereto. It is true, Mary sinned, and should not be exculpated; but her sin was in leaving her maternal roof, yielding, in her unsuspecting innocence, to the dazzling temptations of the young prince Herod. It is not true that she was tempted by ambition and power. She has poured into my ear all her sad and touching story. Prince Herod had but recently returned with his father Antipas, from Rome, and was a youth comely in person, well skilled in the fascinations that easiest win the hearts of the guileless. By accident he saw Mary one morning at the palace of Pilate the Procurator, whither she had gone to deliver the wife of the Governor a piece of embroidery-work which she had done at her command. It would seem, that having made inquiries touching her condition in life, he feigned to be it writer of parchments, and thus readily making the acquaintance of the unsuspecting Lazarus, was readily introduced beneath his roof. Here, as an humble scribe, dressed in plain and coarse apparel, he often came, and succeeded in winning the heart of the lovely girl. At length, in an evil hour, she listened to his temptation secretly to elope with him, to be united to him at his mother's house, he having urged to her that his open marriage would estrange from him the regards of big uncle, a wealthy scribe, who designed, if he married not for seven years, to enrich him with his wealth.

To this tale she listened. But instead of being taken by him to the roof of the mother, of whom he had falsely spoken to her, she found herself seized, and her mouth stopped by the leader of a party of horsemen, who suddenly came up the path, and who, dismounting, placed her on before him. The young scribe, mounting a led horse, headed the band, and the whole escort galloped northward at rapid speed. Ignorant in whose power she was, and fearing for her betrothed husband as well as for herself, supposing that he was forcibly in their hands also, she tried by listening to ascertain what was to be done with her, and who her captors were. To her surprise she heard the voice of her lover giving directions to the horsemen from time to time, which she could hardly believe; but when the moon rose, she succeeded so far in removing her veil as to enable her to recognize him as the leader of the troop.

After riding all night, they stopped at a well, near Samaria, at dawn of day. Here refreshments were offered her, but she refused them, and begged to be permitted to speak to her lover. But he did not come near her. After an hour's rest in the caravansera, they once more proceeded on their route in a northerly course. Leaving Mount Gerizim in the rear, with the Jordan on their right, they at noon reached the base of Mount Tabor. After three hours' repose, they crossed the eastern shoulder of the mountain, from which was a magnificent view of the sea of Galilee. Descending the mountain, they reached, just as the sun set, the gate of a castle that overlooks the town of Nazareth. This they entered, and the portals closed upon her.

But I will not be weary with too minute a narrative, dear father; my object is only to vindicate my cousin Mary from intentional guilt. Ushered into superb apartments, her lover, attired in all the splendor of a prince, soon appeared before her, and acknowledged he had been deceiving her that he was Herod Valerius, the son of the Herod Antipas, Tetrarch of Galilee, and that she was now in one of the palaces of his family. Who can describe the horror, shame, and grief of this cruelly deceived and erring girl! Bitterly did her tears now at the too trusting step she had taken, thus sinning against God. But tears and repentance, implorations and entreaties for permission to return to her humble home, were in vain. As she had sown, she had reaped.

At the expiration of three months, she succeeded in making her escape, and fled to the feet of Mary of Nazareth, the mother of the Prophet Jesus. To her she made known all, and received her sympathy while she bowed her penitent head beneath her reproofs. Here it was that she first beheld the holy Prophet, and received from him the consolations of the forgiveness of heaven for her sin. Led by his noble mother, she bent her steps back again to her father's house. All Bethany knew of her shame -- that is, knew that she had fled with the dissolute prince Valerius, and was living with him in sin at his castle in Galilee but they knew not any extenuating circumstances. So she entered Bethany closely veiled and with hurried step sought the shelter of her mother's arms, if, per adventure, they would be open to receive her.

At length, after many weeks, all who knew her were acquainted with the truth, and their cold censure was softened into pity; and as she went about doing good, as she visited, like an angel, the sick and sorrowing, she won back all hearts, and was loved and honored as before. But the cold world still looked upon her as a guilty one -- as a sinner; but had they known how deep her sorrow was for all the past, they would also have removed the barbs from the sharp arrows of their tongues.

Since then, all the generous care of Lazarus and Martha, and of their friends, has been to make her forget the past; and as it is three years since what I have described happened, the prevailing gentle sadness that now shades her countenance, alone shows to the loving gaze of those around her what she has suffered. It was Jesus who reconciled her to her brother and sister, and hence her deep gratitude to him, which she has shown, not once, but many times, when he has been their guest, by bathing his feet with her tears, and wiping them with the hairs of her head. Her place is ever at his feet. Lovely and guilty one, her tears are her daily offering to heaven, and will atone for deeper guilt than hers, if tears do wash away sins; but she says nothing has given consolation to her heart like the voice of Jesus, when he said to her, "Daughter, thy sins be forgiven thee!" "The words," she added to me, "penetrated my heart, and illuminated the darkness of my soul with ineffable, unspeakable peace!"

I commenced this letter by informing you of the departure of the good and generous, and pious Lazarus. He fell asleep in death as an infant sinks to slumber in its mother's arms, gradually sinking from the loss of blood, growing fainter and fainter till his eyes closed, his pulse ceased to throb, and his noble heart to flutter, like an escaping bird beneath the hand's light pressure.   All too late was Jesus sent for! He is dead! Tomorrow his burial will take place. Alas! how suddenly has perished the noblest young man in Judea!

Farewell, dear father! My heart is full, I can write no more. The day after tomorrow I return to Jerusalem, when I will write you again. You said in your last letter you would soon leave Egypt for Judea, for the purpose of taking me back to my dear native valley of the Nile. The God of Abraham preserve you in your journey, and bring you in safety to the embraces of

Your loving daughter,

ADINA.

LETTER XXVI.

My Dear Father: In my last letter I told you that Lazarus was dead! I write this to say that he that was dead is alive! Lazarus lives! He whom I saw dead and buried, and sealed up within the rocky care of the tomb, he is alive again from the dead: and at this moment, while I am penning this extraordinary account, I hear his voice upon the porch, as he is engaged in relating what has transpired respecting himself to a crowd of wondering people from Jerusalem. Even Pilate, the Roman Procurator, stopped his chariot at the door this morning, to see Lazarus, and have speech of him.

How, my dear father, how shall I find adequate language to tell you all that has happened within the last twenty-four hours! How shall I make you fully believe the marvelous recital which I have taken up my pen to make! I know not how to begin the wonderful narrative, for the joy that prevents me from arranging my thoughts and presenting the facts intelligently to you. God has indeed remembered his chosen people Israel once more, and shown his power among us!

You have already been informed by me how rapidly Lazarus failed after his sudden attack of hemorrhage of the chest, and that he soon died; and that, in hopes that he might avert death, Jesus was sent for at the first to come to him. But Bethabara was a day's journey, and ere the messenger reached him the soul of his friend had fled. The next day he was buried; a very large concourse of people from the town of Bethany, and from Jerusalem, coming to his burial; for he was greatly beloved; even the chariot of the noble lady, Lucia Metella, the good and virtuous wife of Pilate, was present to do honor to the obsequies of him who had no other renown than his virtues.

The funeral procession was so very long, that strangers pausing, asked what great master in Israel, or person of note, was being taken to the sepulcher.

Some answered, "Lazarus, the industrious scribe!" Others said, "a young man who has devoted his life to honor his mother!" Others answered, as Lazarus himself, were he alive, would have had them:

"It is Lazarus, the friend of Jesus!"

This living, was his proudest title; and dead, he would have desired no other. Ah, dear father, may the day yet come when you shall deem such a title greater honor than the gold of Egypt, or all the glory of your proud descent from Abraham and David!

The place where they were to lay him was the cave in which both his father and mother were entombed. It was in a deep, shady vale, that opened into the valley at the Kedron. It was thickly shaded by cypress, palm, and pomegranate trees; and a large tamarind grew, with its stately branches, overclasping the summit of the secluded place of sepulcher, while an abrupt cliff of Olivet hung impending down, like the shaggy brow of a giant looking down upon the spot. Above the tree-tops, in the direction of Kedron, were visible the majestic heights of the distant Temple, and the warlike battlements of the city of David, while the sunlight, glancing upon the dazzling shield of a sentinel who was standing upon its loftiest watch-tower, caused it to gleam like a lesser sun. The remote swell of a Roman bugle from the head of a cohort, which was just issuing from the gate of Damascus, came softly and musically to our ears, as we stood in silence about the grove wherein we were to place the dead. Aemilius, the centurion, was also present, wearing a white scarf above his silver cuirass, in token of grief; for he also loved Lazarus. Of him, dear father, I have not of late spoken for should I begin to write of him, I should have no room in my letter for any other theme. You will soon see him, and judge for yourself how worthy he is of your confidence, and all the love of my heart. I am too grateful to you, dearest father, for not refusing your consent to our union, but only withholding it until you reach Jerusalem. The blessed winds waft your bark swiftly to Jaffa, that I may soon embrace you, and present to you the noble Aemilius, who is as faithful a worshiper of our God as if he were a son of Abraham by birth rather than by adoption.

The sacred observances at the grove being over, they raised the body of the dead young man from the bier, and four youths, aided by Aemilius at the head to support it, conveyed it into the yawning cavern. A moment they lingered on the threshold, that Mary and Martha might take one more look, imprint upon its icy cold lips one last kiss, press once more his unconscious head to their loving and bursting hearts. I also gazed upon him, weeping at their sorrow, and sorrowing to behold so noble a face, beautiful as chiseled alabaster, about to be consigned to the loathsome worm of the charnel-house. He was so good, and excelling all his companions in all things great and pure, and lofty in character; my tears flowed, and I felt that had I not loved Aemilius, I should have loved Lazarus.

The young men moved forward into the gloom of the cave. Mary rushed in, and with disheveled hair, cried:

"Oh, take him not away forever from the sight of my eyes! Oh, my brother, my brother, would that I had died for thee! for I am willing to lie down with the worm and call it my sister, and sleep in the arms of death, as on the breast of my mother! Thou wert happy and honored, and should have lived! I am wretched and heartbroken, and such only should die! Oh, brother, brother, let them not take thee forever from the sight of my eyes! Without thee, how shall life be life!"

Aemilius entered the tomb, and tenderly raising her from the body, on which she had cast herself in the eloquent abandonment of her wild grief, he led her forth, and beckoning to me, placed her in my arms.

Martha bore her own griefs with more composure, but her face expressed how deeply she was moved within, thus to say adieu forever to her only brother, to her beloved Lazarus, who had been the strong rock which had presented ever its front to the shock of the stormy billows of this life, as they threatened her and Mary, and was a tower of strength to them in the day of trouble as well as an exhaustless fountain of holy domestic joy!

The body being placed in a niche hollowed out in the rock, was decently covered with a grave mantle, all but the calm face, which was bound about by a snow-white napkin. Maidens of the village advanced and cast flowers upon his head, and many, many were the sincere tears, both from beneath manly lids and those of virgins, which bore tribute to his worth.

The burial ceremonies being ended, five strong men replaced the ponderous stone door closely fitting the entrance to the cave, and so secured it by letting it into a socket that it would require a like number to remove it.

As we were retiring with heavy hearts from performing this last duty to the beloved dead, the sun sank beyond the blue hills of Ajalon in the west, in a lake of golds gilding the pinnacle of the Temple, and making it appear like a gigantic spear elevated into the sky. From the Levites at evening sacrifice came mellowed by the distance the deep chant of the Temple service, uttered by two thousand voices. The cloud from the altar sacrifice ascended slowly into the still air, and catching the splendor of the sun's last beams, shone like the pillar of cloud and of fire which stood above the tabernacle in the wilderness. The laborers in the harvest were hastening toward the gates, ere they should be shut for the night by the Roman guards; and dwellers in the village were hurrying forth, lest they should by chance be held in the city over night.

There was a sacred hush in the sleepy atmosphere that seemed in sympathy and touching harmony with the scene in which we had just borne a part. With Mary leaning sobbing upon my shoulder, I sat upon a rock near the tomb, giving my heart up to the sweet influence of the hour. We were alone, save Aemilius, who sat upon his horse near by, and seemed to be gazing upon the beauty of the evening scene. Martha and my cousin, with John, had returned to the now desolate home of which Lazarus had been the light and the honor.

"I am calmer now," said Mary, after a while raising her head, and looking into my face, her splendid eyes glittering brimfull with tears: "I am better now! The peace of the sweet holy skies seems to have descended, and entered my heart. The heavens of my soul are as clear and pure, and peaceful, as those above me! The spirit of Lazarus pervades all, and hallows all I see! I will weep no more. He is happy, very happy, and I will try to be holy and go to him, for he cannot come to me!"

At this moment we heard the tramp of horses' hoofs, and Aemilius, startled thereby from his reverie, recovered his seat and laid his hand upon his sword for though the Romans have the mastery in our land, as conquerors, they are not loved; and scarcely a week passes without some conflict between the soldiers of the Legion and the common people among the Jews; and even the officers have been attacked when riding abroad from Jerusalem not sufficiently attended.

Aemilius, therefore, who had with him only his white-haired Celtic servant, Frwynn, prepared to receive a foe or welcome his friends. The next moment, around a rock projecting from the shoulder of Olivet, appeared first, one horseman in the wild, warlike costume of an Ishmaelite of the desert, brandishing a long spear in the air; then another, and another similarly clad and armed and mounted on superb horses of the desert then dashed in sight alone, a tall, daring-looking young man, in a rich costume, half Grecian, half Arabic, though his dark, handsome features were decidedly Israelitish. He rode a superb Abyssinian charger, and sat upon his back like the heathen centaur I have read of in Latin books, which Aemilius has given me to read. Upon seeing me, he drew rein and smiled, and waved his jeweled hand with splendid courtesy but at the sight of Aemilius, his dark eyes flashed, and leaping to his feet in his stirrups, he shook his glittering falchion toward him, and rode with a trumpet-like cry full upon him.

The brave Roman soldier received the charge by turning his horse slightly, and catching the point of the weapon upon the blade of his short sword.

"We meet at last, oh Roman!" cried this wild, dashing chief, as he wheeled his horse like lightning, and once more rode upon the iron-armed Roman knight.

"Ay, Barabbas, and with joy I hail thee," responded Aemilius, placing a bugle to his lips.

At hearing the clear voice of the bugle awaking the echoes of Olivet, the dread robber chief, of whom you have heard me speak before, dear father, said haughtily, and with a glance of contempt:

"Thou, a knight of the tribune, and commander of a legion, call for aid, when I offer thee equal battle, hand to hand, and ask not my own men's swords."

"I know no equal battle with a robber. I would hunt thee as I would do the wolf and the wild beasts of thy desert," answered Aemilius, pressing him closely. At a signal from the robber chief, his four men, who had reigned up a short distance off, near the tomb of Lazarus, sent up a shrill, eagle-like scream, that made my blood stand still, and rode down like the wind to overcome Aemilius.

Hitherto I had remained like one stupefied at being an involuntary spectator of a sudden battle; but on seeing his danger, I was at his side, scarce knowing how I reached the place.

"Retire, dear Adina," he said, "I shall have to defend both thee and myself, and these barbarians will give both my hands enough to do." As he spoke, he turned his horse's head to meet the four-fold shock, and I escaped, I know not how, with the impulse to hasten to Bethany for succor. But heaven interposed its aid -- a detachment of the bodyguard of Pilate, which Aemilius had left in an olive grove to bivouac and refresh themselves and horses, hearing the recall of their chief's bugle, came now threading up the hill, a score strong of armed men, bearded Gauls, who had served in Britain against the Picts. At the sight, Barabbas and his party fled, like wild pigeons pursued by a cloud of Iturean hawks. Barabbas, however, turned more than once to fling back defiance to his foes. Aemilius by this means came up with him, seized the crimson sash which encircled his waist, and held him thus, both fighting as they rode. The troops soon came up with them, and after a desperate battle the celebrated robber chief was taken alive, though bleeding with many wounds, and bound with his own sash to the column of one of the tombs. Aemilius was but slightly hurt; and I never saw such bright joy as sparkled in his eyes, that he had at length captured the bold bandit leader, who had so frequently before escaped him, and to get possession of whom he had made so many attempts. There lay at length in his power the terror of all the country between Jericho and Jerusalem, a bound captive. He smiled still proudly defiant, and looked haughty and wildly noble, even in his bonds. His men were also taken; and giving them, with their chief, into the charge of his soldiers, to convey to the prisons of Jerusalem, Aemilius rejoined Mary and me, and accompanied us to the house of the two sisters.

It appears that Barabbas, emboldened by the rumor that a rich company of merchants were to leave Jerusalem at day-break, for Damascus, had advanced near the city with a few followers, to lie in wait for their coming out, and hang on their path until they should have entered a defile in the mountains of Bethel, where his troop were lying in ambush; and it was while seeking a shelter from notice among the tombs in the vale of Olivet that he came suddenly upon us. Aemilius says that he will assuredly be crucified for his numerous crimes. Dreadful punishment! and for one so young and prepossessing as this desert robber to come to such an ignominious and agonizing death; to hang for hours under the sunbeams by lacerated hands and feet, till death comes from slow exhaustion of all the powers of nature. I am amazed that so polite and humane a nation as the Roman can inflict such a cruel and agonizing death, even upon their malefactors. Last week, as I was walking with my Uncle Amos among the sepulchers of the kings outside of the north gate, being prevented from re-entering the gate by the passage of a Roman

Legion to suppress an insurrection in Samaria, we passed round by the western gate, to reach which we had to pass the foot of the Hill of Calvary, upon which two crosses were erected on one of which hung the still living body of a seditious Jew, executed by order of the Procurator. He writhed fearfully, while his groans penetrated my heart. I cover my eyes and my ears, and begged Rabbi Amos to hurry with me from such a fearful spectacle. Yet it was in full sight of the city, of the road; and many spectators, both of women and men, lingered to gaze. Ignominious, indeed, must the life of a man have been, for him to be justly doomed to suffer such a death.

In this letter, dearest father, I intended to relate to how Lazarus has been restored to life, but it is already taken up with so much, that I defer it to my next. But believe me, that Lazarus is living and well, and thousands are crowding into Bethany, and thronging the house to see this great thing that hath happened. Suffice for me to tell you, at the close of this letter, that is was Jesus who raised him from the dead, the Prophet of God whom you are yet in doubt whether he be the Messias or no! Ah! is he who raised the widow's son of Nain -- who walked on the sea a league to his disciples' boats -- who stilled the tempest by the word of his power -- who fed five thousand men with five pound's weight of bread -- who healed the nobleman Hadad's son -- who raised the dead daughter of the Galilean ruler, Jairus -- who restores the deaf, the blind, the dumb, by a word, a touch, a look -- around whose path and life are gathered together such a multitude of testimonies to his superhuman power, in prophecies, in mighty works, and in glittering miracles -- ah, my dear father, is he only a common man; is he as impostor? Oh, is he not, is he not, the Son of God -- the Messias of the Prophets -- the Lion of the tribe of Judah -- the Deliverer and future glory of Israel? Is he not He whose day of splendor Abraham saw afar off, and was glad? Is He not Shiloh, whom the patriarch Jacob beheld rise up to wield the scepter of Israel? Is He not the mighty Son of God, whom the burning pen of Esaias records in these words of inspiration:

"Unto us a child is born -- unto us a son is given and the government shall be upon his shoulders: and his name shall be called Wonderful, Counsellor, the Mighty God, the Everlasting Father, the Prince of Peace; who shall sit upon the throne of David, and establish it with justice and judgment from hence-forth even forever!"

Think of these things, dear father, ponder them well, and let not the poverty of Jesus be a stumbling-block to your faith in Him as Messiah. That he has raised Lazarus from the dead, is alone proof to me that He is the Son of God.

Your affectionate daughter,

ADINA.

LETTER XXVII.

My Dear Father: Your letter has filled me with joy that I can poorly express by my pen. It was received this morning by the courier from Egypt, with the package, both being safely placed in my hands, nine days only after they quitted your own. I kissed them, and pressed them again and again to my heart, at the thought that they were so lately touched by your fingers. The letter assures me that you are certainly to leave at the new moon, and after a few days' delay at Gaza, will be with me not many days afterward. This letter I shall send so as to meet you at Gaza.

Three years, three long years, dearest father, have passed since I last saw your venerable and kind face. Ah, when you come, how I shall love you, and hang upon you, and watch every look, and catch your every word! It is true, my Uncle Amos has been next to a father to me, all affection and goodness; but no love or care can hold the place of a father's to a daughter.

When I review the interesting scenes I have passed through, the wonderful events which I have witnessed since I first came to Jerusalem, nearly three years ago, with the caravan of Rabbi Ben Israel, I do not regret my long absence from you, dear father for to have been in Jerusalem during the period I have named, is a privilege that Abraham and all the patriarchs and prophets of God would have coveted. During that period the Messias has walked the earth, clothed with divine power, and familiarly gone in and out of Jerusalem before all eyes, performing miracles, and doing mighty works which never man did. I have learned to love and honor that blessed Prophet as the Son of the Highest, and the Anointed of the Lord I have sat at his feet, and listened to his heavenly teachings, and the wisdom at his sacred lips has made me wise.

But I have not yet made known to you the particulars of the greatest miracle of power and love of all those wonders which he has done, viz., the raising up of Lazarus from the dead, and I will here recount them as they occurred.

When Mary and Martha, finding Lazarus given over by the physicians as past possible recovery from his grievous illness, had dispatched the message to Jesus, as I have already stated, they began to be more cheerful with new-born hope, saying:

"If our dear Rabbi, the holy Prophet, comes, he will heal him with a word, as he has done so many of the sick."

"Yes; many whom he knew not, he has restored to health by a touch," remarked Martha, "how much more, Lazarus, whom he loveth as a brother! O that the messenger may press forward with all haste!"

"If Lazarus should die ere he come," hesitatingly remarked my gentle cousin, the betrothed of John the disciple, "he could bring him to life again, even as he did the son of the widow at Nain."

"Yes, without doubt, unless it were too late," remarked Martha, shrinking at the thought that her brother should die; "but, if he be long dead it will be impossible."

"Nothing is impossible with Jesus," answered Mary, her eyes brightening with trusting faith.

Thus the hours passed between mingled hopes and fears and ere Jesus came, the mantle of death was laid over the face of their dead brother. "Lazarus is dead, and Jesus is away!" was the bitter and touching cry made by the bereaved sisters, as they wept in each other's arms.

The next day the burial took place, as I have described already to you, dear father, in my last letter, and yet no messenger came from Jesus. The morning of the third day the messenger returned, and said that he had found the Prophet on the farther bank of the Jordan, where John had baptized, and that he abode in an humble cottage in the suburbs of Bethabara, with his disciples, and was engaged in teaching the things of the kingdom of God, and unfolding the prophecies to many who resorted unto him.

The bearer of the sad tidings from the two sisters delivered his simple and touching message:

"Lord, behold he whom thou lovest is sick!"

"And what said he? -- how did his countenance appear?" asked Martha of the man.

"He betrayed no surprise, but said calmly to me, "Son, I know it! This sickness shall not be unto death, it shall be for the glory of God for hereby will my Father permit me to be glorified, that men may see and believe truly that I came out from God."

"What said he more?" asked Martha, sorrowfully and doubting.

"Nothing more, lady and having given my message, I departed," answered the man.

"Alas he knew not how ill his friend was," said Mary, "or he would not have said it was not unto death, and would have hastened with you."

"Thy Lord should know all things, daughter," said a priest who stood by. "This ignorance of the danger of Lazarus, and his assertion that he would not die, shows that he is an impostor. Is not Lazarus dead and buried?"

At this, Martha's faith seemed for a moment shaken, but Mary eloquently defended her brother's absent friend, and holy Prophet, saying, "That when Jesus should come and speak in person for himself, he would make his words plain, and show them to have been spoken with wisdom."

With what deep sorrow they mourned their brother; and their tears fell the faster in that they felt assured he would not have died had Jesus been there. Their faith and confidence in him underwent a sore trial as day after day passed, and nothing more was heard from him.

"He has forgotten us," answered Martha. "He should be near to console us in our deep affliction, though he came not to heal our brother."

"Nay, sister, do not think hardly of the blessed friend of Lazarus," said Mary, with soothing tones as she caressed her elder sister. "I feel that if he had seen fit he could have raised up our brother, even speaking the word from Bethabara. It was not needful he should see him to heal him; for dost thou remember how he healed Lucius, the Centurion's son, yet at the time he was a day's journey distant from him."

"And why, oh why, did he not save Lazarus" exclaimed Martha bitterly."

"In that he did not, sweet sister," answered Mary gently, "it was for the best. Did he not say to the messenger, his sickness should be to the glory of his power."

"But not his death, Mary, not his death! He is dead four days already; and how can the grave give glory to the power of Jesus? Will he raise him up, since corruption has begun, nay, began ere we laid him in the cold sepulcher? Oh, speak not to me of the cruel prophet. He loved not Lazarus, or he had not the power to save him. Nay; leave me, Mary, to the bitterness of my grief."

"Ah, dear Martha, how soon is thy faith in Jesus when proven, become nought!" said Mary, bending upon her from her dark, earnest eyes, looks of sad reproach. "Shall one day overturn your years of holy friendship for him? Because he answered not our prayer to come to Lazarus, think you he loved him not, and is indifferent to our anguish? He is wronged by your reproof, and injured by your want of confidence in his love and care for us."

"He can heal a proud and rich ruler's son, but he heeds not the cry of the poor and lowly," perseveringly answered Martha, expressing in her looks the intensity of her feelings against Jesus. "The death of Lazarus be upon his head!"

"Ah, sister, God forgive thee, and let thy grief excuse thy words. Though he slay me, I will trust in him," exclaimed Mary, laying her hand on her sister's shoulder, while holy firmness and a resolute light beamed in her shining and tearful eyes.

While they were thus discoursing, one came running swiftly toward the house, and, breathless with haste, cried to them and to the Jews sitting there, who had come to comfort them concerning their brother:

"The Prophet! the Nazarene! He comes!"

Almost at the same moment, Melec, the Gibeonite, entered and said:

"Jesus, the Messias of God, is at hand! He already entereth the village with his disciples."

At this intelligence, the mourners who sat with Mary and Martha in the vine porch rose up to go and meet him but Martha, shrieking with sudden joy, sprang up, and more quickly than they reached the street, and, running with great speed, came where Jesus was.

Mary, who had received the news without betraying any other emotion than the secret and holy joy of a heart that had confidence all along in her Lord, instead of hastening to meet him, rending her hair with grief, like her sister, proceeded to prepare a room for the hospitable entertainment of the beloved Prophet, when he should come in, thus taking Martha's place; and when she had arranged all, she sat down with me in the house, her heart filled with joy, and her face expressive of her calm and quiet happiness.

"I knew he would come! I knew he would not leave or forsake us in our deep sorrow, Adina," she said, two or three times; and, as the confused noise of advancing footsteps fell upon our ears, her heartbeat quicker, and, with the glow that joy and expectation made to enrich her face, I thought she looked more beautiful than ever before.

When Martha came near Jesus, whom she met just entering Bethany, walking with four of his disciples along the dusty road, and looking weary and travel-worn, she ran and threw herself at his feet, crying:

"Lord, if thou hadst been here, my brother had not died!"

Jesus, taking her hand, raised her up, and said with emotion, for he was deeply moved:

"Lazarus sleepeth, Martha. I am now come to awake him out of his sleep."

"Lord, if my brother slept only, he would not have been buried. He is dead, and hath been dead four days."

"I spoke of his death, Martha! Lazarus is dead; but death to those whom my Father loveth is sleep. The good die not, only the wicked. Their death is eternal, where the worm dieth not. I say unto thee, Lazarus is not dead but sleepeth; and he shall rise again!"

"I know, O Rabboni, that he shall rise again in the resurrection at the last day."

Jesus then said unto her, lifting his celestial glances toward heaven:

"I am the resurrection and the life. He that believeth in me, though he were dead, shall he live! and whosoever liveth and believeth in me shall never die! Believest thou this, daughter?"

"Yea, Lord, I believe that thou art the Christ, the Son of God, which should come into the world. I know that whatsoever thou wilt ask of God, God will give it thee, and that even now thou couldst bring Lazarus back again!"

"Corruption and the worm have begun their work," said a proud and unbelieving Pharisee near, on hearing this; "whatever may have been the state of the ruler's daughter, and of the son of her of Nain, Lazarus, the scribe, at least, is dead!"

To this speech Jesus made no reply, but turning to Martha, said softly:

"I am rejoiced that thy faith in me hath come back into thine heart, for thou hast doubted, oh daughter of little faith, in that I came not at thy call. It was needful that thy brother should die, that I might display the power of God in me by raising him up. This day my Father shall be glorified, and the world shall truly know that I come from Him who is Life, and the giver of life. Go, thou, and tell thy sister that I am here, and would have her come and speak with me!"

Martha, then, overjoyed, and wondering that Jesus should have known her thoughts, so as to reproach her for her little faith as he had done, hastened to her sister, and entering, cried:

"I have seen the Lord! He calleth for thee, Mary. Come and see him as he sits by Isaiah's fountain, near the marketplace; for he hath said he will not enter our house until he crosses the threshold with Lazarus by his side!"

Her words made my heart bound with an indescribable thrill! Lazarus to come again into the house alive, walking with Jesus! I buried my face in my hands, overcome with an idea so full of joy, terror, wonder, and supernatural awe. Mary rose quickly, and went out, scarcely supporting herself upon her failing limbs for trembling joy, and a sweet, undefined hope of -- she knew not what -- immeasurable and unbearable happiness about to come upon her. Certain of her Jewish friends from Jerusalem at that moment met her at the door, not knowing that Jesus had entered Bethany and began to comfort her, and to ask her if they also should go with her to weep at the grave of Lazarus; for they said:

"She goeth unto the grave to weep there."

"She goes to see Jesus, the friend of Lazarus, for he calleth her," answered Martha, smiling with eagerness, and speaking with an animation that presented a singular contrast to her late deep grief.

Mary hastened to where Jesus sat by the fountain, bathing his dusty and wounded feet, and discoursing to those about him upon the resurrection of the dead. Upon seeing Mary, he extended his hand, but she sank at his feet, and bathing them with her tears, wiped them with her gleaming black hair.

"Lord," she said, in her sister's words, with great emotion, "if thou, Lord, hadst been here, my brother had not died."

Then bowing her head to the edge of the marble basin, she wept very heavily. The Jews, men and women, who stood about, being touched with her sorrow, also wept, while glittering tears coursed their way down the face of the beloved John, his disciple, who stood near.

Jesus sighed deeply, and groaned in spirit as he beheld her grief, and their mourning with her. His sacred countenance was marred with the anguish of his soul.

"Rise, let us go to the grave where he lieth!" he said to them. "Where have ye laid him?"

"Come, dear Lord, and see," answered Mary, taking him by the sleeve of the robe, and drawing him toward the place of the tombs in the vale of Olivet.

In the meanwhile, at home, Martha had been diligently, and with strange cheerfulness, getting in readiness the room of Lazarus. She swept and dusted it, and garnished it with fresh flowers, which she gathered in the little garden.

"This is the rose he set out and loved. This is the violet which blooms immortal. I will place it upon his pillow," she said with joyous hilarity, softened by the most lovely look of peace; while hope shone in her eyes like twin morning stars ushering in a glorious day. She spoke scarcely above her breath, and moved on tip-toe.

"For whom is this preparation, dearest Martha? For Jesus?" I asked.

"Oh, no! The Lord's own room is ready. Mary has prepared that. This is Lazarus's room, and I am decorating it for him!"

"Dost thou truly believe that he is coming back from the dead?" I asked, between doubt and strange fear.

"Believe! Oh, yes. I know that nothing is impossible with him; I doubt no more. My faith trembles no longer. He will raise up my brother, and this day he shall sit down at our table with us again, and this night rest his head in peaceful slumber upon this pillow which I am strewing with his favorite flowers. Never had house two such guests as we shall have this day -- the Messias of God, and one come back alive from the dead!"

At this moment we heard the noise of the multitude passing by, and it being told us that Jesus was going to the grave, Martha, embracing me with a heavenly smile, drew me gently after her, to follow the blessed Prophet to the tomb. All Bethany was in his footsteps. Wonder and eager expectation were on every face. There was no out cry; no lawless uproar in the vast concourse, but rather a subdued under-current murmur of awe and curiosity.

How shall I describe Jesus, as he then appeared! He wore upon one shoulder, from which it was almost dragged by the eager hand of Martha, a blue garment, woven without seam throughout, the affectionate work and gift of the two sisters. His face was pale and sad, yet a certain divine majesty seemed resting thereon, so that his calm, high fore-head looked like a throne. His large, earnest eyes, richly brown in hue, and darkly shaded by sable lashes, were full of sorrow. His chiseled mouth was compressed, but the swelling of the nether lip betrayed the effort he made to suppress the out bursting of his heart's deep grief.

Slowly he moved onward, and entering the cemetery, he stood before the tomb of his beloved friend.

For a few moments he stood gazing upon the door of the cave in silence. There reigned an expectant hush among the vast throng. Mary knelt at his feet gazing up into his countenance with a sublime expression of hope and trust. Martha drew softly near, and fell upon her knees by the side of her sister. Jesus looked tenderly upon them, and then resting his eyes upon the tomb, he wept. Large, glittering tears rolled down his cheeks, and glanced from his flowing beard to the ground. One of the precious drops struck upon the back of my hand, as I knelt by the side of the sisters.

"Behold how he loved him!" whispered the Jews present. Others said:

"Could not this man, which opened the eyes of the blind, have caused that even this man should not have died?"

Jesus, uttering a deep sigh, now came nearer the grave. It was, as I have before said, a cave, and a stone lay upon it. With a slight movement of his right hand to those who stood by, he said in a tone that, though low, was heard by the whole people, so solemn was the surrounding stillness:

"Take ye away the stone!"

"Lord," said Martha, "by this time he is offensive, for he hath been dead four days."

"Daughter," said Jesus, looking on her, "said I not to thee a little while since, if thou wilt believe that I can raise up thy brother, thou shalt see him alive again. Believe, and thou shalt behold the glory and power of God!"

The men, then, with some difficulty took away the stone from the door of the sepulcher, and stood it upon one side. The dark vault yawned with gloomy horror, and so corrupt was the air that rushed out, all fell back from it, save Jesus and Mary, several steps.

Jesus stood looking into the cave, where, as our eyes become accustomed to the darkness within, we could discern the corpse of Lazarus, covered with the grave mantle, and his face bound with the napkin which was already discolored with the sepulchral damp of the grave.

Raising his hands toward heaven, and lifting up his holy eyes, which were yet moist with tears, Jesus said in a voice of indescribable pathos and earnestness of appeal, and with a manner of the most awful reverence:

"Father, I thank thee that thou hast heard me. And I know

that thou hearest me always; but because of the people which stand by do I offer unto thee this prayer, that they may believe that the power which I have cometh from thee, and that they may believe thou hast sent me. And now, oh Holy Father, may I glorify thee on the earth with the power which thou hast given me!"

He then turned toward the tomb, and stretching forth his hand, he cried with a loud voice, that made every heart quake: "Lazarus, Come Forth!"

My blood stood still in my heart. Scarcely daring to look, I looked and beheld what all eyes also saw, the corpse stared up within the vault, and turning round with its face toward us, come forth, bound hand and foot with grave clothes, and his face bound about with a napkin. His countenance was like marble for whiteness, and his eyes, which were open, looked supernaturally brilliant.

At beholding him, a simultaneous, shriek burst from the bosoms of the people, with a backward rush of all who were nighest the cave.

Martha, uttering her brother's name, fell forward upon her face, and lay insensible.

"Loose him and let him go free!" said Jesus, calmly, to the petrified and amazed men who had taken away the stone. Mary was the first one who had the firmness to approach him, and remove the napkin from the sides of his face, while others, taking courage by her example, hastened to unswathe his arms and feet. In a few moments he was free from his outer grave clothes, and the color of his of his cheek came to him, his lips flushed brilliantly with red, his eyes looked natural, and beamed with wonder and love as he gazed about him. Seeing Jesus, he was about to cast himself at his feet in gratitude (for he seemed to know all that had happened), but the mighty Prophet drew him to his embrace and kissed him. Mary, at first shrinking from awe, now threw herself, blind with tears of joy, into his arms, and Martha was raised up by him to his manly breast, and his loved voice, breathed tenderly into her ear, recalled her to the consciousness of her happiness.

But my pen refuses to find language to express the unspeakable emotions of joy and gratitude, words of love and praise, that filled all hearts. Lazarus, the new-born from the dead, blooming in the rich hues of complete health, walked homeward by the side of Jesus, while the sisters hung upon him with deep thankfulness overflowing their happy hearts.

Now the great Prophet, now Lazarus, and now Jesus again, received the plaudits of the vast throng of people. Hymns were chanted to Jehovah as we passed through the streets, and so many fell down to worship Jesus, that it was long before we crossed the threshold of the dwelling, which Jesus did indeed enter with Lazarus by his side. And Martha did see him sit at the same table, and that night saw his head rest in deep slumber upon the flower-strewn pillow which her faith and love had prepared for him.

Thus, my dear father, have I given you a recital of the particulars of this mighty miracle, the report of which has filled all Jerusalem with amazement, and must lead the priests and the people to acknowledge Jesus to be the Messias of God, him of whom Moses and the Prophets did write. Do you doubt longer, my dear father?

This letter will meet you at Gaza. With the hope of soon embracing you, I remain as ever,

Your loving daughter,

Adina

LETTER XXVIII.

My Dear Father: Your letter from Gaza came safely to my hands this morning, by the courtesy of the Roman courier of the Procurator. I read it with deep grief and feelings of the saddest disappointment. Instead of a letter, I expected to see you in person, and when I heard Melec call out that a horse-man had alighted at the gate, I ran down into the court, crying, "My father, my dearest father!" and when, instead of rushing into your embrace, I was met by the mailed and helmeted figure of an armed Roman, O you may judge of the reaction upon my heart. I read your letter with tears; but you have taught me to bear patiently what cannot be revoked, and I have schooled my impatience till the God of our fathers shall bring you, in his own good time, to your loving and longing daughter. I trust that the two Arabian merchants, from Eziongeber, whom you are delaying to see, will not be long journeying to Gaza, and that on their arrival you will speedily conclude the commerce, which you write it so important to your interests should be effected. In the meanwhile I will try and wait with serenity and peace the day of your coming, and continue to write to you as the only solace which can compensate for not beholding and speaking with you. Like all my letters, dearest father, the theme of this will be Jesus, whom I unspeakably rejoice to hear you are beginning to regard with more favorable eyes, saying in your last letter, these words, which made my heart bound with joy:

"Were I to resist the testimony of the miracles which this wonderful Nazarene Prophet hath evidently done, especially that of raising Lazarus, the scribe, from the dead, I fear I should be fighting against God; for who can restore life and soul to the dead but Jehovah alone! The fame of the raising of Lazarus, as well as many of the other miracles which he has done, has reached me by other channels than your letters, and the accounts fully corroborate all you have so enthusiastically written. Nay, there is now here in Gaza, on his return from Damascus to Alexandria, my friend, Abraham Gehazi, the silk merchant, who was passing through Bethany at the moment, and, halting with his party, witnessed the miracle. He spoke with Lazarus, and confesses to me that Jesus is evidently a mighty Prophet, sent from God! This I am ready to believe, also, my daughter; and when I behold him I am ready to do him the homage I would offer to Isaiah or Daniel, were they now alive. That he is the Christ, I cannot yet believe; for Christ is to be a prince and king, and to sit on the throne of David, and give laws to the nations; before whom every crowned head shall fall prostrate, every knee bow in reverence, and at whose feet the scepters of the earth shall be laid in submission! A humble carpenter's son, prophet of God though he may be, cannot realize the idea of the person of the Messias! Turn to Esaias, and behold how his language glitters with the splendor of the prophecies he enunciates of the power, glory, and dominion on earth, of the Son of David! How can these prophetic words apply to the prophet whom you love to honor? That the hand of the Lord is upon him, and that mighty works show forth themselves in him, doubtless cannot be disputed; but that he is the Shiloh of Jacob, kingly Lion of the tribe of Judah, I cannot, for a moment, entertain the idea; for if I accept him as Messias, neither have I, nor my countrymen at large in Israel, nor the scribes, nor the fathers in Jerusalem, read the Prophets aright, but rather with eyes blindfolded; for to Jesus they do not, cannot aim, else we have altogether misunderstood what is written in Moses and in the Prophets, and in the Psalms, concerning the Christ."

Such, my dear father, is a part of your letter, which I quote, in order to reply to it, if I may do so, without presumption.

You confess, dearest father, that you are at length convinced that Jesus is a Prophet, and that God is with him, for he could not do such great miracles, except the power of God was upon him. Now, if God co-operates with Jesus; if God, so to speak, lends him his power, endows him with his own attributes, so that, like God, he heals, stills tempests, restores lost limbs, raises the dead from their graves alive again, it is because God has chosen him from among men, in order to clothe him with his mighty and divine attributes. Now, that he chose him, and invested him therewith, it is evident that he did so because he delights in him; because he loves him, and would greatly honor him. To be the chosen recipient, by the Lord God Jehovah, of such mighty powers, Jesus must be good, must be holy, pious, and full of those holy virtues in which the Almighty delights in a word, God must approve of his character and be content with whatsoever is done by him.

Now Jesus, thus favored by God, whose power to work miracles you yourself, my dear father, have confessed must be conferred by Jehovah alone, distinctly and everywhere asserts that he is Messias, the Son of God, the Shiloh of Israel, of whom Moses and the Prophets so eloquently wrote. Besides claiming for himself this high character, he was heard, both by my Uncle Amos and myself, in the synagogue at Bethany, two days after he raised Lazarus from the dead, to read from Esaias the words following, and apply them to himself, which he had done also before at Nazareth:

"The spirit of the Lord is upon me, because he hath anointed me to preach the Gospel to the poor: he hath sent me to heal the broken-hearted, to preach deliverance to the captives, and recovery of sight to the blind: to set at liberty, them that are bruised: to preach the acceptable year of the Lord."

When he had read this prophecy, which all our people, dear father, do acknowledge to refer to Messias, when he cometh, he closed the book, and gave it again to the officiating scribe, and sat down. The synagogue was thronged, so that people trod upon one another; for the fame of his miracles had brought people to hear and see him, not only from Jerusalem, but from all Judea, and Decapolis, and beyond Jordan; nay, his fame, it seemeth, is spread abroad in all the world. All eyes are now intent, and all ears are ready to hear what he should speak. He then said unto them, "This day is this Scripture fulfilled in your ears. Ye ask me, oh scribes and men of Israel, to tell you plainly who I am, whether I am the Christ or no. What saith the Prophet of the Messias when he shall come? Ye have just heard his words. If such works as he prophesieth do show forth themselves in me, ye know who I am."

Here a voice cried out in the assembly:

"Tell us plainly, art thou Christ, the Son of the Highest?"

At this direct inquiry there was intense interest shown to hear the reply.

Jesus was about to answer, when a man, who stood near the reading desk, in whom was an unclean spirit, cried out, with a shrieking voice of mingled terror and awe:

"Let me alone! Leave me as I am, thou Jesus of Nazareth! Art thou come hither to destroy me? I know thee who thou art, the Holy One of God?"

Upon this Jesus turned to the multitude, and said: "The very devils bear witness to me, who I am! and if these should hold their peace, these walls would find voices, and speak." Then Jesus rebuked the devil which possessed the man (who was Jaius, a Roman proselyte of the gate, who had long spread terror in the suburbs, by his exceeding madness and ferocity), and said to the devil, in a voice of a master commanding a bond slave:

"Hold thy peace, Satan! The Son of Man needeth not, though thou givest it, thy testimony. Hold thy peace, and come out of the man!"

At this word the man uttered a fearful cry of despair and rage, and foaming at the mouth, cast himself, or rather was thrown down by the devil within him, to the ground; where, after a moment's terrific struggle, with contortions of bodily anguish, he lay senseless as if dead. Jesus took him by the hand, and he stood up, and looking in the face of the Prophet with earnestness and wonder, he burst into tears of gratitude, exclaiming:

"I am escaped as a bird out of the snare of the fowler; the snare is broken, and I am escaped. God hath delivered me out of the hand of my enemy!" He then sat at the feet of Jesus calm, grateful, happy, and in his right mind, while all gazed on him with wonder while from the great mass of the people rose a great shout (for they were all amazed), saying:

"This is none other than the Christ, the son of David! This is the king of Israel!" While the loud shouts of "Hosanna! hosanna! hosanna!" cheered by a thousand voices, "Hosanna to our king!" shook like a passing storm the synagogue.

At this, when the noise had a little subsided, some of the Scribes and Pharisees said, reproving him for not rebuking these cries:

"Who is this that suffereth himself to be hailed as king! This is treason to the emperor!"

At this moment, Aemilius, the Roman knight, appeared at the door of the synagogue, attended by half a dozen soldiers, he happening to be passing at the moment on some duty, and stopped to listen. No sooner did the eyes of these wicked Jews catch the gleam of his helmet, and behold his tall plume rising above the head of his people, than they cried out, with eager loyalty to their conquerors, at the same time looking at Aemilius, to get his approbation:

"We have no king but Caesar! Down with the traitor! He who maketh himself king rebels against our most mighty emperor. Away with him! Arrest him, most noble Roman! Drag him before the Procurator Pilate!"

Aemilius--who well understands these envious Jews, and who is wise in the knowledge of what Jesus teaches, and who loves him as a brother, and reveres him as a father--Aemilius remained quiet, giving no signs that he would do the will of these wicked enemies of the Prophet. Jesus then said, in a loud, clear voice:

"My kingdom is not of this world! I seek not an earthly throne or earthly scepter. My kingdom is from above. Ye say truly, I am king," he added, with indescribable majesty of manner; "and hereafter ye shall behold me sitting upon the throne of heaven, high and lifted up, with the earth my footstool, and before me every knee shall bow, of things in heaven, of things on earth, and things under the earth!"

When he had thus far spoken, he could not proceed farther, on account of the sudden and immense uproar which his words produced. Some shouted "hosannas" others said he blasphemed; one cried for the Roman guard, another for the priests, to eject him from the tribune; many rushed toward him, to cast themselves at his feet, while many, putting their fingers in their ears, hurried forth from the synagogue, crying:

"His blasphemies will cause the house to fall upon us, and crush us!"

Never was such an uproar heard. In the midst of it Jesus conveyed himself away, none knew where; and when I returned to the house of Martha, I heard his low, earnest, touching voice in prayer to God, in his little chamber. He had sought its sacred quiet, to be alone with his Father in Heaven! At times I could hear him praying and supplicating, in tones of the most heart-breaking pathos; at others, the silence of his room was only broken, at intervals, by sighs and pitiful groans, that seemed to come from a breaking and crushed heart! Oh, what hand may remove the veil, and reveal what passed there in that holy retirement, between the Prophet and his God! It was late in the day when he came forth, Martha having softly tapped at his door, to say that the evening meal was prepared, and alone waited for him. When he appeared, his face was colorless and bore traces of weeping, and though he smiled kindly upon us all, as he was wont to do, there was a deep-seated sorrow upon his countenance, that brought tears to my eyes! Aemilius joined us at the table, and with dear Lazarus and with Uncle Amos, we passed a sacred hour for the Prophet ate not, but talked to us much and sweetly of the love of God; and as all listened, the viands were forgotten, not-withstanding Martha more than once ventured to remind her blessed guest that such and such a thing was before him, and that she had prepared it for him with her own hands. But, like him, we all feasted upon the heavenly food, the bread of life, which fell, like manna, from his consecrated lips.

Such, then, my dear father, is the testimony, as you have seen, in what I have above related, which Jesus publicly bears to himself, that he is the very Christ who should come into the world. There can be no further doubt of the fact now that he has so plainly stated it, pointing to the prophecies, which he is daily fulfilling by mighty works, in proof of the truth of his assertion.

Now to what irresistible conclusion, to what inevitable consequence, do we arrive? Is it not that He is the Christ? This result cannot be avoided. Either Jesus is Messias, as he asserts, and his miracles prove, or he is not. Now if he is not, then he is an impostor and a falsifier, as well as a fearful blasphemer of Jehovah! If he is these three, we then have the Almighty conferring upon an impostor his own Almighty attributes, giving him power to heal, to cast out devils, to control the elements, to raise the dead! that is, bearing testimony to the truth of one whom He never sent, empowered, nor authorized to be his Christ, and in, whom there is no truth.

Moreover, the miracles of Jesus, you admit, prove him to have come from God, while you deny his claim to be Messiah. Now, if Jesus truly came from God, as, looking at his miraculous power, you readily admit, he cannot be a sinner: he, therefore, cannot assert of himself what is not true. Yet he asserts that he is the Christ. He, then, either did come from God, or he is a deceiver, and there is no truth in him! But you will not consent to charge such character upon a man who heals with a word, who casts out demons, who raises the dead to life, and who proclaims such pure precepts, and the necessity of holiness in men, in order to enjoy the favor of God! We, therefore, are forced to the irresistible conclusion, that either the miraculous power, with which Jesus is invested, did come from God, and that he is, as he says, the true and very Christ of the Prophets and patriarchs, or that God has endowed a blasphemer of his name, an impostor, with his own powers, and endorses the imposture by continuing these powers to him in every miracle that he performs. Jesus is, therefore, the Christ. Do not, by any artful subterfuge, dearest father, attempt to avoid this conclusion! Jesus is the Christ, or we make both God and the Prophet liars and co-partners in an enormous imposture! Jesus is Christ, and let God be true, though all men be found liars.

Pardon me, dearest father, if I have been too warm and urgent in my efforts to bring you to accept Jesus as the Christ. Convinced, as I am, that he is Messias, I cannot but ardently desire that you, also, should come to the knowledge of this truth. What he is yet to be, how he is yet to develop his majesty and power, is unknown to us all. Some do think that he will enter Jerusalem, ere long, attended by tens of thousands of his followers, and that before him Pilate will peaceably vacate his Procuratorial chair, and retire, not only from the Holy City, but from Judea, with his legions and that Jesus will ascend the throne of David; the glory of the age of Solomon be revived under his rule and with the kingdom of Judah for the center of his power, he will extend the scepter of his dominion from sea to sea, and from the river of Egypt and of the East, to the ends of the earth, till all nations shall fall down before him, emperors and kings sit at his feet, and every tongue and language and speech in the whole world acknowledge him to be the King of Israel, King of kings and Lord of Lords; while under the splendor of his reign Jerusalem and Judah will be more powerful than all the cities and kingdoms that have ever been on the earth, and to the dominion and glory of our people there will be no end.

Such, dear father, is the future of Jesus, as looked for by all his disciples, save one, and this is John, the betrothed of my cousin Mary. He is more closely intimate with Jesus than any other man; and is so beloved by him that he makes known to him many things which he withholds from the rest. John, on hearing our views of the coming glory of the Prophet, looks sadly, and says:

"Not now -- not here -- not in this world! The glory of Jesus you will behold, but first, we must pass through the valley of darkness, the gate of the tomb. His kingdom is not on the earth, but in the heavens. Here, I fear, he will pass through suffering and sorrow, and, perhaps, a painful death, for he has told me that he came to suffer and die, and that he can only win, bleeding from every vein, the kingdom, over which he is hereafter to reign in endless dominion. Prepare your hearts, dear friends," he would say, "to be rent, and your eyes for tears, rather than fill your imaginations with pictures of glory, splendor, and power. He has distinctly said to me, "I must first suffer many things at the hands of men, before I enter upon my reign of glory. The Jews will seek me to kill me, and I shall be taken from among you, but let not sorrow fill your hearts. Death can have no power over me save such as I permit it to hold. I lay down my life, and I take it again. Through much tribulation and sorrow must the Son of God win the scepter of this earth from him who hath the power over the nations, even from Satan, the prince of this world. I shall conquer, but I must first fall. Yet fear not! I shall make death the gateway to Paradise for you all!"

"Such," says John, "are the mysterious and sorrowful words which he has often spoken to me. What they mean, or how to understand them, I know not; for I cannot comprehend how he who can raise the dead can die, or how he who can calm a tempest; can suffer himself to be taken and slain by men, the tempest of whose wrath he could as easily pacify!"

Thus, dear father, do we discourse together about this wonderful Prophet, whose future life is all a mystery, save that, from the prophecies, we know it is to be inconceivably glorious, but from his own lips, first to be inconceivably sorrowful. But, whether on a throne, giving laws to the world, or in the dust, borne down by the deepest woe, I shall still love, honor, reverence Him, and trust in Him, as my Saviour, my Prince, and the Holy One of God!

Your devoted and loving

ADINA

LETTER XXIX.

My Dearest Father: With what emotions of grief and amazement I commence this letter, you can form no just conception. Jesus, the Prophet of God, is a prisoner to the Roman power! He is accused of making himself a king, and of a conspiracy to re-establish the throne of David! And who, think you, have accused him of this noble effort, but the Jews, our own, his own people! men who should glory in seeing the dominion of the Caesars at an end; men who should blush longer to have Mount Zion commanded by a Roman citadel. These base, degraded, and wicked scribes and priests, whom I am ashamed to call my countrymen, have accused the divinely-gifted Jesus, before Pilate, of rebellion and treason! And at this moment, while I write, he is in the ward-room of the Procurator's palace, held a close prisoner.

But I fear not the issue! He cannot be holden of his foes, save by his own free will. He can, with a word, turn his chains into bands of sand, and by a glance render his guards dead men! He will, therefore, escape their bonds! They can have no power over him. But will not the Lord God punish our nation for this sin and enmity against His Christ? You will ask, my father, why, if he possesses such mighty power, hath he suffered himself to be taken prisoner? This question I cannot answer. It troubles me. I wonder, and am transfixed with amazement. Everyone around me asks the same question. Our house is thronged with his friends, who, midnight as it is, have come hither to hear if the rumor is true. Five of his disciples are with Uncle Amos in the court, giving an account of the manner of his arrest, which I will relate to you, although it increases the mystery.

It seems that to-day, after eating the Passover with his twelve chosen friends, he went forth with them toward Olivet, and there seating himself beneath the shade of a tree, he talked with them very sadly, saying that his hour was come, that he had ended his work, and that he was about to be delivered into the hands of sinful men.

John, upon being questioned by cousin Mary and myself,

thus told us: -- It was evening, and the south side of Olivet lay in deep shadow. We were all sorrowful. We felt each one of us, as if some grievous evil was pending over us. The tones of our beloved Master's voice moved us to tears, at much as his words, which latter were full of mystery. We were all present, excepting Iscariot, who had remained in the city to discharge the costs, he being our purse-bearer, of the Passover Supper, and pay for the hire of the room. At that supper Jesus had said very plainly, that one of our number would betray him into the hands of the priests who, since his triumphant entry into the Holy City, preceded and followed by the multitude, shouting hosannas, and proclaiming him Messias, had diligently sought his life. At hearing our Lord say these strange words in accents of touching reproach, we were all deeply moved and Peter and the rest at once questioned him, individually, if it were they. I was resting at the moment, with my cheek on the shoulder of Jesus, and said softly: "Lord, who is it that betrayeth thee? I will forthwith lay hands upon him, and prevent his doing thee harm!" Jesus shook his head and smiling gently said:

"My beloved brother, thou knowest not what thou wouldest do. The son of Man, must needs be betrayed by his own friends, but woe unto him who betrayeth me. See thou who dippeth bread with me into the dish!"

I looked, and saw Judas reach forward, and dip into the dish at the same instant in which Jesus dipped; but in his eagerness, or from conscious guilt, his hand trembled, he spilled the salt on the board, and the sop fell from his grasp into the bowl upon which Jesus gave him the piece he held, saying to him, with a remarkable expression in his clear, piercing eyes: "Judas, what thou doest do quickly!"

We were surprised at the tone and manner in which this was spoken, but supposed the command had reference to some of Judas's duties, little suspecting what fearful awful thing he was to do! Instantly, Judas rose from the table, and without a word, or casting a look at any of us, went out.

For a few moments, after his footsteps had ceased to be heard, there prevailed a heavy silence in the chamber; for a strange fear had fallen upon us; why, we could not tell and looking into one another's faces, and then into our dear Master's, we seemed to await some dread event. His face was placid, and full of affection, as he looked upon us. The momentary cloud, which shaded the noble profile when he spoke to Judas, had passed off, and there was the serenity of a cloudless sky in his face.

"My children," he said, "I am to be with you but a little while longer. The hour of my departure is at hand. Remember my last words -- Love one another! In this shall all men know that ye are my disciples."

"Lord," cried Peter, "we will go with thee! Thou shalt not leave us nor go without us!"

"The priests seek to kill thee, and thy footsteps are watched!" exclaimed Andrew, earnestly.

"Yes, we will not suffer thee, dear Rabbi, to go abroad alone," said James, with enthusiasm; "our hearts and hands will defend thee!"

"Whither wilt thou depart, Lord?" I asked, with emotion. "Thou wilt not trust thyself to the Jews?"

Thus we all, eagerly and tearfully, gathered around him, alarmed and grieved at the words he had said. He regarded us lovingly, and said:

"Little children, I must leave you. Whither I go you cannot come!"

"Though thou wentest to the uttermost parts of the sea, I will follow thee, my Master and Lord!" exclaimed Peter. "Whither goest thou, that we may not follow? I will lay down my life for thee, and so will all these!"

With one voice we asserted our devotion to our beloved Master, and secretly, I asked him whither he intended to go, and why he forbade us to go with him?

"As Abraham bound Isaac his son, and laid him upon the wood, so shall my Father cause me to be bound and laid upon the wood; and shall slay me, a sacrifice for the sins of his people!"

"Not so! not so! Lord," cried Peter. "I will die for thee, ere a hair of thy head shall fall." And the warm-hearted disciple drew his sword, and placed himself by the side of Jesus, as if to defend him.

"Wilt thou die for me, Peter?" said Jesus, gazing on him with a sad, sweet look: "Verily, verily, Peter, thou little knowest thyself. The cock shall not crow twice, heralding the coming morning, ere thou shalt thrice deny that thou knowest me!"

"Deny thee, Lord!" repeated Peter, with amazed grief and horror in his looks.

"Yes, Peter," answered Jesus, firmly, but kindly "deny that you ever knew me for the time draweth near when there will be safety only in confessing ignorance of Jesus the Nazarene.

"And all of you," he added, while his voice grew tremulous, and tears glistened in his eyes, "all of you shall be offended because of me, this night; ye shall be ashamed to confess that you are my disciples, and ye will think me a deceiver, and will be displeased at me. Yea, everyone of you shall desert me; for thus it is written: The Shepherd shall be smitten, and the sheep shall be scattered!"

At hearing these words, we knew not what to answer; but I kissed my dear Lord's hand and said that if danger were hanging over him, as it seemed, I would share it with him!

When he saw that our hearts were troubled, and that we were sad, and that the faithful Philip sobbed aloud, at being supposed capable of abandoning his Master, he added, "Let not your hearts be troubled; I go to prepare a place for you in my Father's house!"

"Thy father, Lord, liveth at Nazareth, and hath but two small apartments in his humble house," said Thomas; "how sayest thou that we are all to lodge there!"

"Thomas, thou canst understand only what thine eyes see. I speak of my Father who is in Heaven. In His house are many mansions."

Jesus then began plainly to tell us that he was to die, and that by his death we should be admitted into a heavenly Paradise, and live forever. We could not understand all he said, but we knew that he was soon to be taken from us; and sorrow filled all our hearts. After discoursing with us in the most touching words, he at length said:

"Come, let us go over to Kedron, to the garden we so much loved to walk in."

We went out with him, inclosing him as a guard, to conceal his person from the Jewish spies, as well as to defend him. Peter and James went before with drawn swords. In this way we passed through the gloomy streets, and forth from the gate, which Pilate suffered to be open day and night, on account of the crowds at the Passover, coming in and going out. The moon shining brightly, and by its light glancing on the face of Jesus, by whom I walked, I saw that it was sadder than its wont, while he spoke but little.

We at length crossed the Kedron, and entered the dark groves of Olivet. Familiar with all the paths, we advanced to a central group of the venerable Olivet trees, beneath which Abraham used to sit, and there Jesus, turning to us, said, in a voice of the deepest woe:

"Friends, the hour of my time of trial is come! My work is ended, I would be alone! Remain you here, and watch, for we shall be sought for. Come with me, Peter, and you, also, James. I am going to pray yonder."

"Not take me, also, dear Lord?" I said sorrow-fully.

"Yes, thou art always with me, beloved," he answered "I will not leave thee now."

So leaving the eight friends to keep watch against the intrusion of his enemies, who were known to be everywhere seeking him, he walked away to the most secluded recesses of the garden. He stopped at the place, near the rock, where Adam is said to have hidden from Jehovah and, saying to us, in a sorrowful tone: "Tarry ye here, while I go apart, and pray to my Father," he went from us about a stone's cast, and kneeled down, where a thick olive branch, hanging low to the ground, concealed him from our view. I was so solicitous lest he should leave us, and we should see him no more, that I soon softly advanced near to the spot, and beheld him prostrate on the ground, while deep groans broke from his heart. I heard his voice murmuring, but could not distinguish the words, broken by grief only the tones were those of strange horror and dread.

As he prayed thus, in great agony, I suddenly beheld a swift light pass by me, as if from the skies, and an angel stood by the side of Jesus, bending over him, and raising him up from the ground. A soft bright glory shone around the spot, so that Peter, seeing it, advanced toward me, supposing someone had entered the garden, bearing a torch. I beckoned to Peter to be motionless, and he gazed with me in speechless astonishment and admiration upon the form of the angel, from whose glorious face was emitted the radiance which illumined the place where Jesus was. As the angel raised Jesus from the ground, we saw that his countenance was convulsed with anguish and upon his brow stood great shining drops of sweat, mingled with blood, which oozed from his pallid temples, and rolling down his marble cheeks, dropped to the ground. Never had we beheld a human visage so marred by sorrow, so deeply graven with the lines of agony.

The angel seemed to utter soothing words and pointed, with his shining hand, toward heaven, as if to encourage him with hope, and give him strength. The face of Jesus grew more serene; he raised his eyes with a divine expression of holy submission, and said, in a strong voice:

"Thy will, not mine, O God, be done!"

The angel then seemed to embrace and kiss him, and rose and disappeared, like a star returning into the blue depths of heaven; while Peter and I stood by wondering, and full of awe, at what we saw.

"How looked the angel?" I asked of my cousin John, interrupting him in his recital.

"As a young and noble youth, with a countenance so dazzling I could not look upon him steadily. He seemed to be clothed in flowing raiment, silvery white and a fragrance, more delicate and grateful than the subtlest attar of roses of India, was diffused by his presence throughout the garden, while the sound of his voice seemed to fill all the air with strange musical vibrations, unlike anything heard on earth."

"Had the angel wings?" asked my cousin Mary.

"Nay, I could not well discern," answered John.

"His robes seemed to shape themselves into wings, as he rose from the earth; and when he stood they flowed with living grace about his god-like form. After the departure of the angel, Jesus seemed calmer, and as we did not wish longer to intrude upon his sacred privacy, we softly returned to where James lay asleep. We remained for some time conversing together upon the wonderful vision we had seen, which confirmed us in the certainty that Jesus came from God, and was in truth the Messias, that should come but at length, wearied with our day's excitements, we must have fallen asleep, for we were suddenly startled by the voice of our dear Master, saying:

"Why sleep ye, children? But the hour is past for watching. Ye may sleep on now, for though your flesh is weary, your spirit is willing. I need your aid no longer!"

But we refused to sleep longer. We then advanced to where the other disciples were, and found them also asleep.

"Arise, let us be going! " cried Jesus, in a tone that roused them to their feet, "they are at hand who seek me!"

While he was speaking, we saw many lights gleaming through the trees, along King David's walk, and the tramp of feet fell on our ears. We soon saw a large party advancing into the midst of the garden, who walked rapidly, and spoke only in undertones. We at once took the alarm, and said to Jesus:

"Fly, dear Master! Let us ascend the hill, and escape by the way to Bethany for these are enemies."

"Nay," answered our dear Master, "I must submit to my Father's will. It must needs be that I deliver myself into the hands of these men; how else shall the Scriptures be fulfilled? Seek safety in flight for yourselves; but I must go whither they will lead me."

"Not so Lord," answered Peter. "There is time for thee to escape; or if not, we will stand by thee, and defend thee!"

So said all the disciples. Jesus shook his head, and said, with a sad smile, "Ye know not now what ye say, or would do. My hour is come!"

While he yet spake, the multitude drew nearer, and those who had the lead, raising their torches high above their heads, discovered us, with Jesus in the midst. To my surprise I beheld Judas acting as their guide, for he alone knew where his Master was to be found at that hour. Upon discovering Jesus, this wicked man ran forward, with expressions of attachment in his face, and kissed Jesus on the cheek, saying:

"Hail, Master! I am glad I have found thee!"

"Judas," said Jesus, "betrayest thou the Son of Man with a kiss?"

When Judas heard this, he turned to the multitude at the head of which I recognized some of the chief priests, and most learned scribes of the Temple, and cried aloud:

"This is he! seize him and hold him fast!"

There upon the crowd, to the number of tenscore men, among whom were the vilest sort of people, rushed forward to lay hands upon Jesus; the moon and torches shedding almost the bright light of day upon the whole group.

At seeing them advance so furiously, with spears, and clubs, and swords, Peter and James placed themselves before Jesus, to defend him, while I, being unarmed, cast myself across his breast, to shield his heart with my body. The more bold men in the crowd coming too near Peter smote one of them with his sword, as he was reaching out his arm to grasp Jesus by the shoulder, and clave off his ear. At seeing this the crowd uttered a fierce shout, and were pressing upon us, when Jesus raised the palm of his hand, and said quietly:

"Whom seek ye?"

Instantly the whole mass rolled backward, like a receding billow rebounding from the face of an immovable rock, and every man fell with his forehead to the ground, where they lay for a minute stunned; and we twelve stood alone, save Judas, who had not been struck down, and now remained gazing with with amazement and terror upon the prostrate enemies of Jesus.

"Lord! " cried Peter, astonished, "if thou canst thus repel thy foes, thou neediest not fear them more. Shall I smite Judas also?"

"Nay -- put up thy sword, Peter! Let him remain to witness my power, that he may see that he nor his have any power over me, save what I give them."

While he was thus speaking, the men rose to their feet, and instead of flying, they seemed to be infuriated at their discomfiture and as the chief priests cried out that it was by sorcery they had been stricken down, they rushed madly forward, and laid their hands upon Jesus, and upon us all. In vain I contended against numbers to rescue Jesus! in vain the sword of the valiant Peter flashed in the torchlight, and fell upon the heads of the captors; overpowered by numbers, we were defeated, and driven from the field of contest, leaving Jesus in the hands of his enemies!

When John had gone thus far in his relation, dear father, our tears and his were mingled. We wondered that Jesus, who could, as he had shown, destroy his enemies with a wave of his hand, should suffer them to make him their prisoner; for in their hands he knew he must die! This amazes and bewilders us. At one moment we are tempted to lose our confidence in him, and believe, as many now begin to say, that we have been following a deceiver, and in the next to trust fully in him, and that he will yet overcome his enemies, and be restored to us. Every step we hear at the door makes our blood bound, for we think it may be our beloved Lord escaped from the hands of his captors. We must wait the issue with hope and faith! Tomorrow will, perhaps, reveal all. The mystery that envelops this Great Prophet is inscrutable. The seeming contradictions that make up his character, bewilder us. But we try and comfort ourselves with the word of his promise:

"Ye know not now; but ye shall know by and by, and shall believe truly, that I came out from God! What seems to you mysterious, shall be made clear as light. Wait, and have faith, and all shall be made known which now you understand not. Let no trials and degradations ye see me pass through cause your faith to fail. I am come into this world to conquer; but it is expedient first that I humble myself; but if I stoop, it is to raise up the world with me, when I rise again!"

Ah, it is stooping, indeed, for this Prince of the Prophets to suffer himself to be led away bound by his foes! But we hope with trembling, dear father, remembering his words!

I have omitted to mention to you what more John related, touching the arrest of the Prophet. As the chief priests bound and laid their hands on him, there was heard above in the air the sound of myriads of rushing wings, and the gathering signal of a trumpet echoing in the skies, as if a countless host of invisible beings were marshaling, armies by armies, in the mid-heaven. At this fearful and sublime sound, all raised their heads, but saw nothing and Jesus said, with a majestic and commanding look, such as I never before beheld upon his face:

"Ye hear," he said to us, "that I am not without heavenly friends!

I have only to pray my Father, which is in heaven and He will bid twelve legions of his angels, now hovering, sword-armed, in the air, and yearning to defend me, descend to my aid! But I may not use my powers for myself. I came on earth to suffer. As a man, I must submit to all things that come upon me; nor make use of more means in my behalf than a man can do! For this I came into the world. I lead on, I go with you!"

Thus, dear father, was Jesus borne away by a fierce multitude, and dragged into the city, followed by a shouting and insulting crowd, who, seeing that, not withstanding his miraculous powers, they could secure and hold him, mocked him only the more, making light of powers which could not prevent the capture of his person. Some even reviled him on the way, and asked him to call down the twelve legions of angels; while others said they were hungry and thirsty, and would have him turn water into wine for them, and give them bread by another miracle of loaves.

John, whose interest in, and affection for Jesus, led him to follow them, disguised in a Roman soldier's cloak, heard all this; but Jesus made no answer, only walking quietly along, patiently enduring all they said and did.

As they entered the Damascus gate, the Roman guard, seeing the immense crowd and uproar, stopped them to learn the cause of the commotion.

"We have here a traitor and conspirator, O Captain of the guard," answered Eli, the chief priest, "a pestilent fellow, who calls himself Christ, a king. We have, therefore, with this band of hired soldiers, taken him, as he was met secretly, with twelve of his fellow conspirators, plotting to overthrow the government of Caesar, and make himself king of Judea."

"Long live Caesar! Long live the emperor!" shouted the Roman soldiers. "We have no king but Augustus Imperator!"

Upon this, many of the soldiers cried, "Take him before the Procurator! He will give him his deserts, who would take his Procuratorship from him! To Pilate! To Pilate!"

"To Annas!" shouted the Jews "First, to Annas!"

Then, with some shouting one thing, and others another thing, and with vast numbers of those who had come up to the Passover pressing to get sight of the Prophet, he was hurried toward the house of Annas, who is the most popular man among our people, and whose influence over them is unbounded. On reaching, with great uproar of voices, and by the light of torches, the dwelling of the High Priest's son-in-law, they called him to the roof of the house, to which he came in his night apparel for it was by this time near the hour of midnight.

When Annas knew that the prisoner was Jesus, he uttered a fearful oath of joy and wicked satisfaction, and coming down into the court, bade them bring the prisoner in. The calm majesty of Jesus abashed him, and checked the course of insulting questions he began to put to him. At length, finding that the Prophet would make him no reply, he caused him to be bound still more closely, and sent him to Caiaphas the High Priest, saying to him:

"Caiaphas will find voice for thy tongue, O Prophet! So, thou wouldst destroy the Temple, and callest thyself the Lord Jehovah! Out, blasphemer! Away with him, or the house will be swallowed up with the presence of one so impious. Away with the blasphemer! Pilate will make thee king in truth, and give thee a Roman throne, to which, so that thou mayest not presently fall from it, he will nail thee, foot and hand!"

At this the crowd shouted their approbation, and many cried:

"To the cross! to the cross with him!"

But others said; "Nay, but to Caiaphas!" While the Roman soldiers asserted that he should be taken before Pilate.

With renewed uproar, they tumultuously pressed forward, their way lighted by the red glare of a hundred torches. John followed, but being recognized as one of his disciples, by a soldier in Aemilius's legion, he was seized, and only escaped by leaving his cloak in the hands of the rude Roman for such was the prevalent hatred to Jesus that they called for his followers, and would have taken them also had it been in their power. Five of the disciples, who have escaped arrest, are now in this house, whither John fled on eluding the grasp of the soldier. We are all sad and anxious. To move in favor at Jesus is only to share his fate, and do him no service; besides, I am pained to say, two or three of his disciples begin to doubt whether he is Messias, since, instead of establishing his promised kingdom, he is now a prisoner, and menaced with death.

Yet, through all, dear father, I trust in him, and hope. I cannot doubt his truth and power. I have seen him bring Lazarus from the grave, and I will not believe but that He can save himself, and will save himself, from their hands. It is only when I shall behold him really no more -- see him really dead, that my faith in his divine mission will waver. If he should be slain, then, alas! not only will perish forever all my hopes, and those of his trembling, weeping disciples, but the hopes of the restoration and glory of Judah; for verily we have believed that it is He which should have redeemed Israel! With eyes blinded with tears, I can scarcely subscribe myself,

Your sad, but loving daughter,   ADINA.

LETTER XXX.

My Dear Father: I know not how to write -- I know not what to say. Dismay and sorrow fill my heart. I feel as if life were a burden too heavy to bear. Disappointment and regrets are all that remain to me. He, in whom I trusted -- He, whom thousands in Judah had begun to look upon as the hope of the nation -- He who, as his now wretched disciples trusted, would have redeemed Israel -- Jesus, has been delivered, this morning, by the Roman Procurator, to be condemned to death, and they have crucified him. Tears of grief unutterable fall upon the parchment as I write, and, more eloquently than any words, tell you how I am smitten by this heavy, heavy blow! Jesus -- the noble, mild, courteous, and wise Prophet, who taught with such grace and wisdom, and whom we believed to be sent from God to be the Saviour of our people, and the Prince who should sit on the throne of David, to restore the former splendor of our nation -- is dead! With him have perished all our hopes! When he bowed his bleeding head on the cross, the necks of weeping Judah bent once more to the dust, to receive the yoke of Rome, from which they believed he would have delivered them. With him has been quenched the rising light of the sun of the Messias, who we hoped and believed that he was. But we hope no more! The daughters of Israel may now sit in the dust, and cover themselves with veils of woe; for he in whom they trusted is dead! Confounded and dismayed, his followers wander in the fields or hide themselves from the multitude who seek their lives also. Alas! I cannot refrain from weeping bitter, bitter tears. How hath the Lord covered the daughters of Zion with a cloud in his anger, and cast down from heaven unto earth the beauty of Israel. "All they that pass by," as saith the Prophet, "will clap their hands at us, who trusted in him, and wag their heads at the daughters of Jerusalem; Is this the man -- the mighty Prophet, whom men called the Son of the Highest, the Messias of God -- the Prince of David -- the excellency of wisdom and the joy of the earth? The punishment of thine iniquity is accomplished, O Daughter of Zion!"

Thus do I weep, and thus do I complain for verily fear and a snare is come upon us, desolation and destruction, O my father! We know not which way to turn! He in whom we trusted has proved as one of us, weak and impotent, and has suffered death without power to save himself. He that saved others could not escape the death of the Roman cross! While I write, I hear the priest Abner, in the court below, mocking my Uncle Amos in a loud voice:

"Your Messias is dead! A famous great prophet, surely, you Nazarenes have chosen -- born in a stable, and crucified as a thief! Said I not that he who could speak against the Temple and the priesthood was of the devil?"

Rabbi Amos makes no reply. Shame and despair seal his lips. Thus our enemies triumph over us, and we answer only with confusion of face. Even the disciples are outlawed, and a reward offered by Caiaphas for their arrest; and all those who, two days ago, were so full of hope, and proud to sit at the feet of Jesus, and to follow him whithersoever he went, now fear to confess that they have ever known or seen him. It is only the high rank, as a priest, of my Uncle Amos, which protects him or his household from arrest.

But, my dear father, to whom I have ever confided all my feelings and thoughts, shall we pronounce Jesus an impostor? Oh, can he whose very countenance was stamped with celestial dignity, whose lips dispensed truths such as the wisest philosophers and holiest prophets have loved to study and teach whose whole life has been blameless, and who has lived only to do good -- can he be, must he be pronounced a deceiver? When I recall the sick he has cured, the indigent he has relieved, the mourners he has comforted, the ignorance he has enlightened, the dead he has upraised, the sublime truths he has taught, his love of God, his respect for the worship of the Temple, the perfect morality of his daily life, the sincerity of all he said, and the universal sympathy which seemed to fill his bosom for all who were in sorrow -- I cannot, oh, I cannot bring my pen to write the word "impostor," in association with his name. But what shall I substitute? Alas! I feel desolate and miserable, like those who, confiding all their heart's treasures to another's keeping, whom they believed good and true, find that he was unworthy of confidence and betrays their trust. Jesus asserted that he came on earth to establish a kingdom, and sit on the throne of David and that all nations would receive their laws from Jerusalem. Where, now, is his power? Where his throne? Where his laws? His power is ended in death! His throne is the Roman cross, placed between thieves and the Roman laws, or rather power, which he was to destroy, have condemned himself to death!

This unexpected, this unlooked-for, startling result has stupefied me! And not only me, but all who have been so led by fascination to trust in him. Even John, the beloved disciple, I hear now pacing the floor of the adjoining room, sobbing as if his noble heart would burst! Mary, my cousin's sweet voice, I catch, from time to time, trying to soothe him, although she is stricken, like us all, to the very earth; for she trusted in Jesus, if possible, with more faith than I did; and hence her dismay at his death, at the sudden termination of all her hopes in him, and of his restoration of Israel is in proportion. We have wept tonight in each other's arms, till we had no more tears to shed and I have left her to pour out my griefs to you. The unhappy John despairingly answers her:

"Do not try to comfort me, Mary! There is no ground for hope more! He is dead -- dead -- dead! All is lost! We who trusted in him have only to fly, if we would save our wretched lives, into Galilee, and return once more to our nets! The sun which shone so dazzlingly has proved a phantom light, and gone out in darkness. He whom I could not but love, I see that I loved too well, since he was not what I believed him to be. Oh, how could he be so like the Son of God, and yet not be? Yet I loved him as if he were the very Son of the Highest! But I have seen him die like a man -- I have gazed on his lifeless body! I have beheld the deep wound made in his very heart by the Roman spear! I cast myself upon him, and implored him, by his love for me, to give some sign that he was not holden by death! I placed my trembling hands over his heart. It was still, still -- motionless as stone, like any other dead man's! The flesh of his corpse was cold and clammy! He was dead -- dead! With him die all our hopes -- the hopes of Israel!"

"He may live again," said Mary, softly, and hesitatingly, as if she, herself, had no such hope. "He raised Lazarus, thou dost remember!"

"Yes, for Jesus was living to do it!" answered John, stopping in his walk "but how can the dead raise the dead! No, he will never move, speak, nor breathe again."

Thus, dear father, are we left to mourn with shame at our delusion, and with utterly wrecked hopes I candidly acknowledge that I have been too hasty to confess Jesus as Messias of God but, oh, what could I do but believe in one who seemed so like an angel from heaven -- a celestial Prince! There is a dreadful and deep mystery in it all. To the last we believed he would free himself, and escape death! For our sins God has suffered this great disappointment to come upon us all.

I try to seek some consolation in recalling all that he was, good and holy; but this retrospect only darkens the cloud of the present; for I irresistibly argue: How could he, who was so good, prove so great a deceiver? I live and breathe, while he, who taught me that he had life in himself, and who I believed could raise me from the dead, if I died, he is now dead and laid in the tomb and yet I live! He, over whom, we fondly believed, Death could have no power, since the doors of sepulchers opened at his voice, and let forth their re-living tenants, he has been conquered by Death, and proved himself only the mortal son of Joseph, and the widowed Mary. She is inconsolable. Her distress is heart-rending to witness. Not only has she lost her only son, about whom all her maternal sympathies were entwined, as the vine encircles the lofty palm, but she is humiliated in the very ashes of shame, that he has died, leaving the thousands who trusted to his word, fugitives for his name's sake, and disappointed in all they expected from him. Even now I hear her heavy sighs, from the couch where she lies, brokenhearted, in my aunt's chamber, to which John led her, after the execution of Jesus, at his request. She asks to be left alone, and I forget my own sorrows when I think upon hers, which are greater than she can bear for, all at once, her son has been hurled from the position in which he drew all eyes up after him, and has died an ignominious death, leaving behind him the stigma of an impostor's fame. This pierces her heart more keenly, than that she has been made childless. "Oh," I heard her say to Rabbi Amos when she came into the house, "oh, that he could have deceived me thus -- he whom I believed to be the soul of truth. Alas! my son -- my son better hadst thou remained in thy humble shop, leading a lowly and useful life, than, for the temporary popularity of a Prophet's name, have held out hopes and promises to thy followers, that thou couldst never realize, and meet with such a death! This has made my heart bleed indeed! My gray hairs will go down to the grave with shame, that I am the mother of him who has deceived Israel."

But I will not dwell on this universal sorrow -- sorrow mingled with mortification -- for the pride of all has been humbled to the dust. I will give you a description, dear father, of what occurred after the arrest for I wish you to be acquainted with every particular respecting him, that you may see how perfectly he sustained the lofty character, which drew all men after him, to the last -- standing before his judges, like a man sublime in the consciousness of innocence, and commanding even the involuntary respect and admiration of his foes. Oh, how could he have been a deceiver? Yet he is dead, and in that he is dead, he has failed in all the glorious things which he promised concerning himself. "His death," says his disciple Peter, who was here to-night, to ask John what should now be done by them, "his death is his infamy!"

But I will not further delay the account of his trial and condemnation for you will be earnest to know how such a man could so fall as to be condemned to a malefactor's death! In my last letter I spoke of his arrest -- through the traitorous part enacted by Judas. Led by his captors, bound by the wrists with a cord, he was taken from the dark groves of Olivet, wherein he had been found at prayer, and conducted with great noise into the city by Caesar's gate. It is near this archway that Rabbi Amos lives. It was the third hour of the night, and I had just gone to my room, which overlooked the street of David, when I was startled by the suddenly heard outcries of fierce men, breaking the night's stillness. Then I heard the quick challenges of the Roman sentinels, the galloping of several horsemen, and a confused tumult; the cries, in the meanwhile, increasing. But I will copy for you Mary's account of it to Martha, just written by her, instead of adding any more to my own.

"I went out upon the basilica, which overlooked the street" says Mary to her sister, in her letter, "and beheld a multitude advancing, with torches flashing and soon they came opposite the house, at least two hundred men, half-clad and savage-looking, with flashing eyes and scowling looks. Here and there, among them, was a Levite urging them on, and I also beheld Abner, the priest, firing their passions by loud oratory and eager gesticulations. Behind rode five Roman horsemen, with leveled spears, guarding a young man, who walked in front of their horses' heads. It was Jesus. His rich auburn locks were disheveled, his beard torn, his face marred, and his garments rent. He was pale and suffering, but walked with a firm step. I burst into tears, and so did Adina, who had come out to see what was passing. He looked up, and said touchingly, "Weep not for me, daughters of Jerusalem, but weep for yourselves."

"He would have said more, but the priest smote him rudely upon the mouth; and the crowd, following his example, would have done him further insult, but for the Roman soldiers, who turned their spears every way, to guard him from violence; for they had rescued him from the terrible rage of the Jews, by their centurion's orders, and were commanded to bring him safely before Pilate. So, thus guarded and escorted, by the men who thirsted for his blood, he was led onward to the Pretorium, where the Roman Procurator resided. Gradually, the whole multitude, horsemen, Jews, priests, torch-bearers, and captive, disappeared in the distance; and silence, a dread and unearthly silence, succeeded. I turned and looked in Adina's face. She was leaning, colorless as marble, against one of the columns of the basilica.

"What can all this mean?" she said, with emotion. "Can it be possible he has suffered himself to be taken -- He who could destroy or make alive with a word? What means this dreadful scene we have just witnessed?"

"I could not answer. It was inexplicable, incomprehensible to me. All I knew was what my eyes just beheld, that Jesus, our Prophet, our King, our Messias, on whom all our hopes and the joy of Israel rested, was dragged, a prisoner, through the streets, helpless and without a helper. I trembled with, I knew not what, unknown forebodings. Suddenly Adina cried:

"He cannot be harmed! He cannot die! He is a mighty Prophet, and has power that will strike his enemies dead! Let us not fear. He has yielded himself, only the more terribly to defeat and destroy his foes. We will not fear what Pilate or the priests will do! They cannot harm the anointed Shiloh of the Lord!"

"While we were yet talking, dearest Martha, a dark figure passed stealthily along beneath the basilica, and seemed to court the shadows of the house. At this moment, my father, Rabbi Amos, opened the outer gate, with a torch in his hand, to follow, at our request, the crowd of people, and see what should befall Jesus. The light glared full upon the tall, spare form of Peter, the Galilee fisherman. His dark, stern features wore an expression of earnest anxiety. In his hand he carried a naked sword, on which were visible drops of blood.

"Is it thou, Peter!" exclaimed my father. "What is this? Who has ordered the arrest of Jesus? What has he done?"

"That hateful and envious man, Caiaphas, seeks to destroy him, and has bribed, with large lures of gold, the baser Jews to do this thing. Come with me, Rabbi, and let us die with him!" and the Galilean pressed eagerly forward at a pace with which my father could not keep up."

"And this was an hour ago, and yet no news has come from the Pretorium; but, from time to time, a dreadful shout from the hill,

on which the palace of Caiaphas stands, breaks upon my ears and the glare of unseen torches illumines the atmosphere high above the towers of the palace. It is a fearful night of agony and suspense. Adina in her painful uncertainty, but for my entreaties, would go forth alone toward the Pretorium, to hear and know all. I can keep myself calm only by writing to you. Adina has also commenced a letter to her father, recording these sad things, but she drops her pen, to start to the balcony at every sound. When will this fearful night end! What will the morrow reveal! Adina is confident nothing can befall the holy Prophet, for he who could raise your brother Lazarus from the dead cannot fear death. Besides, has he not promised that he has come from God, to be king of Israel? If he enters the Pretorium a bound captive tonight, it will be to sit upon the Roman throne within it tomorrow, with Pilate in chains at his feet! I write this, to send to you by Elec at dawn, that you and Lazarus may hasten to come into the city to us.
. .

"It is an hour since I wrote the last line. The interval has been one of agony. Rumors have reached us that the priests insist on Pilate's passing sentence of death on the Prophet. The cries, "Crucify him! crucify him! have distinctly reached our ears. John is now here. About half an hour after Jesus passed he reached the house, nearly destitute of apparel, his clothing having been torn off from him by the Jews, in their efforts to make him prisoner also. He is calm and confiding, saying that his beloved Master can never be injured by them and that he will, ere many hours, deliver himself from his foes, and proclaim himself king of Israel, with power such as man never had before! May the God of Jacob defend him! John has just gone up to the Temple, to get news, in disguise of a priest, wearing my father's robes. I tremble lest he be discovered, and taken; for the Jews are as bitter against the followers as against their Master.

"I have just seen a messenger, passing in great haste along the street and his horse falling, cast him almost upon our threshold. It was the page of Aemilius, the noble Roman knight who is betrothed to my cousin Adina. She hastened to my aid. He was but stunned, and soon was able to say, that he bore a message from Lucia Metella, the fair and youthful bride of Pilate, urging him to have nothing to do with the Prophet, but give him his liberty for she had just awaked from an impressive dream, in which she saw him sitting on the Throne of the Universe, crowned with the stars of heaven, the earth the footstool beneath his feet, and all nations assembled, and doing him homage, while

247

the gods and goddesses of high Olympus cast their glittering crowns and scepters at his feet, and hailed him God!

"Such was the account given by the page to Adina and, remounting his horse, he has continued rapidly on his way toward the Pretorium. This report of the page has filled our hearts with joy and hope inexpressible. Confident that Jesus is the son of God, we will not fear what man can do unto him.

"It is now three hours past midnight, and the dawn is chilly and cold, so that I cannot longer hold my pen. I shall send this as soon as the city gates are opened. Come at once to our comfort for this is no time for the friends of Jesus to be out of Jerusalem."

"My father has returned. It is day. He says nothing can save Jesus but his own divine power. The Jews are in number many thousands, and cry for his blood. Pilate has but a cohort of soldiers, and fears to use force, lest the exasperated people break into open revolt, and take the city from his hands, which they can do if they will unite. "He trembles," said my father, "between fear to condemn the innocent, and fear of the vengeance of the Jews, if he let him go. Nothing can save the Prophet but his own mighty miracle-working power. He who has saved others, will surely save himself."

"While my father was speaking, a man rushed into our presence. He was low in stature, broad-chested, with a stiff, reddish beard, narrow eyes, and sharp, unpleasant visage. His attire was ragged and mean, as was his whole aspect. He grasped in his right hand a small bag, which rung like coin, as his shaking hand held it. He trembled all over, and seizing my father by the arm with the quick, nervous grasp of a lunatic, cried hoarsely:

"Will he let them? will he? will he?"

"Will he what, Judas? Of whom do you speak? Art thou crazed? Thou shouldst well be, after thy deed tonight."

"Will he let them kill him? Will he die? Will he die? Think you he will not escape? He can if he will! Cords, to him, are ropes of sand!"

"No, no -- he is bound hand and foot," answered my father sadly. "He makes no defenses I fear he will let them do as they will with him. He makes no effort to save his life."

"At this, Judas, for it was that wicked man, beat his knotted forehead, in a frenzied manner, with a bag of silver, and, with a look of horrible despair, rushing forth, he cried as he went:

"I will save him! The priests shall have their money again. He shall not die! If I had believed he would not do some miracle to escape them, I never would have sold him. I hoped to get their money, and trusted, if they took him. for him to escape by his power. I did not dream that he would not exert it to save himself. I will save thee, innocent man of God, for I, not thou, alone am guilty! Oh, if I had suspected this -- but he shall not die!"

"With these ravings he disappeared toward the Pretorium, leaving us all amazed at what we had heard."

"Yes," said my father, "I see it now. Judas hoped to secure the money and cheat the chief priests, trusting to his divine power to get away out of their hands. Else the force of conscience! He is now beside himself, with horror and remorse; for he knows that he whom he has betrayed is a man of God, without sin or guile!"

"The sun is up. The fate of Jesus is sealed! The Procurator has signed the sentence of death, and he is to be crucified today! But with Judas, I believe that he cannot die, and that he will signalize the hour by some wonderful miracle of personal deliverance. Thus, tremblingly, we hope and wait."

Here terminates, my dear father, what my cousin has written to Martha and Lazarus, and, as it is very minute, please to receive it as if written by myself, for, during the night, I was too greatly unnerved to write with the composure she had done. But now, that all is over -- now, that Jesus lies dead in the tomb and forever at rest, I have been able to resume my pen.

In my next I will give you an account of his trial, as it was related to me by my Uncle Amos, and by John, one of whom was present to the last. This evening I am going to see the sepulcher, where they have laid him; for, although he has in his death so sorely crushed all our hopes in him, and proved that he was not what he professed to be, yet my heart and affections hover about his memory, and irresistibly draw my footsteps toward his last resting place.

Though we are deceived, I cannot hate his memory. Oh no! I cannot -- I dare not trust myself to say all that I feel. I only wish I could forget him for evermore, and regret that I have ever tried to convince you that he was the Shiloh of the Prophets. Yet never man spake like this man, my dear father! and if Shiloh in truth come, he can do no greater works than he has done. In all things he was the Son of God but in his death! This event dashes all our hopes and our faith in him forever.

Your sorrowing, but loving daughter

ADINA.

LETTER XXXI.

Dearest Father: I have only terminated my last letter, to take up my pen for the beginning of another; for I find relief, only in writing to you, from the deep affliction which has struck me to the earth. If anything can add to my mortification at the death of the Nazarene, Jesus, it is that I should have endeavored so earnestly to make you believe in him also. Forgive me, my dear father your wisdom, your knowledge of the Prophets, your judgment, were far above my own. But who could have believed that he was less than he claimed to be -- the very Son and Messias of God. Oh! I shall never have confidence in a human being again; and the more lovely, the more holy, the more heavenly the character of anyone, the wiser and purer their teachings, the more distrustful shall I be of them. In the grave with Jesus is buried, henceforth and forever, all trust in human virtue -- even when accompanied by amazing miracles. I perceive that a man may teach divine truths, nay, wear upon his lineaments the very impress of an angel, may heal the sick by a touch, walk the sea, raise the dead, and cast out devils, and yet prove in the end a deceiver. Alas for human truth! Alas for poor Israel! which has thus been blinded! They have beheld their idolized Shiloh nailed to a Gentile cross, without power in himself to prevent this ignominy.

But I will turn from these painful thoughts, and, as I promised in my last, will give you an account of what passed at his trial, as you will be desirous of knowing on what accusation his condemnation was founded.

It is now the morning following his crucifixion, and I am calmer than I was yesterday, and will be able to write with more coherency. Twenty-four hours have passed since he was nailed to the cross. His followers have been since hunted like wild beasts of the wilderness. Annas has hired, and filled with wine, fierce Roman soldiers, and sent them everywhere to seize the fugitive Nazarene. John was especially sought out, and the emissaries of Annas came at midnight, last night, to the house to take him, but we assisted him in making his escape, by means of the subterraneous passage, that leads from the dwelling of Rabbi Amos into the catacombs beneath the Temple. Mary of Nazareth, the mother of Jesus, accompanied him, and they got safely out of the city, and are now at Bethany with Martha whence they will go to John's new home, near Gennesaret. Even Lazarus, whom Jesus raised, has been made prisoner, but was released by the influence of Aemilius, the Roman knight, who has conducted him hither, where he now is in safety; and Aemilius has also placed a guard about our house, for fear of further Jewish violence. I therefore can write to you undisturbed. Aemilius is the only one who has any confidence left, since Jesus died, in his promises. He says that Jesus plainly foretold his death, and also that if he died, he would rise again! Peter, also, recollects Jesus' saying this; but Uncle Amos has no confidence, and says:

"It is easy for any man to foretell that he will die, and quite as easy for him to add that he will rise again! But let us see Jesus rise again, and we will believe in him indeed!"

But Aemilius, though only recently a convert from the Paganism of Rome, is firm in his faith, that he will rise again to life; and, instead of giving up all, as we do, he says that he should not be amazed to be suddenly told by the soldiers, whom he left to guard his tomb, that he had burst forth alive from the dead! The confidence of Aemilius has almost inspired me with hope again! But, my dear father, I saw his cleaved side, the torrent of blood and water flow forth from the horrid wound, and saw his lifeless head hang down upon his breast. If he had not been pierced through. I might have hoped that he could yet revive! But that he was pierced, removes all hope that he can be restored. He did not swoon, and thus appear like one dead, or we might trust to his restoration but he was slain, and I saw him lie a mangled corpse at the foot of the cross, bleeding from five wounds, one of which was through and through his heart. I should rejoice to have the faith of dear Aemilius; but I tell him that I have hitherto believed too well, and that when Jesus expired, all faith in my bosom expired with him.

But I have forgotten that I am to narrate to you, dear father, the particulars of his accusation, trial, and condemnation. As I was not present at the Pretorium, I am indebted, for the details which I shall give, in part to John, and in part to Rabbi Amos, who were both there a portion of the night; Peter, and other disciples, as well as Aemilius, have given me additional facts.

As soon as the mob of Jews, who had Jesus under arrest, and which I saw pass the house, reached the house of Rabbi Annas, he, from his window, asked them whom they had in custody; and when they answered that it was the "Nazarene Prophet," he said, with great joy:

"Bring him into the lower court, that I may see him. By the rod of Aaron! I would have him do some notable miracle for me."

And thus speaking, the white-headed old man hastened to the court, which, on reaching, he found thronged with the infuriated multitude, mingled with the Roman soldiers. It was with difficulty he made a passage to where Jesus stood, both imprisoned and defended by a glittering lattice of Roman spears. After regarding him attentively, he said, with curiosity, yet with sarcasm:

"Art thou, then, the King of the Jews? Hast thou come to reign on the throne of David? Show me a sign from heaven, and I will acknowledge thee, O Nazarene!"

But Jesus stood calm and dignified, making no answer. Annas then angrily plucked him by the beard, and a messenger at the same moment arrived to say that Caiaphas, the High Priest, who had married the beautiful and haughty Miriam, the daughter of Annas, demanded to have Jesus brought before him. Upon this he said, in a loud voice:

"Lead him to the Palace! Caiaphas, my son-in-law, would see the man who would destroy the Temple, and rebuild it in three days."

There now arose a dreadful shout from the priests and people who, rushing upon Jesus, attempted to grasp his person and in protecting him, as they had been commanded to do, the Romans wounded several of the Jews. Hereupon there was a great cry of:

"Down with the Roman eagles! Down with the barbarians! Death to the Gentiles!"

These cries were followed up by a fearful rush of the mass of men, upon the handful of guards. They were forced back, their spears broken like straws, or turned aside, and Jesus successfully wrested from their power. But in the height of the battle, Aemilius, who had heard the tumult from the castle, appeared with a portion of the legion of which he was Prefect, and instantly charging the people, who fled before the breasts of his horses, rescued the Prophet, but not without the sacrifice of the lives of three of the foremost.

"Rabbi," said Aemilius to the Prophet, with compassionate respect, "I know thou hast power from God to disperse, as chaff, this rabble of fiends! Speak, and let them perish at thy divine command!"

"Nay, my son! I am come into the would for this hour," answered Jesus. "This, also, is a part of my mission from my Father. It becomes me to endure all things, even death."

"You cannot die, my Lord!" said Aemilius warmly. "Did I not see thee raise Lazarus from the tomb?"

"To die I came into this world; but not for myself. I lay down my life, and I can take it again. These men could have no power over me, except my Father did grant it to them: and what my Father doth, I do also. Seek not, my son, to deliver me. This day was seen by Esaias, who wrote of me. I must fulfill the Prophets. There remains only that I be delivered to judgment and to death!"

These words passed between them beneath the portico, as Aemilius was loosing the sharp cords from the bleeding wrists of the youthful Prophet.

"To Caiaphas! to Caiaphas!" now cried the multitude, who had been for a moment awed by the bold charge of the Roman horse, but now grew bolder, as some men removed the dead and wounded out of sight "To the palace with the blasphemer! for he who calls himself God is, by our law, to be punished with death. To the High Priest with him!"

"I can rescue you, Great Prophet!" said Aemilius resolutely "Give me the word, and you are mounted on my horse, and safe in the castle of David."

"The High Priest has sent for me He must be obeyed," answered Jesus; and Aemilius, surprised at his refusal to escape, reluctantly escorted him to the palace. The windows already glared with the torches; and the superb Hall of Aaron, within the Palace, was alight with a hundred flambeaux. The Romans entered, guarding their prisoner, and followed by a tumultuous throng, which, each moment, fearfully increased in numbers. Caiaphas was already upon his throne, although it was the hour of midnight, an unwonted time for him to sit in the council-chamber; but his desire to have Jesus brought before him, of whose arrest in Olivet he had been an hour before apprised by one of his emissaries, led him to hold an extraordinary court. A score of the elders and chief priests were standing about him, their dark, eager faces earnestly watching the entrance, to get a look at the approaching Prophet. Among the most eager of all these was Caiaphas himself, who regarded the eloquent Nazarene as his rival in the eyes of the whole people, and had, therefore, long thirsted for his destruction. As Jesus serenely entered, led by the sorrowful Aemilius, Caiaphas bent his tall, gaunt form forward, thrust his neck and huge black head in advance, and, with keen eyes, and sharp, scrutinizing glances, surveyed his youthful rival.

The multitude, pressing in, soon filled all the vast hall, and even crowded upon the rostrum, upon which were seated the scribes, elders, and many of the principal priests. The Roman soldiers, with clanging steel, marched in, and arrayed themselves on either side of the High-Priest's throne, leaving Jesus standing alone before its footstool. The scene must have been striking, and full of painful interest, to the most unconcerned present. The arched ceiling of the chamber, supported by seventy columns of porphyry, represented the deep blue heavens, studded with glittering constellations in starry gold. The walls were of jasper, superbly colored, with precious stones inlaid, representing every variety of fruit and flower, in all their native tints and varied forms of grace and beauty. The hundred flambeaux, reflected a thousand times from the polished surfaces of the columns, shed a magnificent light overall. The gorgeous robes of the High-Priest, his dazzling tiara and priceless breastplate, refracted the radiant beams with indescribable prismatic splendor. The steel spear-heads and polished cuirasses of the Roman guard, catching the light upon points and bosses, gleamed like flames of fire while the silver crest of the helmet of Aemilius shone among all this glory like a lesser sun.

Contrasting this brilliancy, surged, and heaved, and moved below the dark masses of the people, in their gray and brown caps and cloaks, for the night was cold, and they wore their winter garments and all this dark ocean of human forms gleamed with ten thousand eyes, flashing like the phosphorescent stars, that glitter on the surface of the up heaving sea, when the shadow of the storm cloud hangs above it, and the winds are about to be unbound, to lash it into fury. So seemed this terrible sea of human heads -- Jesus, the center of their looks and of their hate, the Pharos at who's feet these foaming billows of passion broke with terrible power. He alone, of all that countless host, he alone was calm -- serene -- fearless! Caiaphas gazed upon him, as he stood before his footstool, betraying admiration mingled with resentment. The scribes and priests also gazed and talked together, with looks of unusual interest. Caiaphas now waved his hand, with a gesture for silence, and addressed Jesus:

"So, then," he said, with haughty irony, "thou art Jesus, the far-famed Galilean Prophet! Men say thou canst raise the dead! We would fain see a miracle. Thinkest thou if we put thee to death presently, thou canst raise thyself?"

"Jesus," said Rabbi Amos, who just entered, and stood near, and saw all, "Jesus remained unmoved. His bearing was marked by a certain divine dignity, and an expression of holy resignation sat upon his features. He looked like Peace, incarnate in the form of man! A soft influence seemed to flow from his presence, and produce a universal, but momentary, emotion of sympathy. Caiaphas perceived it, and cried, in his harsh, stern voice:

"You have brought this man before me, men of Jerusalem! Of what do ye accuse him?"

"He is a malefactor, or we would not have brought him," responded a fierce voice from the multitude.

"Let those who have accusations come forward and make them. He is a Jew, and shall have justice by our laws."

"Ye Jews have no power to try a man for his life, most noble Caiaphas!" said Aemilius. "The lives of all your nation are in the hands of Caesar, and of his tribunals. You can put no man to death!"

"This said Aemilius, in hopes that if Jesus could be brought before Pilate, the Roman Procurator, he might be by him released, for he knew Pilate had no envy or feeling against the Prophet."

"Thou sayest well, noble Roman," answered Caiaphas "but for crimes of blasphemy against the Temple, we are permitted by Caesar to judge our people by the laws of Moses. And this man, if rumor comes nigh the truth, has been guilty of blasphemy. But we will hear the witnesses."

"Hereupon several of the chief-priests and scribes who had been going in and out among the crowd, brought forward certain men, whose very aspect showed them to be of the baser sort. One of these men testified that he had heard Jesus say, that he would destroy the Temple, and could again in three days rebuild it more magnificently than it was in the days of Solomon the Mighty.

"Upon this testimony all the priests shouted, "Blasphemer!"

and called for him to be stoned to death; and the passionate Abijah, the most virulent of the scribes, cast his iron ink-horn violently at him, but one of the soldiers turned it aside with his lance; at which there was a deep murmur against the Romans, which Caiaphas, with difficulty, silenced.

"A second witness was now produced by Abijah, who testified, that Jesus had taught in Samaria, that men would soon no longer worship in the Temple, but that the whole earth would be the temple, for Jews and Gentiles.

"This was no sooner heard, than some of the men gnashed at Jesus with their teeth, and, but for the gestures and loud voice of the High-Priest, they would have made an attempt to get him into their power. The noise of their rage is described as having been like the roaring of all the wild beasts of the wilderness, rushing to the banquet of a fresh battlefield.

"A third witness, a man who had been notorious for his crimes, now came up. He carried on his wrist a cock, with steel gaffs upon the spurs, as if just brought up from the cock-pit to bear testimony for such were the sort of fellows suborned by the priests. He testified that Jesus said, that the day would soon come when not one stone should be left upon another of the Temple; that he had called it a den of thieves, and the priests blind guides and deceivers; the scribes foxes and the pharisees hypocrites!"

"But the fourth and fifth witnesses contradicted each other; neither did the testimony of two others agree; one, who asserted that he heard him call himself the Son of God, was contradicted by others, who asserted that it was only the Son of Man; and in another instance, one said he heard him say, that he and God were One, while the other testified that what he said was, that God was greater than he. Neither did other witnesses agree together.

"Such opposite testimony perplexed and irritated Caiaphas, and confounded the chief-priests and scribes. The High-Priest now began to perceive that Jesus would have to be released, for want of testimony against him. All the while the prisoner had remained standing before him bound, with his hands tied across his body, his countenance mild, but heroic -- the firmness and composure of innocence, as Aemilius described his bearing to be.

"What! Galilean and blasphemer of God and His Temple! answereth thou nothing?" cried the High-Priest; "hearest thou not what these witnesses say against thee!"

"But Jesus remained silent. Caiaphas was about to break the silence by some fierce words, when a voice was overheard the other side of the columns, on the left of the throne, where was a fireplace, in which was burning a large fire, about which stood many persons. Rabbi Amos at once recognized, in the violent speaker, Peter, who had come in with him and John the latter of whom, in the disguise of a priest, stood not far from Jesus gazing tenderly upon him, and listening, with the most painful interest, to all that they testified against him; but Peter stood farther off, by the fire, yet not less eagerly attending to all that passed.

"Thou art one of the Nazarene's followers!" cried the voice of a maid, who brought wood to feed the fire. "Thou needst not to deny it. I am of Galilee, and knew thee when thou wert a fisherman. Seize him, for he is one of them."

"Woman, I swear by the altar and ark of God, and by the sacred Tables, I know not the fellow! I never saw Galilee!"

"Thy speech betrayeth thee, now thou hast spoken!" cried the woman "thou art a Galilean, and thy name is Simon Bar Jona. I know thee well; and how, three years ago, you and your brother Andrew left your nets, to follow this Nazarene!"

"May the thunders of Horeb and the curse of Jehovah follow me, if what thou sayest be true, woman. Thou mistakes me for some other man. I swear to you, by the head of my father, men and brethren, that I never saw his face before!"

"As he spoke," said John, "he cast his angry looks toward the place where Jesus stood. He caught his Master's eyes bent upon him, with a tender and reproving gaze, so full of sorrowing compassion, mingled with forgiveness, that I saw Peter stand, as if smitten with lightning. He then pressed his two hands to his face, and uttering a cry of anguish and despair, that made the High-Priest start, and which went to every heart, he rushed out, by the open door, into the darkness, and disappeared. As he did so, the cock, which was held tied upon the wrist of the third witness, crowed twice, in so loud a tone, that it caused some persons in the gross crowd to burst into laughter, and to imitate him, greatly to the annoyance of Caiaphas, who for some time could not still the confusion. I then remembered the words of Jesus to Peter, spoken but twelve hours before: "This night, even before the cock crow the first watch of the morning, thou shalt thrice deny that thou knowest me!" "Upon this," added John, "my confidence in my Master came back, full and strong, and I felt that he would not, could not, be harmed for, that he foreknew all things that could happen to him, and would escape danger of death."

"At length, when order was restored, so that Caiaphas could be heard, he again addressed Jesus, saying, but with more respect than before:

"Art thou the Christ, the Son of the Blessed? I adjure thee, by the living God, tell us plainly!"

Jesus then elevated his princely form, and bending his eyes upon the face of the High-Priest, with a look so brightly celestial that Caiaphas involuntarily dropped his eyelids to the ground, answered, and said:

"If I tell you, O Caiaphas, ye will not believe! If I prove it to you from the prophets, and by my works, ye will not listen! If I say that I am Christ, Ye will not then acknowledge me, nor let me go free! I have spoken openly to the world, in the Temple, and in the synagogue. I have concealed nothing. Ask them which heard me, what I have said. Nevertheless, I say unto you what I have before taught, that I am the Christ, the Son of the Blessed; and hereafter ye shall behold me sitting on the right hand of the power of God, and coming in the clouds of heaven."

"Art thou the Son of God?" cried several of the priests at once, while Caiaphas held up his hands in horror."

"Ye have said that which I am," answered the Prophet, without changing, except to a sublimer look, the expression of his countenance, which," says John, "seemed to shine, as he had seen it in the Mount, when he was transfigured before him."

"Men of Israel and Judah, ye hear his words!" cried the High Priest, rending down the blue lace from his ephod. "Hear ye his blasphemy?"

"Said I not, son of Aaron, that you would neither believe me nor let me go, if I told you who I am?" said Jesus firmly. "I tell you the truth, and ye call it blasphemy!"

"Answerest thou the High Priest so!" cried Abner furiously, the chief officer of the Temple! striking him with the palm of his hand across the mouth.

Jesus calmly answered, with the blood trickling from his lips: "If I have spoken evil, bear witness of the evil, and judge me by our law but if well, why smites thou me?"

"Ye have heard his blasphemy," said Caiaphas, extending his hands toward the people. What think ye? Need we any further witness than his own mouth?"

"He is guilty of death!" cried Abner, in a hoarse voice, his eyes, red with being up all the night, glaring like a leopard's and advancing to where Jesus stood, bound and bleeding, he spat in his face thrice.

"This was followed by a loud outcry for his death; and several vile fellows also spat upon him, and pulled him by the beard, and for some minutes it seemed to be the only thought of all, who were any ways near him, to do him some ignominy; and, but for the protection of Aemilius and his soldiers, they would have torn him to pieces.

"Is this Jewish justice?" cried Aemilius indignantly to Caiaphas. "Do you condemn and kill a man without a witness? Stand back, hounds, for Romans are not used to see men condemned without law. Back fellows -- or your blood shall flow sooner than his for which you thirst!"

"At this determined attitude they gave back for a moment, and left Jesus standing in the midst, sad but serene.

John ran to him, wiped the blood and uncleanness from his lips, and cheeks, and beard, and gave him water, which the woman who had recognized Peter, compassionately brought in a ewer.

"Master, use thy power, and escape from them!" whispered John.

"Nay -- tempt me not, beloved," he answered. "My power is not for my deliverance, but for that of the world. For you I can do mighty works; but for myself I can do nothing. I came not to save my life, but to lay it down! Mine hour is at hand!"

"Let not a handful of Romans frighten you, men of Jerusalem!" cried Abner. "There is not a legion in all the city. Here we are master, if we will it! To the rescue! Let me hear the Lion of Judah roar in his might, and the eagle of Rome will shrink and fly away. To the rescue!"

"Hold! men and brethren!" cried Caiaphas, who had judgment enough to see that the first blow would be the beginning of a revolution, that would bring down upon the city the Roman army quartered in Syria, and end in the destruction of the nation. "Hold, madmen!"

"But his voice was drowned amid the roar of the human tempest. Aemilius and his men were borne away on the crest of the surge, and so pressed by the bodies of the Jews that they could not make use of their weapons. In the wild confusion, Jesus was carried, by fierce hands, to the opposite end of the council-chamber; while Caiaphas strove to appease the wrath of Aemilius, who insisted that the fate of Jesus should be left with Pilate, the Procurator.

After brief consultation with the chief-priests, elders, and scribes, Caiaphas consented; though knowing that Pilate, would not heed a charge of blasphemy, he resolved with the rest, that nothing should be said of that before him, but that he should be accused of sedition, and setting up a kingdom in opposition to the universal empire of Caesar.

"When Aemilius, aided by the authorities of Caiaphas, at length came where Jesus had been dragged, they found him standing blindfolded among a crowd of the basest of fellows of Jerusalem, who were amusing themselves by slapping his cheeks, and asking him to tell, by his divine knowledge of all things, who did it. They would also hold money before his blinded eyes, and ask him to name its value or inscription; and when he still kept silence, they struck him, beat him with their hands, and cruelly smote him with their staves to make him respond.

"We will let thee go, Nazarene," said one, "if thou wilt tell how many hairs I have in my beard!"

"Nay, let him divine!" cried another, "what I gave for my Passover lamb, in the market, and the name of the Samaritan of whom I bought it!"

"Out with your lambs, Kish!" shouted a third fellow, thrusting himself forward, "let me hear him prophesy! It is a rare quail, a prophet, in these dull times. What, Galilean, silent and sullen! I will make thee speak, and sing, too!" and he let a blow of his staff fall upon the head of Jesus, which would have felled him to the earth, but for the voice of Caiaphas, which arrested, in part, its force.

"Men of Israel!" he cried aloud, "that this pestilent Nazarene is a blasphemer, we have heard with our own ears; and, by our law, he ought to die, because he hath made himself to be the Son of God! But Caesar hath taken the power of life and death out of our hands! We can put no man to death, but the Romans only. That he has spoken against Caesar, and is a seditionist can be proved. Let us take him before Pilate with this accusation; and if he be found guilty of death, as he will be, unless the Procurator wink at a usurper's rising up in his government, which he will not dare to do, we shall have the Nazarene hanged on a Roman cross, ere the sun reaches the mark of noon on the dial of the Temple."

"This speech pleased the people, and having rebound Jesus, more securely, they cried, all with one voice: To Pilate! To the Pretorium!"

The multitude then poured out of the gates of the palace, like a foaming and chafing river, which hath overflowed its banks, and with terrible cries which we heard, startling the dawn, even in our house, took the direction toward the Pretorium. Of the hundreds of thousands of Jews from the country, who crowd Jerusalem like a bee-hive at this holy season, not one slept that night, or was absent from that scene; and the noise of the tramp of that multitude shook the very foundations of Mount Zion, while the murmur of voices was like the sound of many waters.

It was with difficulty that Aemilius could protect the Prophet in safety up the hill, and to the entrance of the Pretorium, while he entered with his prisoner, just as the sun gilded the loftiest pinnacle of the Temple, and the trumpets of the Levites sounded to prayers.

In another letter, dear father, I will continue the account of his trial, the remembrance of which, while I now write of it, almost rekindles again all my love, faith, devotion and confidence in him; for who but a man, God-sustained, could have borne so meekly all his pain, insult, ignominy, and shame?

ADINA.

LETTER XXXII.

My Dear Father: This is the evening of the Great Day of the Feast, and the second day since the ignominious execution of him whom we all believed to have been a Prophet sent from God -- nay, more than a prophet, Christ, the Son of the Blessed! Yet he still lies dead in the tomb, and his splendid prophecies of his future glory, as King of Israel, have perished with him. Alas! that one so good, and noble, and wise, should have been a deceiver! Henceforth I have no faith in goodness. I have wept till I can weep no more.

I will now resume my narrative of his trial; for I would, by showing you how like a true prophet he bore himself, even before his judges, in some degree excuse myself to you, for being carried away by him, and accepting him for all that he professed to be -- the very Messias of Jehovah.

It is now the close of the High Day of the Feast. The slanting rays of the setting sun linger yet upon the gilded lances that terminate the hundred lesser pinnacles of the Holy House of the Lord. The smoke of incense curls lazily up the sky from its unseen altar, and the deep voices of the choir of Levites, increased by those of the tens of thousands of Judah, who crowd all the courts of the Temple, fall upon my ears like muffled thunder. I never heard anything so solemn. Above the Temple has hung, since the crucifixion yesterday, the cloud of the smoke of the sacrifices, and it immovably depends over all the city like a pall. The sun does not penetrate it, though its light falls upon the earth outside of the city; but all Jerusalem remains in shadow; and, shooting over the cloud, the setting sunbeams, catching the lofty pinnacles, make the gloom beneath only seem the more somber. The cloud is a fearful sight, and all men have been watching it, and talking of it, wondering. It seems to be in the form of a pair of black gigantic wings, spreading a league broad over Jerusalem.

There it hangs, visible from my window; but we are in some

sort used to its dreadful presence, and cease to fear; but we are lost in wonder! This morning, when a high wind arose, blowing from the great sea eastward, everyone expected and hoped to see the cloud sail away before it in the direction of the desert. But the only effect the wind produced was to agitate its whole surface in tumultuous billows, while the mass still retained its position over the city. The shadow it casts is supernatural and fearful, like the dread obscurity which marks an eclipse of the sun.

And this reminds me, my dear father, to mention what, in the multiplicity of subjects that rush to my pen for expression, I have omitted to state to you; and what is unaccountable, unless men have, in very truth, crucified, in Jesus, the very Son of God. At the time of his death, the sun disappeared from the mid heavens, and darkness, like that of night, followed over all the earth, so that the stars became visible; and the hills on which Jerusalem stands, shook as if an earthquake had moved them, and many houses were thrown down and where the dead are buried, outside of the city, the earth and rocks were rent; tombs broken up, and the bodies of the dead were heaved to the surface, and exposed to all eyes; and some arose, and went alive into the city, where many saw them, and on all sides shrank away from them in terror. Others of the dead bodies have lain all to-day, for the Jews dare not touch them to rebury them, for fear of being defiled. All this is fearful and unaccountable. What will be the end of these things is known only to the God of Abraham. Never was so fearful a Passover before. Men's faces are pale, and all look as if some dread calamity had befallen the nation. Can the death of Jesus be the cause of all these things? If so, he was the Son of God, and men have done unto him whatsoever they listed. If he be the Blessed Christ, whom Caiaphas and the priests have had crucified, the retribution of God's vengeance upon our city and nation is but just begun. But if he were the Christ, why did he not save himself?

My last letter, my dear father, closed with the termination at the examination of Jesus before Caiaphas, the High Priest, who, not being able to convict him of anything save alleged blasphemy, and not having the power in his hands to condemn him to death on this charge, resolved, in order unfailingly to secure his execution, to charge him before Pilate, the Procurator, of sedition and treason against Caesar. But for the fact, that the Romans had taken the power of death from the

Jewish nation, Jesus would have been then stoned to death for blasphemy, by order of Caiaphas; but a more ignominious death, as a revolutionist and usurper of Caesar's crown, was in reserve for him, at the hands of the Roman law.

Guarded by Aemilius, who was his true friend to the last, and followed by the envious Caiaphas, the fierce Abner, the captains of the Temple, Scribes, Pharisees, Sadducees, Herodians, and a mixed rabble of the Jews, artisans, peasants, robbers, beggars, and all the off-scourings of the nation that pour into the city at the Passover season, he was led to the house of Pilate.

The Praetorian gates were shut by the Roman guards, as the tumultuous crowd advanced, for Pilate believed the Jews were in insurrection, and was prepared to defend his palace; for so few are the troops with him in the city, that he has for some weeks held only the name of power, rather than the reality. But when Aemilius explained to the captain of the guard, that the Jews desired to accuse Jesus, the Nazarene, of sedition before the Procurator, he was admitted, with the chief men of the city, into the outer court of Antiochus; but none passed beyond the statue of Caesar, lest they should defile themselves; and, at their call, Pilate came forth to them. When he saw the vast concourse of people with Caiaphas and the chief priests, and many rich Sadducees, and the leading men of Jerusalem in the advance, and Jesus bound, and disfigured by the insults he had undergone, and Aemilius and his few soldiers enclosing him with their protecting spears, and heard the loud voices of the multitude, as of wolves baying for the blood of a defenseless lamb, he stood with amazement for a few moments, surveying the scene.

"What means this, Aemilius?" he demanded, of the young Prefect. "Who is this captive?"

"It is is Jesus, called the Christ, my lord; the Prophet of Galilee. The Jews desire his death, accusing him of blaspheming their God; and ---"

"But I have no concern with their religion, or the worship of their God. Let them judge him after their own way," said Pilate indifferently, and with an indolent air.

"But, most noble Roman," said Caiaphas, advancing to the portico on which the Procurator stood, "by our law he should suffer death; and thou knowest though we can condemn, as we now have done, this Galilean, we have no power to execute sentence of death!"

"This is well said; but would you have me put one of your nation to death for blaspheming your God? So far as that is concerned, O priest," added Pilate, smiling contemptuously, "we Romans blaspheme him daily for we worship him not, and will have nought to do with your faith. Let the man go! I see no cause of death in him!"

He then spoke to Aemilius, and desired him to lead Jesus to the spot where he stood. Pilate then regarded him with mingled pity and interest. After surveying him a moment, he turned to one of his officers, and said aside: "A form divine, and fit for Apollo, or any of the greater gods! His bearing is like a hero. Mehercule! The chisel of Praxiteles, or of Phidias, ne'er traced the outlines of limbs and neck like these. He is the very incarnation of human symmetry and dignity."

The courtiers nodded assent to these cool criticisms of the indolent and voluptuous Italian. Jesus, in the meanwhile, stood motionless before his judge, his eyes downcast, and full of a holy sadness, and his lips compressed with immovable patience. Pilate now turned to him, and said:

"Thou art, then, that Jesus of whom men talk so widely. I have had curiosity to see thee; and thanks, Caiaphas, to thee, for this privilege. Men say, O Jesus, that thou art wiser than ordinary men; that thou canst do works of necromancy, and art skilled in the subtle mysteries of astrology. I would question thee upon these things. Wilt thou read my destiny for me in the stars? If thou answerest well, I will befriend thee, and deliver thee from thy countrymen, who seem to howl for thy blood."

"My lord!" cried Caiaphas furiously, "thou must not let this man go! He is a deceiver, and traitor to Caesar. I charge him and formally accuse him, before thy tribunal, of making himself king of Judea!"

To this the whole multitude assented, in one deep voice of rage and fierce denunciation, that shook the very walls of the Pretorium.

"What sayest thou?" demanded Pilate "art thou a king? Methinks if thou wert such, these Jews have little need to fear thee." And the Roman cast a careless glance over the mean and torn apparel, and half-naked limbs of the Prophet.

Before Jesus could reply, which he seemed about to do, for his lips parted as if to speak, there was heard a sudden commotion in the lower part of the court of Gabbatha (for thus the outer court of the Pretorium, where they were, is

266

called by the Jews), and a loud, hoarse voice was heard crying. "Make way -- give back! He is innocent."

All eyes turned in the direction of the archway, where a man was seen forcing his path toward the door of the Judgment Hall, in front of which Pilate was standing, with Jesus a step or two below him.

"What means this madman!" cried the Procurator. "Some of you arrest him!"

"I am not mad -- he is innocent. I have betrayed the innocent blood!" cried Iscariot, for it was he, leaping into the space in front of the portico. "Caiaphas, I have sought thee everywhere!" he exclaimed, on seeing the High Priest. "Take back thy money, and let this holy Prophet of God go free! I swear to you he is innocent and if thou harm him, thou wilt be accursed with the vengeance of Jehovah! Take back thy silver, for he is innocent!"

"What is that to us? See thou to that," answered Abner, the priest, haughtily for Caiaphas was too much surprised at this open exposure of his bribery of Judas to speak, his eyes falling under the withering glance of the Roman Procurator.

"Wilt thou not release him if I give thee back the pieces?" cried Judas, in accents of despair, taking Caiaphas by the mantle, and then kneeling to him imploringly.

But Caiaphas shook him off; Abner and the chief-priests also spurned him from them, as he approached them, when, at last, in a frenzied manner, he threw himself at the knees of Jesus, and cried, in the most thrilling accents:

"Oh! Master! Master! thou hast the power! Release thyself!"

"No, Judas," answered the Prophet, shaking his head, and gazing down compassionately upon him, without one look of resentment at his having betrayed him, "mine hour is come. I may not escape. For this I came into the world."

"I believed thou wouldst not suffer thyself to be arrested when they should find thee in Olivet, my Master, or I would not have taken their money. It is my avarice that hath slain thee! Oh, God! Oh,God! it is too late!" Thus crying, he rose and rushed, with his face hid in his cloak, forth from the presence of all, the crowd of men giving back hastily, as he advanced through their midst toward the outer gate.

This extraordinary interruption produced a startling effect upon all present; and it was a few moments before Pilate could resume his examination of Jesus, which he did by entering the Judgment Hall, and taking his seat on his throne. He then repeated his question, but with more deference than before: "Art thou a king, then?"

"Thou sayest that which I am -- a king," he answered, with a dignity truly regal in its bearing; for all the time, bound and marred as he was by the hands of his enemies, pale with suffering, and withstanding a sleepless and fearful night upon his feet, exposed to cold and to insults, yet he had a kingly air, and there seemed to float about his head a divine glory, as if a sunbeam had been shining down upon him; yet no sunshine that day penetrated the dark-winged cloud, that hung suspended low above the city.

"Thou, thyself, hearest him!" exclaimed Caiaphas, standing upon the threshold of the Judgment Hall of the Gentile governor, which he would not enter for fear of defilement.

"He hath, also, sought to prevent the people from paying tribute to Caesar!" cried Abner, shouting through an open window, for he also would not, on account of the holy feast, be profaned by entering a Gentile house.

"He has everywhere publicly proclaimed that he has been ordained of God, to re-establish the kingdom of Judah, and overthrow the power of Caesar in Jerusalem," added the Governor of the Temple, lifting his voice so as to be heard above the voices of the priests and scribes, who, all speaking together, vehemently accused him of many other things, which we all knew not to be true. Pilate at length obtained comparative silence, and then said to Jesus:

"Hearest thou these accusations? Hast thou no answer to make? What defense hast thou, Sir Prophet? Answerest thou nothing? Behold how many things they witness against thee!"

Pilate spoke as if he had taken a deep interest in Jesus, and would give him an opportunity of defending himself.

"He hath perverted the nation -- a most pestilent and dangerous fellow! " exclaimed Caiaphas. "He is a blasphemer, above all men."

"I have nothing to do with your religion. If he has blasphemed your gods, take ye him and judge him according to your laws," answered Pilate.

"Thou knowest, O noble Roman, that we have no power to execute to the death -- therefore do we accuse him before thee."

"I am no Jew, priest! What care I for your domestic and religious quarrels. He hath done nothing, that I can learn, for which the laws of Imperial Rome, which now prevail here, can adjudge him to death. I, therefore, command his release, as having done nothing worthy of capital punishment. Aemilius, unbind thy prisoner, and let him go. I find no fault in him, that he should be longer held in bonds."

Upon this the Jews sent up a cry of unmingled ferocity and vindictiveness. Caiaphas, forgetting his fear of defilement, advanced several steps into the Judgment Hall, and shaking his open hands at Pilate, cried:

"If thou lettest this man go, thou art not Caesar's friend. Thou art in league with him. He that sets himself up as a king, in the wide bounds of Caesar's dominions, wars against Caesar, as well at Jerusalem as at Rome. If thou release this man, I and my nation will accuse thee to thy master, Tiberius, of favoring this Galilean's sedition. He hath stirred up all Jewry, from Galilee to this place, and yet thou findest no fault with him!"

When Pilate heard the name of Galilee, he asked if the prisoner were a Galilean? Upon beings answered in the affirmative by the excited priest, he said to Aemilius:

"Hold -- loose not his bonds just now! Herod, the Tetrarch of Galilee, last night came up to the Passover feast of his God, and is now at the old Maccabean palace, with his retinue. Conduct your prisoner to him, and let Herod judge his own subjects. Present him with this signet in token of amity. Tell him I will not interfere with his privileges, and that I desire he would take and judge the man as if he were in his own tetrarchate."

The chief priests and scribes now shouted with approbation at this decision, for they began to fear that Pilate would release him; and they knew that the vacillating and reckless Herod would do whatsoever would gain popular applause.

"If he sends us to Herod with him," said the priest Abner, "his doom is sealed -- his blood is ours!" And the multitude without hailed the reappearance of Aemilius, and his unresisting captive, from the Judgment Hall, and followed them across the marble pavement of Gabbatha into the streets, crying:

"To Herod! -- to the Tetrarch of Galilee with him!"

But Caiaphas, frowning and dissatisfied, remained behind, and Pilate, glad to get rid of the delicate affair of condemning an innocent man, to gratify the envy of the Jews, by sending him to his enemy, Herod, smilingly came out, and spoke to the gloomy High Priest:

"Thou wert something sharp upon me just now, my lord

Caiaphas. Thou knowest I can condemn men only for crimes committed against the laws of the Empire. This Jesus has done nothing worthy of death were he called before a tribunal in the capital of the world itself, Caesar his judge."

"Noble governor," answered Caiaphas, stopping in his angry strides up and down the porphyry floor of the outer portico, "thou forgettest that I brought him not before thee on this charge of blasphemy alone but for sedition. By the altar of God! this is a crime known to thy laws, I wot! "

"True. You charge a young, defenseless, quiet, powerless man, destitute for money, men, or arms, an obscure fisherman or carpenter of Galilee, of setting up a throne and kingdom against that of Tiberius Caesar, the ruler of the earth! The idea is absurd. It should be treated only with ridicule. So will Herod say, when he understands the affair."

"So will not Caesar say, my lord," answered Caiaphas, with a sneer upon his curled lip, "if you let this man go (for Herod will not, surely, accept your courtesy, and judge him within your jurisdiction), the Jewish nation will draw up a memorial, accusing you to the Emperor, of protecting treason. You will be summoned by the Senate to answer the charge and though you succeed in clearing yourself, you will have lost your government, given to another, and for your fair name, you will live, ever after, under Caesar's suspicions!"

Here the High Priest, said my Uncle Amos, who heard all that passed, looked with concentrated maliciousness into the eyes of the Italian ruler, who turned pale, and bit his lips with vexation.

"My lord priest, thou art bent, I see, on this innocent man's death. I am no Jew, to understand how he has drawn upon himself thy terrible wrath, and that of thy nation. It must have been something I am incapable of comprehending. I will see what Herod will say, who, being a Jew, if familiar with your customs. But it seems to me, O Priest, that the testimony of the wretched man whom, I see, you bribed to betray his master into your power, would now release him!"

Pilate now reseated himself upon his throne.

While he spoke, a youth threw himself from his horse, at the door of the court, and drew near the Procurator.

"What aileth thee Alexander? " demanded Pilate, on seeing blood on his temples, and that he seemed faint.

"But a trifle now, my good lord. I was thrown from my horse, who was startled at a burning torch, lying on the ground; and was detained at a hospitable house until I was able to remount, which brings me hither late."

"And why come at all? What news sends my fair wife, that she should dispatch you from my house in Bethany at this early hour? No evil tidings, boy?"

"None, my lord -- save this note."

The Greek page then handed his master a small roll of rose-tinted parchment, tied with scarlet thread. He cut the knot with his dagger, and reading the contents became deathly pale. Caiaphas watched him closely, as if he would read, reflected in his eyes, the contents of the note which had so deeply moved him.

"Caiaphas," said the Procurator, "this prisoner must be released!"

"It is either his destruction, proud Roman or thine!" answered the High Priest, turning and walking haughtily away.

Pilate looked after him with a troubled air, and then re-entered the Hall of Judgment, and seating himself upon his throne, again read the parchment, ---

--- "Have thou nothing to do with this just man," he read, half aloud, "for I have suffered many things this day in a dream because of him! The very gods seem to take sides with this extraordinary young prisoner," he exclaimed. "Would to Jove that Herod may have sense enough to release him, and relieve me of this unpleasant business. One might better keep in subjection a province of painted and savage Scythians, than these fierce Jews. I should be well rid of my Procuratorship; but I will not lose it by accusation from them! I must save both Jesus and myself!"

While he was yet musing with himself, unconsciously, aloud, so that those who stood about heard him, among whom was El Nathan, the brother of the maid Mirza, who dwells in our household, and from whom I received this portion of the narrative, there was heard a great noise of voices, in the direction of the Maccabean Palace and as it grew nearer and more distinct, Pilate started up, and cried:

"It is as I feared -- Herod gives them no satisfaction, and they come again to me! Oh, that the gods would give me wisdom and nerve for this trying hour, so that I condemn not the innocent, nor bring myself into the power of an accusation to Caesar from these wicked Jews!"

At this moment the multitude, increased, if it were possible, in numbers and in vindictiveness, reappeared, pressing Jesus before them. This time he was alone, Aemilius having been separated from him in the palace, and kept by the crowd from rejoining him. He was now unbound, and upon his head was a crown of thorns, piercing the tender temples, till the blood trickled all down his face; upon his shoulders was clasped an old purple royal robe, once worn by Herod, in his state of petty king; and his hand held a reed, as a scepter; and as he walked along, the bitterest among the priests, as well as the vilest of the common fellows, bent the knee before him, crying:

"Hail! King Jesus! Hail, Royal Nazarene! All hail!"

Others went before him, carrying mock standards -- while others, acting as heralds, ran, shouting:

"Make way for the King of the Jews. Do homage, all men, to Caesar! This the great Tiberius, Emperor of Nazareth! Behold his glittering crown! Mark his royal robes, and see his dazzling scepter! Bend the knee -- bend the knee, men of Judah, before your king!"

When Pilate saw this spectacle, and heard these words, he trembled, and was heard to say:

"Either this man or I must perish! These Jews are become madmen with rage, and demand a sacrifice. One of us must fall!"

Oh, that I could write all I feel! but I am compelled, my dear father, to end here.

Your affectionate child,

ADINA.

LETTER XXXIII.

My Dear Father: In this letter, which I write in the solitude of my chamber, while all in the house have sought repose, will be continued my account of the trial, if such it can be called, of Jesus. I have already shown you how he was first taken to Annas, and thence dragged before Caiaphas, who, unable to execute upon him the sentence of death, sent him to the Procurator Pilate, charged with conspiracy; and he, shrinking from condemning a man whom he knew to be innocent of any crime, and yet fearing to release him, lest he should be impeached by the Jews to Caesar, sought to shift the responsibility upon Herod, in whose tetrarchy lay Nazareth, where Jesus ordinarily dwelt.

John the faithful, and yet trusting disciple whom Jesus loved, still kept near his captive Master, and sought to cheer him by affectionate looks, and, where he could do it with safety, by kind acts. More than once he was rudely thrust aside by the fiercer Jews, and once several men seized upon him, and would have done him violence, as a follower of the Prophet, if Caiaphas, to whom John is remotely related, and who knows him well, had not interposed. Indeed, it was through this protecting influence of the High Priest, that the disciple was allowed to remain near Jesus. And while John was thus doing all that he could to soften the asperity of his friend's treatment, we at home were exerting ourselves to soothe the maternal solicitude of Mary of Nazareth, his noble and heart-broken mother, whom with difficulty we could restrain from rushing to the palace, and casting herself at the feet of the Procurator, to implore him to interpose to save her son -- her only son --

273

from the hands of his own countrymen! Thus a twofold scene of anguish, at the palace and in the house of Rabbi Amos, was passing. Mary, Martha, and Lazarus, were also with us, having come into the city as soon as my cousin Mary's letter reached them; and, besides, there were with us four or five of the disciples, who had come in, one by one, secretly, for fear of being seized by the Jews, and were anxiously waiting here the result and firmly believing that Jesus would yet free himself by his divine and miraculous power. At every approach of a footfall at the door, they eagerly cried: "It is the Lord!" But ah, in vain their hopes and all our anticipations!

Herod, the Tetrarch of Galilee, who occupied the old palace of the Maccabees, which Alexander, the Macedonian, had built for Seleucus, was breaking his fast with fruit and wine, at a table overlooking, by a window, the street of the Gentiles, when the noise of the advancing thousands of the Jews, who were bringing Jesus before him, reached his ear. He started from the table, and said:

"These people are surely up in insurrection against Pilate!"

"No, great Prince," answered the lad Abel, his cup-bearer, who is a cousin to John, and has told me many of these things "they have taken the Nazarene Prophet, Jesus, and are trying him for sedition."

"This uproar proceeds from no trial, but a wild mob in motion, and they seem to be approaching," was his answer to him.

As Herod spoke, he went to the lattice of his basilica, and beheld the head of the multitude, just emerging into the street, from that which descended from the hill of the Pretorium. At first, he could not make out of the confused mass any individual objects.

"There are spears and Romans in the van -- and I see priests and peasants mixed together. I now see the cause of all the tumult -- a mere youth, bound and soiled, and pale as marble! What, sirs, this is not the Great Prophet, of whose fame I have heard?" he said, turning to his officers. "What mean they by bringing him hither? Yet, per Bacchum! I am glad to get a sight of him!"

The crowd, like the swelling Nile, flowed toward the gates, roaring and chafing like its mighty cataracts, so that there was something fearfully sublime in this display of the power of human passions. Aemilius, with difficulty, succeeded in getting his prisoner into the piazza of the palace, so closely pressed the crowd of Jews around and upon him. At length he stood with him before Herod in his banquet-hall, at the further end of which was a dais, or throne, where the Tetrarch sat down, while the Jews filled all the vast room with a billowy sea of eager faces.

"Most royal Prince," said Aemilius, kneeling before Herod, and presenting the signet, "I am sent by his Excellency, Pontius Pilate, the Roman Procurator of Judea, to bring before you this person accused of blasphemy! Ignorant of your customs and faith, the Governor desires that you, who are of his nation, would examine him: and, moreover Pilate, learning that he is a Galilean, and a subject of your jurisdiction, courteously declines interfering with your authority."

When Herod Antipas heard delivered so courteous a message from the Procurator, with whom he had been some time at enmity, partly on account of Herod's cruel murder of John the Baptizer, whom Pilate thought much of, he was pleased.

"Say thou, Sir Knight, to his Excellency, the most liable and princely Governor of Judea, that I appreciate his extraordinary civility, and that nothing will give me more pleasure, in return for such dignified courtesy, than to be considered by him his friend: and that I regret any occurrence that has hitherto estranged us. Convey to him my assurances of the high estimations in which he has ever been held by me."

Aemilius, upon receiving this answer, arose, and bowed, and then said, with the boldness which characterizes him:

"Most noble and royal king, I pray you heed not the charges of these Jews, touching this prisoner. They have conceived against him a bitter hatred, without just cause. He has done nothing worthy of death! Pilate could find nothing, whatsoever, in him deserving of the attention of the dignity of a Roman tribunal."

"Let thy prisoner fear not," answered Herod, regarding Jesus attentively, as he stood before him, in the calm majesty of innocence. "I will not take Pilate's prerogative of judgment out of has hand, so handsomely tendered to me. If he hath blasphemed, Mehercule! the High Priest, the priests of the Temple itself," he added, laughing, "do that every day of their lives: for religion is at a low ebb among the hypocritical knaves. I have nothing to do with their charges of blasphemy, or I would have them all stoned to death, without mercy. I will first see some miracles wrought by thy far-famed prisoner, good Aemilius, and then send him back to my noble friend Pontius, whom his gods prosper in all things."

Herod, then fixing his eyes curiously upon Jesus, who had stood silently before him, seemingly the only unmoved person in the vast concourse, heaving and murmuring around him, said to the soldiers:

"Unbind him! Someone bring water, to remove the blood from his cheeks and beard. By the staff of Jacob: he hath been roughly handled. Men of Israel, it becomes not such as you to do violence to a man before he is condemned; and then if it be proved he have done aught deserving chastisement, let the law punish him. This man is a Galilean, and I am bound to see him have justice, and to protect him from wrong."

While he was speaking, water was brought, and John, with a napkin, wiped away the stains of blood, which flowed from the wound on his temple, inflicted by the staves of the Jews; and, also, removed the spots from his princely beard and golden hair. He also arranged his mantle about his form. Herod regarded, with interest and looks of compassion, the pale and divinely-serene countenance of the prisoner; and seemed struck with the indescribable majesty of his aspect and bearing, and the purity of soul that beamed from his holy eyes.

"Art thou the Nazarene, Jesus, of whom I have heard so much?" he asked, in deferential tones.

"I am he," was the quiet answer of the captive.

"Then gladly do I meet thee for I have long time desired to see thee and I would fain behold thee do some miracle. Men say thou canst heal the sick, restore the maimed, and raise the dead! Does rumor belie thy powers? What! Art thou silent? Dost thou not know who it is that speaks to thee? Come hither, fellow;" he called to a Samaritan muleteer, who stood in the crowd, whose oval face and Jewish eyes showed him to be both of Assyrian and Israelitish descent, whose arm had been taken off by a sword, in a contest with Barabbas and his robbers: "Come hither, and let this Prophet prove his power and mission, by restoring thy arm whole, like as the other!"

The man alertly came forward, and all eyes were directed eagerly upon him, and upon Jesus; but he thrust the stump of his arm, by Herod's order, in vain before Jesus. The eyes of the prophet moved not from their meditative look upon the ground.

"Art thou mocking us, thou false Christ!" cried the Tetrarch angrily; "wilt thou neither speak nor act? If thou art not an impostor, do a miracle before us all, and we will believe in thee!"

Jesus remained motionless, yet with a firm and majestic countenance, that made him look more kingly than Herod.

"He is a deceiver! He performed his works through Beelzebub, who has now deserted him!" cried the priests.

"Nazarene," said Herod, "I am a Jew also. If thou wilt prove to me, by a sign that I will name, that thou art the Christ, I will not only become thy follower, but will let thee go free. Your silence is an insult to my power. I warn thee that my patience is not divine -- I make no pretensions to superior sanctity. Thou seest yonder marble statue of Judas Maccabeus. Command the sword in its hand to wave thrice above its helmeted head, and I will bend the knee to thee! Nay -- wilt not? I will give thee something easier to do! Seest thou the carved pomegranates in the entablature of the wall? Bid the one which hangs over this column to trim into ripe, natural fruit, and fall at my feet! No?"

"He has no power -- his friend Beelzebub hath given him up into our hands! Death to the necromancer!" were the words which now made the hall tremble.

"He is an accursed blasphemer! He would destroy the Temple! He calls himself the Son of God! He breaks the Sabbath-day! He is a foe to our religion!" was shouted by Abner, the priests, and the scribes.

"See the whirlwind thou hast raised, O Nazarene!" cried Herod, rising; "if thou art a Prophet, no harm can they do thee and if thou art an impostor, if they kill thee, thou deserves thy fate! I give thee up into their hands! Save thyself, if thou be the Christ!"

Scarcely had Herod spoken these words, relinquishing Jesus into the hands of his foes, than, with a savage cry, as the famished jackals in the desert rush upon their prey, they rushed upon their victim. Aemilius could not protect him: nay, some of Herod's soldiers, whom the Jews had half-intoxicated with wine, joined them as soon as they saw their master Antipas had cast him off, and began to scoff and mock him, and one of them thrust a helmet on his head, and pulled the visor down over his eyes!

"Nay," said Herod, on seeing this, "as he calls himself a king, crown him, and robe him royally, and place a scepter in his hand; and yonder block will make him a proper throne! We must show Pilate how we Jews serve men who usurp the power of his master Caesar!"

No words could have better pleased the people, save such as would have sentenced Jesus to death. With a glad response, they began to put into execution the hint he had so wickedly given them. One of his men of war brought a cast-off robe of purple, which belonged to Herod, and, with loud shouts of laughter, and coarse jests, they robed him in it, unresisting as the lamb wreathed for the sacrifice. Someone then untwined the creeping thorn, which grew on the outer wall, and twisting it into the shape of a crown, handed it over the heads of the men to Abner, whose hatred against Jesus proceeded from the well-known fact, that among the changers of money, whom he drove from the Temple, was a younger brother, who was making, by his business, great gains for the avaricious priest who, therefore, never forgave this act of the Prophet.

When Abner saw the crown, he smiled with malicious gratification, and nodding approvingly to the man, said:

"This is what we needed! Nothing could have done better;" and with his two hands he placed it upon the head of Jesus, pressing, cruelly, the sharp thorns into his temples, till the blood trickled from a dozen wounds. Jesus made no complaint, but the pain forced large, bright tears from his eyes, which rolled down his cheeks, and fell along the purple robe like glittering pearls.

"Here is also a scepter for our king!" exclaimed the man with one arm, rising this one to reach a piece of reed, from which a Passover-lamb had been slung, to those who were arraying Jesus. This was thrust into his grasp, and he held it patiently. His submission, his silence, his endurance of pain, his constant dignity, the majestic indifference which he seemed to manifest to all their insults and tortures, brought tears into the eyes of Aemilius; and John, unable to benefit his dear Master, kneeling at his feet, bathed them with his flowing tears, nor stirred though men trampled upon him, and smote him but he desired to suffer with his master, and, as he said to me, would gladly have borne in his stead all his indignities. Even Herod stood amazed at such God-like forbearance, and said to his chief-captain: "If this man is not the Son of God, he is worthy to be deified. Such sublime patience is more than human -- it is divine! You Romans, Aemilius, would make a hero of such a man, and when he died worship him as a god!"

"Then, mighty Prince, why suffer him to be thus entreated?" asked Aemilius.

"It is his own choice. I have entreated him fairly! I asked of him but one of those miracles men say he works, as proof of his Messiahship, and he works me none -- shows me no sign! The inference is, that he can do none, and, therefore is an impostor. Else why not prove to me his pretensions by working a miracle?"

"Most royal Prince," said Abner aloud, "thou now beholdest the King of the Jews crowned, robed, and sceptered!" and he pointed to Jesus.

"Hail! most puissant and potent sovereign of Galilee! Hail! King of Fishermen!" cried Herod, mocking him, and seemingly greatly amused at the jest. "If thou wilt tell me in what part of cloud-land thy capital lies, I and my court will pay thee a visit. Doubtless, thou hast a brave army of Galilee fishermen, and a mighty fleet of fishing boats! Hail! powerful king! What, fellows, men-at-arms, and all ye gapers! bend ye not the knee before this royal personage? Do homage to your king!"

Upon this all who were around him kneeled and some, mockingly, prostrated themselves before the Prophet; but he stood so very like a monarch, that others, who were about to mock him, refrained; and Herod even turned away, with a troubled look, saying abruptly:

"Take him back to the Procurator!"

Once more the vast multitude were in motion, and, with cries and insults, escorted Jesus from the presence of Herod, back to the Pretorium, as I have already stated in my previous letter.

When Pilate beheld their return in this manner, and understood how that Herod declined exercising his privilege in the matter, he was greatly vexed. When, once more, Jesus stood before him, arrayed, as I have described, in the gorgeous robe and crown, Pilate, turning toward Caiaphas and the priests, said angrily:

"What more will ye have? Why bring this man again before me? Ye say he perverteth the people. Behold, I have examined him before you, and have found no fault in him. You proved nothing by your witnesses, touching those things whereof ye accuse him. I then sent you with him to Herod, and lo! the Tetrarch of Galilee, one of your own nation, finds nought in him worthy of death! Doubtless he has said something about not paying tribute, and deserves for this a light punishment, but not death. I will chastise him, and charge him that he be more cautious, and let him go."

"If thou let this man go, thou art an enemy to Tiberius,"

answered Caiaphas: "see thou what a commotion he has raised in the city? If he is released there will be a revolution, and Caesar will come and take away our place and nation. Is it better that all Judea should perish than one man? It is expedient that either he die or the people perish. Nothing less than his life will now be received."

"In the name of Olympian Jove, O Nazarene, what hast thou done to incense these Jews? If thou art their king, prove it to them or to me," demanded Pilate, greatly troubled.

"My kingdom is not of the earth" answered Jesus. "If my kingdom were an earthly one, then would my servants fight, that I should not be delivered to the Jews; but my kingdom is not of this world."

"Then thou confessest thyself a king!" exclaimed Pilate, with surprise.

"Thou sayest that which I am -- a king. To this end was I born, and for this cause came I into the world, that I should bear witness to the truth."

"Truth! What is truth?" asked the Roman but, without waiting for Jesus to reply, and seeing that the Jews outside the Hall were becoming more and more impatient, he hurriedly went out to them, and said:

"I find in the prisoner no fault at all. But ye have a custom, that I should at the Passover pardon a criminal out of prison, as an act of clemency, in honor of the day. Will ye, therefore, that I pardon and release unto you this King of the Jews?"

No sooner had Pilate made this proposal, than they all, with one voice, and furious gestures, cried:

"No! -- no! -- not this man! We will not have him released. We will have the vilest malefactor thy prison holds, rather than he!"

"Whom shall I then release unto you? " demanded Pilate, in a tone of disappointment.

"Barabbas! Barabbas!" was echoed, and re-echoed, by ten thousand voices.

This Barabbas, dear father, is the same fierce bandit, of whom I have spoken in one of my earlier letters, two years ago. He has recently been taken captive, while heading a revolt, in the hill country south, and lies now under condemnation of death, and was on that day to have been crucified, with two of his lieutenants. But, at the loud demand of the people, Pilate was forced to send to the officer of the wards, to let him go free; and it was but a short time before he was escorted from his cell to the front of the Pretorium in great pomp, and became presently one of the most active in hostility to Jesus.

Pilate, therefore, finding that the Jews would be content with nothing less than the blood of Jesus, returned, sorrowfully, into the Judgment Hall, where he had left him seated upon the lower step of his throne for he could no longer stand for weariness, and for the heavy treatment he had undergone.

The residue of my narrative of the condemnation and crucifixion, I will give in the morning, dear father,

Your loving daughter,

ADINA.

LETTER XXXIV.

My Dearest Father: I now resume the narrative of the condemnation, or rather sentence of Jesus, after he had been brought a second time before Pilate. The Procurator, finding that the Jews would have the Prophet's life, and that, if he resisted further, he, himself, would be reported to Caesar, as protecting a revolutionist and usurper, vacillated, and showed an indecision that became not a Roman Governor. His sense of justice revolted at sacrificing, to the hatred of the people, an innocent man, against whom no accusation had been proven; and he feared for his own name and fame, should Tiberius, who is always jealous of his Oriental Governors, believe their statement of the case.

Jesus, as I stated in my last, had, from weakness, sunk upon the steps of the throne of the Hall of Judgment. John knelt by him, bathing the wounds in his temples, from which he had boldly taken the crown of thorns. When Pilate, after giving the order to release the robber-chief, Barabbas, came again where Jesus was, he stopped, and regarded him attentively, and with an expression of sorrow and admiration. The youthful beauty, the dignity, even in his humiliation, the patience, and air of innocence, that enveloped him, deeply impressed him. At length he spoke:

"If thou be indeed a god, O heroic young man, as thy patience would seem to prove thee to be, thou neediest not to fear these blood-hounds, that bay so fiercely for thy blood. If thou art an impostor and a seditionist, thou verily meritest death. I regard thee but as a youthful enthusiast, and would let thee go free but I cannot protect thee. My soldiers are reduced, by sending them to garrison Jericho and Gaza, to less than three hundred men; and of these enraged Jews there are half a million in the city. It is only by moral force, and a show of power, that I keep them in subjection. If I release thee, not only thou, but all my troops, will be massacred; for we are but a handful in their grasp. Tell me truly, art thou the son of Jupiter!"

When Jesus, instead of replying, remained silent, the Procurator said sternly:

"What, speakest thou not unto me? Knowest thou not that I have power to crucify thee as a malefactor, and power, if I choose to meet the risk, to release thee?"

Jesus looked up, and calmly said:

"Thou couldst have no power against me except it were given thee from above. Therefore, he that delivered me into thy hand hath the greater sin!"

And as Jesus said these words in an impressive tone, he glanced fixedly at Caiaphas, who was looking in at the door, as if designating the High Priest. Upon this Pilate pressed his hands against his forehead, and paced several times, to and fro, before the Judgment-seat, as if greatly troubled. Caiaphas seeing his irresolution, cried harshly:

"If thou let this self-styled king go, O Governor, thou art not Caesar's friend! Our whole nation charges him, before you, with setting himself up to be our king over us, when Tiberius is the only king to whom we can owe allegiance. Release the Usurper, if thou darest, and I would not give two brass mites for thy head!"

Pilate's brow grew dark. He took Jesus by the hand, and leading him to the portal, and pointing to him, said aloud:

"Behold your king! What will you that I should do with him? Looks he like a man to be feared?"

"We have no king but Caesar!"

"Crucify him!"

"To the Cross with the false Prophet!"

"Death to the Usurper! Long live Caesar! Long live Tiberius! Death to the Nazarene! To the Cross! -- to the Cross with him! Let him be crucified!"

These were the various cries from ten thousand throats, that responded to the Procurator's address. Impressed, as he has since said, with the innocence of Jesus, and remembering the warning message sent him by his young and beautiful wife, who held great influence over him, he trembled with indecision.

"Why will you compel me to crucify an innocent man? What evil hath he done?"

"Crucify him! Crucify him!" was the deafening response.

"I will chastise him, and let him go!"

"At your peril, release him, O Roman!" exclaimed Caiaphas, in a menacing tone. "Either he or you must die this day for the people. Blood must flow to appease this tempest!"

The tumult was now appalling. The voices of the chief priests and people kept up a ceaseless uproar, calling for his crucifixion; and in vain Pilate appealed to their humanity and justice. They drowned his voice with their own; and his gesticulations for silence only increased the roar of the human whirlwind.

When the Procurator saw that he could prevail nothing, but that rather the tumult increased, he called for water, which was brought to him in a basin, by his page; and, in the presence of the whole multitude, he washed his hands, saying:

"I am innocent of the blood of this just person. See ye to it, oh, Jews, ye and your High Priest!"

"His blood be upon us, and on our children," answered Caiaphas; and all the people re-echoed his language:

"Aye on us and on our children, rest the guilt of his blood!"

"Be it so," answered the Procurator, with a dark brow, and face pale as the dead. "Take ye him and crucify him, and may the God he worships judge you, not me, for this days deeds."

Pilate then turned away from them, and said to Jesus, who stood unmoved, with the same heroic and celestial serenity which he had manifested throughout the storm raging about him:

"Thou art, I feel, an innocent man; but thou seest that I cannot save thee! I know thou wilt forgive me, and that death can have no terrors for one of fortitude like thine!"

Jesus made him no answer; and Pilate, turning from him, with a sad countenance, walked slowly away, and left the Judgment Hall. As he did so, one of his captains said to him:

"Shall I scourge him, according to the Roman law, which commands all who are sentenced to die to be scourged?"

"Do as the law commands," answered the weak-minded Roman.

His disappearance was the signal for a general rush toward Jesus, chiefly of the rabble, who, indifferent about Gentile defilement, crossed the threshold into the hall, which Caiaphas and the chief priests had refrained from doing. These base fellows seized Jesus, and aided by the men-at-arms, dragged him forth into the outer or common hall. Here they stripped him, and, by order of the chief captain, scourged him with forty stripes, save one. They then re-arrayed his lacerated and bleeding form in the torn, kingly robe, which John had removed when he had taken off his crown but now they replaced both the crown and the robe, and once more went through the mockery of homage, kneeling, and hailing him, "King of the Jews."

All this Jesus still bore with godlike majesty. Not a murmur escaped his lips; not a glance of resentment kindled the holy depths of his eyes, which, from time to time, were uplifted to Heaven, as if he sought for help and strength from thence.

Not only Aemilius, but John, was now separated from him but my uncle, the Rabbi, stood near, in order to see what would follow; and to use his influence, if possible, to induce the chief priests to abandon the idea of killing him.

"Good Rabbi," said Jesus to him, "let them do with me what they list! My Father hath given me into their hands. I die, but not for myself; I can keep or yield up my life, as I will."

"Oh, then, dear Master!" cried my uncle, "why not save thyself? Why shouldst thou suffer all this, and death also, if thou hast the power over thy life?"

"If I die not, then were ye all dead! The Scripture must be fulfilled, which spoke of me: He was led like a lamb to the slaughter."

Here Rabbi Amos could speak no more to him, for the crowd dragged him off out of the court of Gabbatha, and so down the steep street, in the direction of the Gate of the Kings, that leads to the Hill of Calvary, the public place of execution, where the Romans since they have been masters of Jerusalem, have executed criminals by their cruel mode of crucifying. At the gate, a Roman Centurion took him into custody, under arms, and escorted him, followed by the vast multitude.

Rabbi Amos accompanied the multitude, keeping as nigh to Jesus as the Roman soldiers, who marched on each side of him, would let him. On the way, as they crossed the open space where once stood the palace and statue of Antiochus Seleucus, the eyes of the Rabbi were attracted by the cries and pointed fingers of many of the people, to the body of a man lying dead at the foot of a withered fig-tree. Upon drawing nearer, he recognized the features of Judas, who had so basely betrayed his Master. The spectacle which he exhibited was revolting, and horrid to look upon. About his neck was wound a fragment of his girdle, the other half being still secured to a limb of the tree, showing how he had met his fate. The cord had broken by his weight, and being a fleshy man, he had, most dreadful to relate, in the fall burst asunder, and the hungry dogs that infest the suburbs, were feeding upon his bowels. With cries of horror, several of the Jews drove them away, and the Roman Centurion, whom Pilate had ordered to crucify Jesus for the Jews, directed four of his soldiers to convey the hideous corpse from sight, and see that it was either burned or buried.

"If," said Rabbi Amos to John, who now rejoined him, "if the accusers of Jesus are to be punished like this man, this will be a fearful day for the men of Jerusalem. Judas, the betrayer, dies before his victim dies, and by his own hand. This looks like Divine retribution, and, as if Jesus were, in truth, the favored Prophet of the Highest."

By this time, the people, who were dragging Jesus to death, were got out of the gate, where a cross of heavy cypress was obtained by the Centurion, from a yard near the lodge, wherein stood several new crosses, awaiting whatsoever victims Roman justice might, from day to day, condemn to death. Two others were also brought out, and laid upon the shoulders of two men, the lieutenants of Barabbas, who were also that day to be crucified. The released Barabbas was himself present, and the most active, in laying the cross upon the back of the already faint and drooping Jesus.

By the time the great crowd had passed the gate, it was known throughout all Jerusalem, that Pilate had given orders for the crucifixion of the Nazarene Prophet; and, with one mind, all who had known him, and believed in him, or loved him, left their houses, to go out after him, to witness his crucifixion; for, I forgot to say, that Caiaphas had promised, if Jesus were delivered up, his followers should not be molested. Therefore, every person went out of the gate toward Calvary. Mary, his mother, my cousin Mary, Martha and her sister, Lazarus, John, and Peter, and Thomas, and some women, his relatives from Galilee, and many others also went. When we had got without the walls, we seemed to leave a deserted city behind us. As far as the eye could embrace, there was a countless multitude moving along the vast space, between the Gate of the Kings and Mount Calvary. Jesus was borne in front, where we could now and then catch the gleam of a Roman spear. We hastened to get near him, and, with difficulty, made our way to the head of the throng; both foes and friends giving back, when they saw his weeping mother among us.

At the ascent of Calvary we found that, from some cause, the course of the mighty current of human beings was checked. We soon learned the reason. Jesus had, at length, sunk to the ground, under the weight of the wooden beams on which he was to die, and fainted.

"He is dead!" was the cry of those about him but, as we drew near, he was reviving, someone having offered wine to his lips, and poured water upon his brow. He stood up, and looking mildly around, and meeting his mother's gaze, he said touchingly:

"Weep not! Remember what I have often told thee of this hour, and believe! The sword pierces through thy soul, but it is held in my Father's hand. Mine hour is come."

Thus speaking, he smiled upon his mother, and upon us, with a certain look of Divine peace illuminating his countenance.

Barabbas, the robber-chief, who had, in some degree, taken the lead of the mob, now, with the aid of three men, raised the cross to the shoulders of Jesus, and ordered him to move on. But the young victim sank at once beneath the load. Upon this they were at a loss what to do; for it is ignominious for Jew or Gentile to aid in bearing a malefactor's cross, and not a Roman would touch it; and the Jews would not for fear of defilement, which would compel them to be set apart afterward for many days' purification. Barabbas again raised Jesus to his feet, and began to scourge him, to make him drag the heavy beams up the steep of Calvary. But he had no strength to advance three steps with it, though he made the effort to obey his tyrannous executioners. At this crisis they discerned a Syro-Phoenician merchant, Simon of Cyrene, a venerable man, well-known to all in Jerusalem, and father of the two young men, Rufus and Alexander, who were followers of Jesus, having sold, the last year, all they had, in order to become his disciples, and sit at his feet, and listen to his Divine teachings. Their father was, for this, or some other reason, particularly obnoxious to Caiaphas, and, on seeing him, he pointed him out to the Centurion, "as one of the Nazarenes," and suggested that he should be compelled to bear the cross after him.

The Cyrenian merchant was at once dragged from his mule, and led to the place where the cross lay, believing he was about to be himself executed. But when he beheld Jesus standing, pale and bleeding, by the fallen cross, and knew what was required of him, he burst into tears, and kneeling at his feet, said:

"If they compel me to do this, Lord, think not that I aid thy death! I know that thou art a Prophet come from God! If thou diest to-day, Jerusalem will have more precious blood to answer for than the blood of all her prophets."

"We brought thee here not to prate, old man, but to work. Thou art strong-bodied. Up with this end of the cross, and go on after him!" cried the chief priests.

Simon, who is a powerful man, though threescore years of age, raised the extremity of the beam, and Jesus essayed to move under the weight of the other but he failed.

"Let me bear it alone, Master," answered the stout Simon "I am the stronger. Thou hast enough to bear the weight of thine own sorrow. If it be a shame to bear a cross after thee, I glory in my shame, as would my two sons, were they here this day."

Thus speaking in a courageous and bold voice, and looking as brave as if he would as gladly be nailed to the cross for his Master, as carry it after him (for Simon had long believed in him, as well as his sons), he lifted the cross upon his shoulders, and ascended the steep after Jesus, who, weak from loss of blood and of sleep, and weary unto death, had to lean, for support, against one arm of the instrument of death.

Ah, my dear father, what a place was this, up which we climbed! Skulls lay scattered beneath our footsteps, and everywhere human bones bleached in the air; and we trode in heaps of ashes, where the Romans had burned the bodies of those whom they crucified.

At length we reached the top of this hill of death, on which five crosses were already standing. Upon one of them a criminal still hung, just alive, who had been nailed to it the noon before. He called feebly for water, but some derided, and all passed him unheeded. There was an empty space on the summit, and here the Centurion stopped, and ordered the crosses to be set in the rock, where deep holes had been already cut for them. The crosses carried by the thieves were now thrown down by them; by one with an execration, by the other with a sigh, as he anticipated the anguish he was to suffer upon it.

The largest cross of the three was that for Jesus. It was taken by three soldiers from the back of the old Cyrenian merchant, and thrown heavily upon the earth. It was now that a crisis approached, of the most painful interest. The Centurion ordered his soldiers to clear a circle about the place, where the crosses were to be planted, with their spears. The Jews, who had crowded near, in eager thirst for their victim's blood, gave back slowly and reluctantly, before the sharp points of the Roman lances, pushed against their breasts; for the Centurion had with him full threescore men-at-arms, besides a part of Herod's guard. So great was the desire of the Jews to get near, that helpless females could not be otherwise than crowded away from the immediate scene. John, however, held his place close by his Master. He relates that Jesus continued to evince the same sublime composure when the Centurion commanded the crucifiers to advance and nail the malefactors to their crosses. The robber-lieutenant, Ishmerai, who was an Edomite, upon seeing the man approach with the basket containing the spikes and hammers, scowled fiercely upon him, and looked defiance. He was instantly seized by four savage-looking Parthian soldiers, of the Roman guard, and stripped, and thrown upon his back upon the cross. His struggles, for he was an athletic man, were so violent, that it took six persons to keep him held down upon the arms of the cross, and his palms spread open, to receive the entering nail; which one of the crucifiers, with naked and brawny arms, by pressing one knee upon the wrist, drove in, through the flesh and wood, with three quick and powerful blows, with his short, heavy-headed hammer. Ishmerai gnashed his teeth as the nail entered the quivering flesh. The other hand, in like manner, was fastened, with difficulty, to the other arm of the wood and then, both feet being lapped together, a long, sharp spear-nail was driven through both into the timber, while a shriek, mingled with curses, bore testimony to the agony suffered by the wretched man.

Thus secured, he was left, bleeding and writhing, by the six crucifiers for there are four to bind the victim, one to hold the spikes, and the sixth to drive them home with his hammer; and from the glance I caught of their half-naked and blood-stained figures, they were worthy to hold the dreadful office, which made all men shun them as if they were leprous.

They now approached Omri, the other robber, who was a young man, with a mild look, and a face whose noble lineaments did not betray his profession. He was the son of a wealthy citizen in Jericho, and had, by riotous living, spent his patrimony, and joined Barabbas. He had heard Jesus preach in the wilderness of Jordan, and had once asked him, with deep interest, many things touching the doctrines he taught. John, who had seen him talking with Jesus, a few months before, at Bethabara, now recognized him, and saw him regard the Prophet with reverential looks; and more than once heard the latter speak kind words to him as they climbed the hill.

When the crucifiers, with their cords, baskets, nails, and iron hammer, drew near him, he said:

"I will not compel you to throw me down, I can die as I have lived, without fear! As I have broken the laws, I am ready to suffer the penalty of the laws."

Thus speaking, he stretched himself upon his cross, and extending his palms along the transverse beams, he suffered them to nail him to the wood, uttering not a moan. He glanced toward Jesus at the same time, with an expression of courage, as if he sought to show him that the pain could be borne by a brave man. And, perhaps, indeed, Jesus looked as if he needed a heroic example before him to show him how to die without shrinking, for his cheek was like the marble of Paros, in its whiteness, and he seemed ready to drop to the earth from weakness. His youth -- his almost Divine beauty, which not even his tangled hair, and torn beard, and blood-streaked countenance, could wholly hide -- the air of celestial innocence that beamed from his eyes, drew upon him many glances of sympathy, even from some of his foes. The Centurion, who was a tall man, with a grizzly beard, and with the hardy exterior of an old Roman warrior, looked upon him with a sad gaze, and said:

"I do not see what men would hate thee for, for thou seemest more to be a man to love; but I must do my duty, and I hope thou wilt forgive me what I do. A soldier's honor is to obey."

Jesus smiled forgiveness upon him so sweetly, that the stern Roman's eyes filled with tears, and he placed his gauntleted hand to his face, to conceal his emotion.

"Pilate would not do this crime, were there another legion or two with him. It is the fewness of his men-at-arms that compels him to please these howling Jews."

This was spoken to Jesus, who made no reply for, at this moment, the crucifiers drew nigh, to prepare him, by stripping, for the cross, lying at his feet.

But, my dear father, I can go on no farther now with my narrative. I am weary, weeping at the sad recollections it calls before me, and at our present affliction. In my next I will give you an account of the unhappy crucifixion of the Prophet of Nazareth, and with him, the crucifixion and death of all our hopes in him as Messias of God.

Your affectionate daughter,

ADINA.

LETTER XXXV

Jerusalem, third morning after the Crucifixion.

My Dear Father: It is now dawn, and I have arisen early, as I shall leave the city to-day, with my Uncle Rabbi Amos, and the whole family, to go to Bethany, to escape the Jews, who are diligently seeking the arrest of all in Jerusalem who were followers of the slain Prophet. As an hour or two will elapse before all is ready for our safe departure, I will occupy the interval in completing my narrative of the crucifixion of Jesus; especially as Rabbi Amos, finding I have been so careful, heretofore, in recording all things concerning him, desires me not to omit any particulars; as my account may hereafter be convenient to refer to, and, perhaps, if necessary, be laid before Caesar, in defense of such as may be sent to Rome on charges of sedition. I feel that my poor letters, dear father, are only valuable to you, and those I love; but, if they can aid in explaining anything for the exculpation of the poor Nazarenes, who are now so despised, and vigilantly hunted, they are at the service even of the mighty Tiberius himself. Their only merit is accuracy of detail and truthfulness, so far as circumstances have enabled me to ascertain the truth.

As I now resume my pen, to continue the particulars of the crucifixion of the unhappy son of Mary, who, widowed and childless, still remains with us, mourning over her slain son, my heart involuntarily shrinks from the painful subject, and bleeds afresh. But there is a fascination associated with all that concerns him, even now that he is dead, and has proved himself as weak a mortal as other men, which urges me to write of him, and which fills my thoughts only with him.

I have just alluded to his grief-smitten mother. Alas! there is no consolation for her. Her loss is not like that of other mothers. Her son has not only been taken from her by death, but has died, ignominiously, on a Roman cross, executed between two vile malefactors, as if he, himself, were the greatest criminal of the three; and not only this, but executed as a false prophet -- as a deceiver of Israel -- with a thousand glittering promises of Judea's future glory through him, on his lips which now, as his death proves, were vain promises, and that he made them to deceive his countrymen, for the temporary fame of drawing all men after him. She thus mourns, not as other mothers, and refuses to be comforted.

Yet her love for her son -- that deathless maternal love, which seems immortal in its nature, is not buried with him. She, with dearest Mary and Martha, have just gone out, secretly before the Jews are astir, to pay the last duties to his dead body, ere we depart for an asylum in Bethany. They have taken spices, myrrh, and aloes, and sweet herbs, for the purpose of embalming the body; for his mother hopes to get permission of Pilate to remove it sometime to Bethlehem, to be laid in the tomb of his fathers. Until they return from this sad mission of love, I will continue my subject.

When the Centurion, to whom was committed, by Pilate, the charge of conducting the crucifixion of Jesus, gave orders to bind him also to the cross, which lay upon the ground, like an altar awaiting its victim, the four Parthian soldiers, his brutal crucifiers, laid hold upon him, and began to strip him of his garments, for his enemies had put on him his own clothes, when they led him out of the hall of Pilate. He wore a mantle of spotless white, woven without seam, by Mary and Martha, and which had been a present to him, by the sisters, as a token of their gratitude, for raising from the dead their brother Lazarus.

When I saw them remove this robe, which was a visible attestation of his former power over death, I could not believe that he could be himself killed; but would yet break away, by some mighty miracle, from his foes, and, scattering them, like dust before the wind, proclaim himself, with power, the very Son of God! But when I perceived that he stood, calmly and sorrowfully, letting them do what they would, I lost all hope, and turned away weeping. His mother, supported by John, could no longer gaze upon her son, and was borne afar off, crying thrillingly:

"Oh let me not hear the crashing of the nails into his feet and hands! My son -- my son! Oh, that thou wouldst now prove to thy mother that thou art a true prophet!"

"What means this wailing?" cried the fierce Abner "who is the woman?"

"The mother of Jesus," I answered indignantly.

"The mother of the blasphemer. Let her be accursed!" he cried in a savage tone "thou seest, woman, what is the end of bringing up an impostor, to blaspheme Jehovah and the Temple. Thy hopes and his, O wretched woman, have this day miserably perished! So die all false Christs and false prophets! Thou seest, if he were the Christ, he would not stand there, and be crucified, like a common malefactor!"

Mary buried her face in her hands, and wept on my shoulder. She felt that it was too true! I could not look toward the place where Jesus stood. I dreaded to hear the first blow upon the dreadful nails, and as she stopped her ears, I would have closed mine also, but that my hands supported her. I could hear the awful preparations--the rattling of the hard cord, as they bound him to the cross, and the low, eager voices of the four busy Parthians; and then the rattling of the spikes: and then a silence like that of the grave! Suddenly a blow of a hammer broke the moment of suspense! A shriek burst from the soul of his mother, that echoed far and wide, among the tombs of Golgotha!

I could see -- hear no more! John has told me the rest. Leaving the stricken mother with me, he and Lazarus drew near to where they were enrobing the Prophet, in order to bind him to the wood. They caught the eyes of their Master, who gazed upon them calmly and affectionately. They said they had never before beheld him appear so majestic and great! He looked, as the Centurion afterward said, "Like a god surrendering himself to death, for the safety of his universe!"

Nothing but the ferocious madness of the Chief Priests and Jews could have prevented them from being awed by the majesty of his presence. And, besides, there sat upon his brow heroic courage, with a certain divine humility and resignation. Not the rough hands of the barbaric soldiers, not the indignity of being stripped before the eyes of thousands, not the sight of his cross, nor of the thieves, nailed and writhing on theirs, moved him to depart, by look or bearing, from that celestial dignity which, through all, had never left him.

He made no resistance when bound upon the cross, but resigned himself, passively, into the hands of his executioners, like a lamb, receiving its death. "Father," he said, raising his holy eyes to Heaven, "forgive them, for they know not what they do." But his heroic soul could not prevent the natural emotions of humanity at pain. The piercing nails, rending his tender flesh, made it quiver, and caused him to turn deadly pallid, while a deep sigh escaped his breast. Unlike the first robber, he did not resist unlike the second, he did not steel himself to indifference; but he met his fate like a man who fears not death, yet does not brave it!

"Great drops of sweat, when they nailed his feet to the wood, stood upon his forehead," said John, who remained near, to see his Master die, and to comfort and strengthen him "and when the four men raised him and the cross together from the earth, and let the end drop into a hole a foot deep, the shock, bringing his whole weight upon the nails in his hands, tore and lacerated them, nearly dislocating the shoulders at the same time, while every sinew and muscle of his arms and chest were drawn out like cords, to sustain this unwonted weight upon them. The first thief fainted from pain, at the shock caused by the setting of his own cross and the second, cool and defiant as he had been, uttered a loud outcry of agony. But Jesus made no moan, though the unearthly pallor of his countenance showed how inexpressible was his torture."

Ah, my dear father, I would draw a veil over this scene -- for it is too -- too painful for me to dwell upon. To the last, John believed his Master would not die -- that he could not suffer! But when he saw how that pain and anguish seized heavily upon him, and how that he suffered like other men, without power to prevent it, he greatly wondered, and began to believe that all the miracles that he had seen him perform must have been illusions. He could not reconcile the calmness and dignity, the heroic composure and air of innocence, with which he came to the cross, with imposture; yet his death would, assuredly, seal as imposture all his previous career.

The three crosses, that of Jesus in the midst, as the place of chief dishonor, being raised into the air, and fixed in the sockets of the rock, the Centurion commanded the adjacent space to be cleared, and that the malefactors be left to die.

Oh, what a fearful death for Jesus! for him whom we knew so well, and whom we still loved, although he had deceived us. There, thought we, he might linger two or three days, dying slowly, as some have done, and exposed to the fierce sun by day, and the chilly winds of night, while about them hovered, on steady wings, the savage birds of prey, impatient for their feast.

Much of the residue of the account I have from John, who remained at the last close to the cross, while we stood afar off, with his weeping mother, Mary of Bethany, Martha, Lazarus, and Mary, the mother of Salome, and other women, our friends from Galilee, who also had hope in Jesus. There we waited, in expectation of seeing him do some mighty miracle from the cross, and descend unharmed, showing to the world, thereby, his title to be the Messias of God.

The Centurion having placed a guard about the crosses, to keep the friends of the crucified from attempting their rescue, stood watching them. The soldiers, who had nailed Jesus to the tree, began to divide, with noisy oaths, his garments among themselves, as well as those of the two thieves, these being, by the Roman law, the fee of the executioner. This division being made, after some time, but not without high talking, and drawing of their long Syrian knives upon each other, they were at a loss what to do with the large white mantle, without seam, which the sisters of Lazarus had woven for the friend of their once dead brother. A group of the Roman guard being seated near, astride upon the four arms of a fallen cross, playing at dice, suggested that the Parthians should decide by lot whose it should be. This the latter consented to, and taking the dice-boxes in their bloody hands, each of them threw thrice. The highest number fell to the most ferocious of the four fellows, who, taking the mantle, wrapped it about his huge form, and, pacing up and down before the people, called, in a loud voice, himself a great prophet, and asked, in his broken, barbarous tongue, some of the Jews if they would like to have him foretell their fortunes. At this they began to cry out upon him, and stone him, as a blasphemer -- and but for the interposition of the Centurion, a tumult would have been made. The soldier then proposed to sell the cloak, which John joyfully purchased of him, by means of the jewels of several of the women, who gladly took rings from their ears, and bracelets from their arms, I giving, dear father, the emerald which you bought for me at Cairo. But I could not see the robe, which Jesus had worn, thus desecrated; for still, oh, yes! still we love him, even in his death, which death was his and our infamy! The mother of Jesus received the robe with deep emotions of gratitude to us all. But now, my dear father, how shall I describe the scenes and events that followed?

After Jesus had hung about an hour upon the cross Aemilius came from Pilate, and bore the inscription, which it is usual to place above the heads of malefactors, showing their name, and the crime for which they are crucified. Above the head of Ishmerai was written, in Syriac:

"Ishmerai, the Edomite."
" A Robber."

Above that of Omri was inscribed, also, on a leaf of parchment, in the same tongue, his name, and the nature of his crime, which was that of robbery and blood-shedding.

Above the head of Jesus, by means of a small ladder, was placed this inscription, in Greek, Latin, and Hebrew:

"This is Jesus,
The King of the Jews."

When the wicked Abner read this, he turned angrily to the Centurion, and to Aemilius, who stood sadly near the cross:

"Write not, O Roman, that he is King of the Jews, but that he said that he was King of the Jews!"

"I have placed above him what Pilate has ordered to be written," answered the Centurion.

Abner, upon this, mounted a mule, and hastened into the city to the Procurator, and laid his complaint before him.

"What I have written, I have written, sir priest," we have heard that the Procurator coldly answered.

"But you, then, have crucified this man for being our king, which we deny," retorted Abner.

"I will take his word, before that of all the Jews in Caesar's empire," answered Pilate, angrily. "He said he was a king and if ever a king stood before a human tribunal, I have had a true and very king before me to-day; and I have signed the warrant for his execution. But his blood be on your heads for I was compelled to do this deed, or lose my Procuratorship; for else you would have had me before Caesar as a traitor. Leave my presence, Jew! Have I not, against my own convictions of justice and humanity, consented to gratify your thirst for this innocent person's blood? What more do you demand? Is he not hanged? If you approach my presence more on this subject, by the gods of Rome, I will crucify you, and ten score more! I will pile a hecatomb to his manes!"

Abner left his presence abashed, and returned to the hill of the crucifixion. The Jews, in the meanwhile, mocked Jesus, and wagged their heads at him, and reminded him of his former miracles and prophecies.

"Thou, that raisedst Lazarus, save thyself from death!" said a Pharisee.

"If thou art the Son of God, prove it, by coming down from the cross!" cried the leader of the Sadducees, Eli.

"Thou, who saidst if a man kept thy sayings he should never see death -- let us see if thou canst avoid death thyself!" said Iddo, the chief of the Essences.

"He saved others -- himself he cannot save!" mocked Ezekias, one of the chief priests.

Aemilius, finding it impossible to save the Prophet from crucifixion, had come out to guard him from the usual insults of the rabble, while he was dying. He had now lost faith in Jesus as a Prophet, but he loved him still as a man, and pitied him for his sufferings. He talked with him, and earnestly prayed him, as he hung, if he were indeed a god, to show his power. Jesus made no reply: but, shortly, said, in a faint voice;

"I thirst."

The generous knight ran and filled a sponge with the preparation of sour wine and hyssop, usually given to malefactors, after they have suffered a while, in order to stupefy them, and render them insensible to their sufferings. While Aemilius was affixing a sponge, dipped in this vessel of vinegar, upon a reed, split at the end to hold it firmly, Ishmerai, who all the while, as he hung, had uttered execrations upon his crucifiers, and upon Pilate, called, howling fiercely, to Jesus:

"If thou be the Son of God, save thyself and us! If thou didst raise a man once from the dead, thou canst, surely, keep us from dying! Thou art a vile wretch if thou hast power as a prophet, and wilt not use it for me, when thou sees how heavy I am of body, and how my great weight tortures me, with infernal racking and rending of every joint."

But Omri, rebuking his fellow, said:

"Dost thou not fear God, seeing thou art in the same condemnation? We suffer justly for our crimes, and today do receive the due reward of our transgressions; but this young man hath done nothing amiss, save to preach against the wickedness of the priests, and for being holier than they. Lord, I believe that thou art the Son of God! None but the Christ could do the works thou hast done, or suffer patiently, as thou art doing. Lord, remember me when thou comest into thy kingdom, for I know thou wilt go from this, thy cross, to thy throne, and there reign forever and ever. I have listened to thy teaching on the banks of Jordan, and now believe."

Jesus turned his bleeding head toward him, and, with a smile of ineffable glory radiating his pale face, said:

"Verily, I say unto thee, this day shalt thou be with me in Paradise."

Omri, upon this, looked inexpressibly happy, and seemed to rise superior to his sufferings. The other cursed the Prophet aloud, and gnashed at him with his teeth, with demonical hatred.

At this moment, Aemilius came near with his dripping sponge, and presented the reed upward to the parched lips of the suffering Jesus. When he tasted it, he would not drink, for he perceived it was the opiate which was usually given in compassion, to shorten the anguish of the crucified.

The robber, Ishmerai, now eagerly cried for the sponge, and the prefect giving the reed to a soldier, the latter placed it to the mouth of the robber, whose swollen tongue protruded, and he drank of it with a sort of mad thirst. The other man, also, gladly assuaged his burning fever with it, and soon both of them sunk into insensibility, hanging unconscious of their situation, and showing no other signs of life than the heavings of their chests, and, from time to time, the involuntary twitching of their muscles. But Jesus retaining his senses, in all their clearness, suffered all that such a fearful death imposes upon its victim.

All at once, just as the sixth hour was sounded from the Temple, by the trumpets of the Levites, a cloud, which, formed by the smoke of the numerous sacrifices, had hung all day above the Temple, was seen to become suddenly of inky blackness, and to advance toward Calvary, spreading and expanding in the most appalling manner, as it approached us; and in a few minutes, not only all Jerusalem, but Calvary, the Valley of Kedron, the Mount of Olives, and all the country were involved in its fearful dark- ness. The sun, which had before been shining with noon-day brilliancy, became black as sackcloth of hair, and a dreadful, unearthly, indescribable night overshadowed the world. Out of the center of the cloud, above the crosses, shot forth angry lightnings in every direction. But there was no thunder attending it only a dead, sepulchral, suffocating silence.

Of the thousands who had been gazing upon the crucifixion, everyone was now prostrate upon the earth in terror! Jerusalem was blotted out from our view: only an angry spot of fire-red light, as it were the terrible eye of God itself, was visible above the Temple, over the place of the Holy of Holies.

The crosses soon were no longer visible, save by the fearful shine of the lightnings, flashing fiercely from the dread and silent cloud. The form of Jesus, amid the universal gloom, shone as if divinely transfigured, and a soft halo of celestial light encircled his brow like a crown of glory; while the dark bodies of the two robbers could scarcely be discerned, save by the faint radiance emanating from his own.

The darkness continuing, many of the multitude at length ceased their moans, and the beating of their breasts, and rending their garments, and arose to their feet; but moved not; for none could stir from his place, for the midnight depth of gloom. They talked to each other in whispers. An undefinable dread was upon each mind. The sudden overspreading of the darkness was unaccountable as it was frightful. Mary, his mother, and Lazarus said, with awe, both speaking together:

"This is his power. He has produced this miracle!"

"And we shall behold him next descend from the cross," said Rabbi Amos. "Let us all take courage; and let what dismays his enemies fill us with joyful expectation."

Three hours -- three long and awful hours, this supernatural night continued and all that while the vast multitude remained fixed, and waiting they knew not what. At length the cloud above the cross parted, with a loud peal of thunder, while a shower of terrible lightnings fell, like lances of fire, all around the hanging form of Jesus, which immediately lost its halo and its translucent radiance. His face, at the same time, became expressive of the most intense sorrow of soul, and he seemed, to all eyes, to be the central point of this fierce wrath at the heavens.

A hundred voices exclaimed, with horror:

"See! he is deserted, and punished by the Almighty!"

We, ourselves, were amazed and appalled. Our rising hopes were blasted by the livid lightnings, which seemed to blast him. His mother gave utterance to a groan of agony, and sank upon the ground, satisfied that her son was truly accursed of God. At this moment, as if to confirm all our fears, he cried, in the Hebrew tongue, with a loud voice, that, in the deep silence, reached the ears even of the Roman guard on the citadel:

"Eloi! Eloi! My God, my God, why hast Thou forsaken me!"

Upon this some ran to give him wine and hyssop.

"Nay, let him live -- let us see if Elias will save Him!" answered Abner.

Jesus then turned his head, and looked affectionately upon his mother, and committed her to the tender care of John, who stood supporting her near the cross.

Suddenly the darkness, which had filled all the air, seemed now to concentrate, and gather about the cross, so that he became invisible. From the midst of it his thrilling voice was once more heard, as clear and strong as it rang over the waters of Galilee, when he preached from a boat to the thousand thronging the shore:

"It is finished! Father, into thy hands I commend my spirit!"

As he uttered these words, a supernatural glory shone around him and, with a deep sigh, he bowed his head upon his breast and gave up the ghost.

The general exclamation of surprise that followed these clear, trumpet-tones, was suddenly checked by a terrible trembling of the earth beneath our feet, so that vast numbers of people were cast down; the rocks of the hill of Calvary were rent, and thrown upwards, while the whole city shook with the convulsive throes of an earthquake. The temple seemed on fire, and above its pinnacle appeared a flaming sword, which seemed to us to cleave the walls to their foundations and while we looked, the sword changed into the shape of a cross, of dazzling light, standing high in the air, over the altar; and from its golden beams poured rays so bright, that all Jerusalem, and the hill country, for a wide extent, became as light as noon-day. The ground still continued to rock, and the sepulchers of the kings, with the tombs of ancient prophets, were riven by vast chasms, and the green earth was strewn with the bones and bodies of the dead. The dark cloud, which had begun to form first with the smoke of the Temple, was now dissipated by the light of the fiery cross, and the sun reappeared. Before it the glorious vision over the Temple gradually faded out and disappeared. The natural order of things gradually returned; and men, smiting their breasts, began to move toward the city, filled with awe and dread at what they had witnessed. The Centurion, who stood watching these fearful things, said, aloud, to Aemilius:

"This man spake the truth. He was a God!"

"Truly," responded Aemilius, "this was none other than the Son of God -- the very Christ of the Jewish Prophets. All things in the air and on the earth sympathize with his death, as if he were the very God of nature who has expired."

Sad and weeping, we left the dismal scene, hanging our heads in despondency, having, while wondering at these mighty events associated with his crucifixion, abandoned, forever, all hope that this was He who should have redeemed our nation, and restored the royal splendor of Judah, the throne of the house of David.

I am, my dear father, your loving daughter,

ADINA.

LETTER XXXVI.

Jerusalem, Third Morning after the Crucifixion.

My Dearest Father: I closed the last letter, but to resume in another the sad narrative which I have been writing to you. It is now half an hour to sunrise, and as the party who went to the sepulcher have not yet returned, I will still continue my painfully interesting subject. The mother of Jesus, who I thought went with the two Marys and Martha, remained at home unable to bear the sight of her dead son.

On the day on which the wonderful events took place, which I have detailed at large in my last letter, that day which can never, for its signs and wonders, be forgotten in Jerusalem, the chief priests, at the head of whom was Abijah, met Pilate as he was riding forth from the city, attended by a score of men-at-arms, to survey the deep rents made by the earthquake, and to hear from the mouths of all the people the particulars of the marvels which attended the crucifixion of Jesus. When they came near him, they besought him that he would command his soldiers to take down the bodies, as the next day was a high-day, and that it was contrary to their customs to have criminals executed or left hanging on that day.

"What think ye?" demanded Pilate, reining up and soothing his Syrian war-horse, which, startled at the dead bodies that lay near (for they were crossing the place of open tombs), had for some time tramped and plunged madly: "What think ye, priests? Have you crucified a common man! -- or a God? We think these mighty wonders tell us that he was more than a man! All nature sympathizes with his death! The sun veiled his brightness, the heavens clad themselves in mourning, the gods sent forth angry lightnings; and the earth herself heaved and rocked as if sharing the universal woe!"

The priest looked troubled, and seemed unable to answer: but Tereh, the chief priest of the house of Mariah, answered, and said:

"My lord, these were wonderful phenomena, but they would have happened if this Nazarene had not died! Here is a famous astrologer from Arabia, who studies the skies, who says that the darkness was caused by an eclipse of the sun, and the dark cloud was but the smoke of the sacrifices, and the earthquake was but a natural and usual occurrence!"

"Stay, sir priest," answered Pilate: "we at Rome, though called barbarians by you polished Jews, have some scholarship in astrology. We know well that an eclipse of the sun can take place only when the moon is new! It is to-day, on this thy feast day, at its full, and will to-night rise opposite the sun! It was no eclipse, sir priest, and thy Arabian is a false astrologer. These events occurred because that man, your king, has been executed."

"Why not for the two robbers as well?" demanded Abner, with an incredulous sneer on his lip.

Pilate made no answer, and was riding on, when Tereh, in behalf of the chief priests, asked permission to have the bodies of the crucified removed from the crosses and buried.

"He cannot be yet dead, since it is only seven hours since he was nailed to the cross," said Pilate "I will see for myself."

Thus speaking, the Roman Procurator spurred as toward the top of the hill, followed by his bodyguard; now avoiding an open grave; now leaping one of the freshly opened chasms; now turning aside from some body cast up by the earthquake. When he came in front of the crosses, he saw that Jesus hung as if dead, while the thieves still breathed, and from time to time heaved groans of anguish, although partly insensible from the effects of the opiate which had been administered to them.

"Think you, Romulus, that he has any life in him?" asked Pilate, in a subdued tone of voice, gazing sorrowfully, and with looks of self-reproach, upon the drooping form of his victim.

"He is dead, an hour ago," answered the Centurion. "He

expired when the earthquake shook the city, and the flaming sword was unsheathed in the air above the Temple! It was a fearful sight sir, and the more wonderful to see it change in the shape of a cross of fire. I fear, sir, we have crucified one of the Gods in the shape of a man."

"It would appear so, Centurion," answered Pilate, shaking his head. "I would it had not been done! But 'tis past! The Jews desire their bodies to be removed before their great Sabbath. Caesar's orders are that they shall be humored always in all things touching their religion, which do not militate against the Imperial laws. Let them have their desire. The robbers are not yet dead!"

"Nearly so. I will break their legs and remove their bodies, your excellency," answered the Centurion.

Pilate then turned his horse and rode slowly and sadly away from the spot. Romulus then gave orders to his soldiers to remove the bodies. One of them with a battle-ax approached the robber Omri, and at two blows broke his knees. With a shudder that shook the cross, he ceased to move. The first blow upon the limbs of Ishmerai caused him to open his eyes and to growl a half-intelligible execration; but at the second stroke his huge head fell upon his hairy chest, and, muttering a curse upon his executioners, he the next moment hung there dead! When the soldiers came to Jesus they saw that He was already dead. He seemed like a Phidian statue of the whitest marble of Paros. His polished limbs were shaped with celestial symmetry; his golden hair was tossed by the evening breeze about his brow and shoulders; his divine aspect death could not mar; and the contrast he presented to the rough forms of the two malefactors between whom he hung, struck even the rude soldiers.

"Let us not break his legs," said one to the other, "it were sacrilege to mar such a manly form."

"Yet, we must insure his death ere he be taken away," responded the other. "I will pierce him to make sure!"

Thus speaking, he directed his spear to the side of Jesus, and cleaved the flesh to his heart. John, who stood near, and saw and heard all, upon seeing this done, bowed his head to the earth in total abandonment of hope! Until that moment he had believed that Jesus would revive and descend from the cross; for to the last all our faith in his power to save himself was firm, though greatly tried when we saw him in the hands of the Roman soldiers. Even when we beheld him nailed to the cross we did not give up hope, for we had all seen him raise Lazarus from the dead, and felt that he could free himself from the cross alive also. And, although after the earthquake, we left the hill and returned, sorrowing and smiting our hearts, into the city, we often lingered and looked back to where he hung, expecting to see him descend from it, and proclaim himself, by such a mighty miracle, the Son of God. John, first having delivered the mother of Jesus to our care, and many of the women and others who had loved and followed him, remained long watching him, and expecting some great event.

But when the unhappy disciple saw the Roman spear pierce his side, his own heart seemed to be pierced also. Hope perished forever! Jesus was dead -- dead, and thus proved a deceiver. Yet his emotions were not of anger, but of sorrow for he greatly loved him.

When he raised his head to gaze upon his crucified Master, he saw flowing from the rent in his side two fountains together, one of crimson blood, the other of crystal water. He could not believe what he saw, until the soldiers and the Centurion also saw it, and expressed aloud their wonder at such a marvel.

"Never was such a man crucified before," exclaimed the Centurion. "He is without doubt one of the immortal Gods, and therefore have the heavens and earth been moved with amazement at the deed!"

When John saw that Jesus was indeed dead, and all hope of his restoration to life was destroyed, he drew near, and asked permission of the Centurion to be allowed to have the body; for he had promised the mourning mother of the dead son that he would recover it, if possible, for sacred burial. But the Centurion, though a kind and generous man, answered that he could deliver the body to no one without an order signed by the Procurator's own hand.

Upon this, John, after getting the promise of the Centurion that the body should not be taken down until his return, ran rapidly toward the city to ask the consent of Pilate. But in the meanwhile, Rabbi Joseph, the counselor of Arimathea, whom my dear father, you have, many years ago, well known to be a man of probity and honor, and who stands high in favor with Pilate, met him as he was skirting the wall of the city with his cohort, and asked him if, when Jesus should be pronounced to be dead, he might take down the body and give it sepulcher. Pilate did not hesitate to give his ready consent to this request, and taking from his purse a small signet engraved with his cipher, he placed it in the hands of the rich Rabbi.

"Go and receive the body of this wonderful man," he said. "Methinks thou art one who knew him well. What thinkest thou of him, Rabbi?" Joseph perceived that Pilate asked the question with deep interest, and seemed very greatly troubled in mind and he answered him boldly:

"I believe that he was a Prophet sent from God, your excellency, and that to-day has died on Calvary the most virtuous, the wisest, and the most innocent man in Caesar's empire"

"My conscience echoes your words," answered Pilate gloomily; and putting spurs to his horse, he galloped forward in the direction of the Gethsemane Gardens.

John, therefore, did not see Pilate, and on returning from the city weary and disappointed, he met the ruler, Nicodemus, who, attended by one of his Gibeonite slaves, was hastening into town to purchase spices and linen to wrap the body in, as our manner is to bury. From him John learned, with great joy, how that Rabbi Joseph had seen Pilate, and obtained from him permission to take down and remove the body.

When John reached the cross, he found that Joseph, by the aid of Lazarus, Simon Peter, Mary, Martha, and Rabbi Amos, had taken it out of the socket in the rock, with its precious burden, and gently laid it upon the ground with the body still extended upon it. With many tears and lamentations they drew forth the copper spikes from the torn hands and bleeding feet, and with water from the brook Kedron, washed the enmarbling blood away, and wrapped the alabaster limbs in the spices and white linen, which Nicodemus presently arrived with.

The bodies of the robbers in the meanwhile were taken, or rather torn down by the soldiers, and cast together into one of the yawning chasms rent by the earthquake, and covered by fragments of stone, which the soldiers, assisted by some of the baser Jews who still lingered about the place, cast down upon them.

In the still, holy twilight of that dread day, the west all shadowy gold and mellow light, the air asleep, and a sacred silence reigning in heaven and on earth, they bore away from the hill of death the body of the dead Prophet. The shoulders of Nicodemus, of Peter, of Lazarus, and of John, gently sustained the loving weight of Him they once honored above all men, and whom, though proved by his death, to have fatally deceived himself as to his Divine Mission as the Christ, yet they still loved for his sorrow so patiently borne, for his virtues so vividly remembered.

Slowly the little group wound their way down the rocky sides of Golgotha, the last to leave that fearful place in the coming darkness. Their measured tread, their low whispers, the subdued wail of the women who followed the rude bier of branches, the lonely path they trode, all combined to render the spectacle one of touching solemnity. On reaching the valley between the hill and the city, the shades of evening were gathering thick around them. They took secret ways for fear of the Jews. But some that met them turned aside with awe when they knew what dead corpse was borne along; for the impression of the appalling scenes of the day had not yet wholly passed away from their minds. At length they reached a gate in the wall of the garden attached to the noble abode of the wealthy Rabbi Joseph, who went before, and with a key unlocked it, and admitted them into the secluded enclosure. Here the thickness of the foliage of olive and fig trees created complete darkness; for by this time the evening star was burning like a lamp in the roseats west. They rested the bier upon the pavement beneath the arch, and awaited in silence and darkness the appearance of torches, which Rabbi Joseph had sent for to his house. The servants bearing them were soon seen advancing, the flickering light from the flambeaux giving all things visible by it a wild aspect in keeping with the hour.

"Follow me," said Joseph, in a low voice, that was full charged with great sorrow, as the servants preceded him with their torches.

The sad bearers of the dead body of Jesus raised their sacred burden from the ground, and trode onward, their measured foot-falls echoing among the aisles of the garden. At its farther extremity, where the rock of Moriah hangs beetling over the valley, and forms at this place the east wall of the garden, was a shallow flight of stone steps leading to a new tomb hewn out of the rock. It had been constructed for the Rabbi himself, and had just been completed, and in it no man had ever been laid.

The torches flashed brightly upon its massive door, and upon a dark cypress tree, the branches of which drooped in majestic gloom around it. It seemed the very temple and shrine of death, so secluded -- so solemn -- so funereal was all!

The servants, by command of Joseph, rolled back the stone, and exposed the dark vault of the gaping sepulcher.

"How is it, most worthy Rabbi," said a Roman Centurion, suddenly apprising them of his presence by his voice, "that you bury thus with honor a man who has proved himself unable to keep the dazzling promises he has allured so many of you with?"

All present turned with surprise at seeing not only the Centurion, but half a score of men-at-arms, on whose helmets and cuirasses the torches brightly gleamed, marching across the grass toward the spot.

"What means this intrusion, Roman?" asked Rabbi Joseph.

"I am sent hither by command of the Procurator," answered the Centurion; "the chief Jews have had an interview with him, informing him that the man whom he had crucified had foretold that after three days he would rise again. They therefore asked a guard to be given them to place over the sepulcher till the third day, lest his disciples secretly withdraw the body, and report that their master is risen. Pilate, therefore, has commanded me to keep watch to-night with my men."

While the Centurion was speaking, several of the priests whom Joseph knew drew near, bearing torches; and also a company of women and relatives of Joseph and Mary, who had heard where they were entombing the body, came to see the place wherein he was laid.

"We bury him with this deference and respect, Centurion," answered Rabbi Joseph, "because we believe him to have been deceived, not a deceiver. He was gifted by God with vast power, and therefore doubtless believed he could do all things. He was too holy, wise, and good to deceive. He has fallen a victim to his own wishes for the weal of Israel, which were impossible by man to be realized. We do this honor to the memory of one whom to know was to love, even though we are disappointed in seeing him establish the kingdom in Judah."

The body of Jesus, wrapped in its shroud of spotless linen, and surrounded by the preserving spices of Arabia, was then borne into the tomb, and laid upon the table of stone which Joseph had prepared for his own last resting-place. By the light of the torches all present took a last look of the body, even the women of Galilee also, and ere they closed the tomb, Mary of

Bethany, her sister Martha, and Lazarus, also appeared, to gaze a tearful farewell upon the immovable features of the dead Prophet, for a Prophet since the remarkable phenomena attending his death, we are all now assured he must have been; and that we have misunderstood, from their divine depth, many of his sayings and prophecies concerning himself. Simon Peter was the last to quit the side of the body, by which he knelt as if he would never leave it, and shedding all the while great tears of bitter grief. John only at last drawing him gently forth, enabled the Centurion and soldiers to close the heavy door of the tomb. Having secured it evenly by revolving it in its sockets, he placed a mass of wax melted by a torch upon each side of it over the crevices, and stamped each with the signet of the Procurator, which to break is death.

The Jews which were present, seeing that the sepulcher was thus made sure by the sealing of the stone, and by the presence of the vigilant Roman guard of eighteen men, took their departure. Rabbi Joseph, Nicodemus, and the rest of the friends of Jesus, then slowly retired, leaving a sentinel pacing to and fro before the tomb, and others grouped about beneath the trees or on the steps of the sepulcher, playing at their favorite game of dice, or gazing upon the broad moon and singing their native Italian airs yet with their arms at hand ready to spring to their feet at the least alarm or word of alert. The tall, mailed figure of the Centurion standing motionless, leaning upon the hilt of his long, straight sword, in a meditative attitude above the tomb, was at length shut out from the view of the retiring disciples, by the angle in the path which turned in the direction of the gate. [Something fearful must this instant have happened for the house has just shaken as if with an earthquake. What can be the meaning of these wonders?] Such, my dear father, is the history of the arrest, trial judgment, crucifixion, death, and burial of the mighty Nazarene Prophet. I have been thus particular, not only to enable you to see, as if you had been present at all that passed, but also at the request of my uncle, Rabbi Amos, and to give vent to my own fullness of emotion. It was also due to myself who have believed in him so firmly, to show that, although he was crucified and is dead, the extraordinary events which accompanied his crucifixion attested that he was more than a man, if not the true Messias; and that, therefore, there is excuse not only for me, for being his disciple, but for all others who followed him. You can also perceive, my dear father, from the honorable manner in which he was buried by the eminent counselor, Rabbi Joseph, of Arimathea, that he was deemed by him innocent of any crime worthy of such a death; and that he believed him to have been deceived rather than a deceiver.

It is this view of his character, combined with his patience, his dignity, his forbearance, his air of divine innocence on his trial, which makes us all still think and talk of him with tenderness and tears. All that remains to us of him is his body, and to this we have paid the homage of our reverential affection.

This morning Mary and Martha, with others, have gone to visit his tomb in Joseph's garden (as I have already said), for the purpose of embalming it; and on their return we are to go to Bethany for a few days until the violent hostility of the Jews to his followers subsides. The Procurator is daily looking for four legions of Roman soldiers from Syria as a re-enforcement, when he will be able to protect us, and maintain completely the supremacy of the Roman power. Oh, that these forces were here on the day of the crucifixion, for then, says Rabbi Amos, Pilate, conscious of military strength, would have acted freely, and saved Jesus from their hands.

I hear now the voices of Mary and Martha, in the court of the street returning from the tomb. They are pitched to a wild note of joy! What can mean the commotion -- the exclamations -- the running and shouting all through the corridors and court! I must close and fly to learn what new wonder has occurred.

In haste, your affectionate daughter,

ADINA.

LETTER XXXVII.

Jerusalem, First Day of the Week.

Father, My Dear Father; How shall I make known to you in words, the marvelous, joyous, happy, happy, and most wonderful news which I have to tell! My heart beats, my hand trembles with rapture, while a sense of profound awe impresses all my soul. Jesus is alive! Jesus has risen from the dead! Jesus has proved himself to be the Son of God! Oh, now we know that Jesus is, indeed, the Messias who should come! Oh, that I could have doubted! Alas! that I should have written to you such words of disbelief and of doubt, and have thought him in my heart a deceiver! But I have seen him, and he has forgiven me! None of us understood his words, which he spake to us before his crucifixion, concerning his death, and hence all our consternation and despair. But now we clearly perceive the meaning of all, and are amazed at our dullness and disbelief. His death, to our benighted apprehensions, seemed the seal to a life of falsehood; the proof that he was a false prophet, rather than, as we now know it to be, a proof of his being the Son of God, by his resurrection from the dead!

I can scarcely hold my pen for joy and wonder, or collect my thoughts, for very amazement, at what has transpired. But I will try, and calm my emotions, in order, my dear father, to make known to you the mighty events which have come to pass today.

My last letter to you abruptly closed, as I was interrupted by loud exclamations of gladness, and great confusion, of running and calling, in the court and corridors below. Upon hearing my name called by Mary, and others, in eager, joy-trembling tones, I hastened to go down. On reaching the staircase I met my cousin Mary, ascending, almost flying. Wonder, love, and happiness inexpressible, beamed from her beautiful countenance. Meeting me, she threw her arms about my neck, and essayed to utter something, but her heart was too full, and bursting into sobs, she wept convulsively upon my bosom, in an ecstasy of delirious joy.

Amazed and confounded, not knowing what had happened, I held her to my heart, and tried to soothe her emotion. The voice of Martha now reached my ears from the foot of the stairs, talking rapidly to Rabbi Amos, who answered with loud exclamations!

"What -- what hath happened? Speak, dear Mary!" I asked, unable to wait longer in suspense.

She raised her head, and through her tears and smiles, at length said brokenly:

"He -- He -- is -- risen -- oh, He is risen from the tomb!"

"Who?" I cried, half-believing, yet doubting."

"The Lord! Our Mighty Master -- Jesus -- the very Son of God, the Blessed! He is alive, Adina -- alive and well!"

"You have seen a vision, or your grief, at his death, Mary, has shaken your reason," I answered.

Upon this she released herself from my arm, and fixing upon me her large, earnest eyes, said:

"Adina, be not faithless, but believing. Jesus is risen from the dead. He is alive, and walking! I have seen Him -- he has spoken to Mary of Bethany, Lazarus's sister, and also to me! Oh, joy, joy! He is the very Son of the Highest, and we have not been deceived; but we have been blind, and deaf, and ignorant, not to have understood that he must die, and rise again the third day! Come -- delay not! I have flown into the city to tell thee; and Mary has told Peter and John, whom she met at the door, and who, doubting, as thou hath done, yet have run to see if these things be so. They will find the sepulcher empty. Haste thee to go with us!"

While overwhelmed with wonder, and trembling with joy, I was preparing to accompany her, Martha appeared, her face radiant with celestial happiness:

"You have heard the tidings of great joy, O Adina!"

"Can they be true, Martha?" I asked earnestly.

"Yes, for I have seen him walking, heard his voice, and touched him! You, also shall see him, for he hath sent us to tell his disciples."

At the gateway we met Mary of Bethany, who had been telling John and Peter the news, and had also made it known to Rabbi Amos and Nicodemus. They were talking together in the court, upon the crucifixion, when she burst in upon them with the cries I had heard -- "He is risen -- He is risen!"

We three now hastened together toward the garden of Joseph, I wishing my feet wings, that I might reach the sepulcher sooner, fearing that the vision of Jesus would be vanished ere I arrived. As we were going out of the gate, we were met by four or five Roman soldiers, who, with aspects stamped with fear, were running past us into the city.

"What means this flight and terror, men?" cried the captain of the gate. "You fly as if you were in full retreat from an enemy. Speak, Marius, you seem to have your senses!" he demanded, of the youngest of the soldiers.

We paused to hear what he said.

"Per Dian, captain -- we have been terrified beyond measure," answered the soldier. "My heartbeats yet, as if it were an alarm-drum. You see, we were a part of the guard left in charge of the sepulcher of this Jewish Prophet, crucified three days ago. Before dawn this morning, as I was pacing to and fro before the tomb, and my comrades were reclining about at ease, and while I was idly gazing at the morning star, fading into the dawn, there suddenly shone round about us a light, like a descending meteor, accompanied by a rushing, like a legion of wings. The men started to their feet in amazement! On looking about us I saw a dazzling form, in the mid heavens, with broad wings of gold, sparkling with myriads of stars, every feather a star, and clad in raiment white and gleaming as the summer's lightning. This terrible presence, like that of one of the Dii Immortales, made us fear exceedingly, beyond any terror we had before experienced. But when we saw this mighty being descend straight toward the tomb, and beheld the resplendent majesty of his celestial visage, which blinded us, our hearts failed within us. The angel, or god, alighted amid a blaze of radiance at the door of the sepulcher; and as his foot touched the earth, it trembled, as if with a great earthquake. The soldiers shook with terror, and fell to the ground, before his presence, as dead men. I stood, unable to move, frozen by fear to a statue. He touched the great stone with one of his fingers, and it rolled outward at his feet, as if a catapult had struck it, and like a Jove taking his throne, he sat upon it!

"But one thing more," continued the soldier, "was wanting to fill my cup of terror to the full. And it followed. I saw the crucified Prophet rise up from the slab on which he was laid, and stand upon his feet, and walk forth alive, with the tread of some mighty conqueror! The celestial being, so terrible in his majestic splendor, veiled his face with his wings before his presence, and prostrated himself at his feet, as if in homage to one greater than himself!

"I saw no more, but fell, insensible with terror, to the earth. When, at length, I came to myself, the tomb was filled with dazzling forms of resplendent beauty; the air rung with music, such as mortals never before heard; and I fled, pursued by my fears, the rest of the soldiers rising, and following me, each man fearing to look back."

"This is indeed marvelous," answered the captain of the gate "I saw the light, and felt the tremor of the earth but I thought it was a thunderbolt which had struck the ground near the hill of Calvary. Go, let the Prefect of Aemilius, or Pilate himself know what has happened."

The soldiers hurried forward into the city while confirmed now in the certainty that Jesus was risen, I hastened, with Martha and Mary, in the direction of the garden.

"Thou believest now, Adina?" said Mary of Bethany, to me, as we flew along.

"Yes -- only let me behold him face to face, and I shall then be willing, at that hour, to meet death. How did the risen Lord look, Mary?" I asked.

"There was the same benign and holy expression -- the same divine majesty, the same loving words, and celestial dignity."

"How and where did you behold him, Mary?" I interrogated, as we drew near to the steep path leading to the gate of Joseph's garden.

"When we reached the tomb, with our spices and precious ointments, to embalm the body, we found it open, and the soldiers, who had guarded it, lying about upon the ground like dead men. Upon the stone sat the archangel, but the resplendent light of his apparel and countenance were so tempered to our eyes, that, although we believed that it was an angel, we were not terrified, for his looks were kind, and the aspect of his face divinely beautiful, combined with a terrible and indescribable majesty. We shook with fear, and stood still, unable to move, gazing on him in silent expectation.

"Fear not, ye," he said, in a voice that seemed to fill the air about us with undulating music, "fear not, daughters of Abraham. I know that ye seek Jesus, which was crucified! He is not here, but is risen, as he foretold. Lo! see the place where the Lord of Life, and Conqueror of Death hath lain!"

"We then timidly approached and looked in, and saw the sepulcher empty; but a soft light filled the whole place.

"Go and tell his disciples, that the Lord is risen," added the angel "and that he will go before them into Galilee. There shall they see him not many days hence!"

"When the angel had thus spoken to us," continued Mary, "we departed quickly from the sepulcher with fear and great joy, and ran to go into the city, to bring his disciples word, according to the command of the angel. But I had not advanced so far as the gate of the garden, being behind the rest, when I beheld Jesus himself standing in my path. I stopped, between terror and joy.

"All hail! daughter of Israel," he said. "Be not afraid. I am living, that was dead! It was needful that I should die, and rise again, that I might raise up from the dead all who die in me, to life immortal. Go, Mary, and tell my mother and my brethren, and Peter, and John, and Lazarus, that I am risen, and that I have spoken with you. Behold my wounded hands, that it is I myself! Be not afraid! I am the resurrection and the life!"

"I then cast myself at his feet, and worshiped him; and when I looked up, he was gone."

"The others did not see him. We now continued on to the city, as if we had wings; yet, rapidly as we went, some of the same Roman watch whom we met coming in just now, passed us, in their flight and alarm; for they fled at first in different parties, different ways. But see! we are now at the gate of the garden," added Mary of Bethany, in a low tone of awe. "He must be near us."

But we approached the tomb without seeing any man, having arrived before Peter and John, who had been delayed some time at the Jaffa gate, which route they took, as being nighest; but it was not opened when they reached it, and they were detained. We, therefore, found no one at the sepulcher. It was open, and empty. The stone in front, on which the archangel sat, was vacant. As we drew near, a bright light suddenly shone out from the tomb; and upon going nigher I beheld two angels, clothed in white robes, and with countenances of Divine radiance, seated, one at the head and the other at the foot of the slab of marble, on which the body of Jesus had lain. At the sight of these noble and beautiful beings, which we knew were sons of God, come down from heaven, we were affrighted. I sank upon the stone which had been rolled away, and remained without power of motion.

"Be not afraid, daughters of Jerusalem," said one of the angels, speaking to us in the Hebrew tongue "He whom ye seek, liveth -- and dieth no more! He is risen from the tomb, which could not hold him but through his consent; for Jesus is Lord of Life, and Victor over Death and Hell, forevermore! Go your way, and tell his disciples that he awaits them at Nazareth, at the house of Mary, his mother, by the sea-side."

The angels then vanished from our sight and at the same moment John and Peter came running, and seeing the stone rolled away, John stooped down, and looked in, and said that he saw the linen clothes in which the body of Jesus had been wrapped, lying folded together, and also the napkin which had been bound about his head. Peter now coming up breathless with eagerness and haste, no sooner saw the tomb open, than he went boldly in, and carefully examined all for himself. He then called to John, who also went in, and both were convinced that their Lord had indeed risen from the dead and when we made known to them what the angels had said to us, that Jesus would go before, and meet them in Galilee, they rejoiced greatly, and shortly afterward departed, to hasten into Galilee, no longer doubting, but believing. I also returned with them, to convey the news to Mary, the mother of Jesus, who had not left the house, and scarcely her bed, in her great sorrow, since the day of the crucifixion. Mary of Bethany, however, remained, lingering near the tomb, hoping that Jesus had not yet left the garden, and that she might once more behold him.

Seated upon the steps of the tomb, weeping for joy at his

resurrection, and wishing once more to behold him, she heard a footstep behind her, and, turning round, saw a man standing near her. It was Jesus himself, and kneeling, she was about to clasp his feet, when he said to her:

"Touch me not, Mary, I am not yet ascended to my Father. But go and tell Lazarus, and my brethren, and my mother, that I ascend, ere many days, unto my Father and your Father, and unto my God and your God."

Jesus then vanished out of her sight; and she came and told all these things to us, and to the disciples; and we all, once more, believed that Jesus was the Messias and Christ, the immortal Son of the Blessed. Such joy as filled the bosoms of his friends was never before experienced by human beings. Our happiness and exultation now were in proportion to our depression before his resurrection.

But what pen can describe, my dear father, the amazement and consternation of Caiaphas, and the chief priests, and the rest of his enemies! The soldiers who had kept guard of the sepulcher had entered the city by different ways, and spread the report of the mighty miracle of the resurrection through every principal street in Jerusalem, as they fled through it.

Caiaphas hearing the uproar, sprang from his couch to inquire the cause of it, and on being assured by his servants, "Jesus has burst his tomb and risen alive from the dead!" he quaked, and became deadly pale. But he soon rallied, and sending for two or three of the soldiers, who were describing vividly what they had witnessed to a large concourse in the street, he questioned them closely upon the facts. The soldiers' testimony agreed together, and could not be gainsaid.

When Pilate received the account from the Centurion of the guard, he said:

"We have crucified a God, as I believed! Henceforth I am accursed!" and leaving his Hall of Judgment, he went and shut himself up in his own room, which he has not since left. But men say he neither eats nor sleeps, and that a dread fit of gloom has settled upon his soul.

Caiaphas and the priests in the meanwhile assembled together in full Sanhedrim, and hearing the testimony of the Centurion. Were convinced that the fact could not be concealed of Jesus' resurrection.

"Who hath seen him alive?" demanded the High Priest.

PRINCE OF THE HOUSE OF DAVID

"I have seen him, my lord," answered the Centurion, -- "I saw his pierced feet and hands as he walked past me and the morning breeze blew aside his mantle and exposed to my eyes the open wound made by the spear of my soldier Philippus. He was alive, and in full strength of limb!"

"Thou sawest a vision, Roman," answered Caiaphas. "Come then aside with us, and let us talk with thee."

In a few minutes afterward the Centurion left the court of the High Priest's palace followed by a Gibeonitish slave, bearing after him a vase of Persian gold. He has told everyone since that he must have seen a spirit, for that the disciples of Jesus came by night and stole away the body of their master, while they slept, overcome with watching. His soldiers have also been bribed to tell the same tale.

Such is the false version that now goes about the city, my dear father; but there are few that give it credence, even of our enemies. As Aemilius, who is filled with great joy at the resurrection of Jesus, today very justly says:

"If these soldiers slept on guard, they merited death therefor by the military laws of the empire. If, while sleeping, their charge -- the dead body of Jesus -- was taken away, they deserve death for failing to prevent it. Why, then, are they not placed under arrest by Pilate's orders, if this story be true? Because Pilate well knows that it is not true! He knows, because he has privately examined many of the soldiers, that Jesus did burst his tomb, and that angels rolled away the stone without breaking his seals, which could not have been left unmarred, but by a miracle. He knows that Jesus has arisen -- for it is believed that he has also beheld him; at least such is the rumor of the Pretorium. It was the form of Jesus visible before him, doubtless, that drove him in such amazement from his Hall to his secret-chamber for it was remarked that he started, turned deadly pale, and essayed to address the invisible space before him, as if he saw a spirit. Therefore his soldiers are not molested -- and their exemption from arrest, is proof that the body of Jesus was not stolen away while they slept. Besides, if they were asleep, these soldiers, how could they tell that it was stolen away, and declare the persons who did it?"

This is the unanswerable reasoning of the Prefect Aemilius; and thus you see, dear father, that Caiaphas can gain little by his briberies and diligently circulated falsehood. That Jesus of Nazareth is alive from the dead is true, and if I had not seen him, the evidence is complete enough to convince me of the fact.

Besides the facts which I have stated, is the increasing testimony of the thousands, who, today, have gone out of the city to see the sepulcher where he was laid. They say, both enemies of Jesus as well as our friends, that it was impossible for the door to have been opened by any human being, not by Pilate himself, without marring the seals. They also assert that to remove the stone by night, which would require four men, and to bear forth the body, would have been impossible if the guard had been present; and if they had been asleep, they must have awakened them with the heavy noise made by rolling the massive door along the hollow pavement outside the sepulcher.

"If," say the common people, "the watch slept, why does not the Procurator put them to death?"

This question remains unanswered, and the watch go about the streets unharmed! My dear father, remember no more my unbelief, but with me, believe in Jesus, that He is the Son of God, the Savior of Israel, the immortal Christ of the Prophets.

Your affectionate daughter,

ADINA.

LETTER XXXVIII.

*Bethany, House of Mary and Martha,
one Month after the Passover.*

I deeply regret, my dearest father, the delays which have
detained you so long from arriving at Jerusalem, but I trust that
ere many days, the caravan for which you wait will reach Gaza,
and that you will be enabled to resume your journey to the
Holy City. I am now at Bethany, where I have been some time
making it my home, for such was the hostility of the Jews,
incited by the chief priests, against us, that, by Pilate's
command, we were compelled to leave Jerusalem on the day
of the resurrection, to remain until their hatred had in some
degree subsided; for he said that the continued presence there
of the disciples of Jesus, kept up constant occasion for tumult
and interposition of the Roman authority.

Uncle Amos has retired for the present to his farm, near
Jericho; but will be here to-morrow to remain with us.
Therefore when you come near to Jerusalem, instead of going
directly into the city, turn aide by the road leading past the
king's garden and go up the brook of Kedron, into the way of
Bethany. I pray that God may preserve you in safety, and soon
permit me the happiness of once more embracing you, after
three long years of separation.

And what events have transpired, and to which I have been
a witness in these three years! From the preaching of John the
Baptizer and the baptism of Jesus by him, unto the glorious
resurrection of the mighty Son of God! Favored, indeed, have I
been to have been a dweller in Judea, during this eventful
period, and to have seen and heard these things, which no
other age of the world can parallel! But so far as one could

know them, who was not an eye-witness, you, my dear father, have been faithfully informed of them through my letters. You have, therefore, before you the same testimony as I have, and those who have seen and now believe. Once more, my dear father, read carefully over the whole narrative, from the first letter, and thus, until all the facts fresh in your mind, answer to yourself this inquiry:

"Was not this man the Son of God? Was not he the very Christ, the divine and long-looked for Messiah? Was he not that mighty Prophet which should come into the world? If he were not, who is He? Who is He at whose birth the air was filled with angels, over whose couch hung a celestial star; before whose infant feet the three wisest men of the world, Shapha of Egypt, the son of Ham, Beltazar of Assyria, the son of Shem, and Thoropha, of Grecia, the son of Japhet, representing the family of mankind, bowed in adoration and worship, as to a God! Who is He for whom Herod the first slew three hundred and two score children in Bethlehem, in order to reach his life? Who was He whom John the Baptizer proclaimed the "Lamb of God," whose blood was the only fountain for sin? Who was he at whose baptism the heavens were opened above his head, and the spirit of God descended upon him in the form of a dove of light, while the voice of the Lord, like the voice of many thunders, proclaimed from the depths of the cloudless skies, "This is my beloved Son?" Who was He, my dear father, at whose word the tempest became still the billowy waves placid; the winds hushed? Who was He that healed the sick and leprous by a word; who restored a lost arm or leg by touch who by a look reanimated the lifeless limb of the paralytic; who raised the daughter of Jairus healed the Centurion's servant; restored to life the son of the widow of Nain; cast out a legion of devils from Beor, the Levite; restored the deaf and dumb nephew of the Governor of Syria to hearing and speech; gave to his disciples also the same power to do miracles; feeds at one time four thousand men, and another time five thousand, from a few pounds of bread and a few fishes, which a lad could carry in a basket; whom Moses and Elias came from the regions of the blessed, shining in resplendent glory, bright from the presence of the Father, to visit and hold communion with; who calls forth from the tomb of corruption Lazarus to life and health; who once while praying, was answered by a voice from Heaven in the hearing of many people, "I have glorified My name, and will glorify it again?"

Who was He, my father, at whose trial nothing could be found against him, and who, when delivered to execution by Pilate to save himself and appease the Jews, was publicly declared to be an innocent man, by the act of the Procurator, in calling for water and washing his hands, and saying that he was clear of his blood, for he found no fault in him? Who was He at whose crucifixion the heavens grew black as sackcloth, the sun withdrew its light, the stars shot from their spheres, the lightnings leaped along the earth, the earth itself quaked, and this dead sprung from their graves? Who was He who the third day burst the bars of the tomb, received as he walked forth the homage of an archangel, whose servants were a seraph and a cherubs, waiting behind him in the tomb; who appeared alive to his mother -- to the women of Galilee -- to Mary of Bethany, to Martha and Lazarus, and last of all to me also? Who was this wonderful person, my father -- who was He but the Christ? Oh, read, reflect, compare the prophets that speak of Messias, with the life, and words, and deeds of Jesus; and the life of Jesus with the prophets. There thou wilt see that he has proven himself to be the very Christ, by what we in our ignorance looked upon as the seal affixed to an impostor. Isaiah prophesied of the Christ whom he saw afar off, that "he should be a man of sorrow;" that he should be "despised and rejected of men;" that he should be brought "as a lamb to the slaughter;" that he should be "taken from prison and judgment, and but off from the land of the living;" that he should be "numbered with the wicked in his death, and make his grave with the rich!" How light, how clear, how plain, all these prophecies now are to me, and to us all! How wonderfully in their minuteness they have been fulfilled, you already know.

His resurrection also was foretold by himself, but we did not understand his words until now. When he spoke of destroying the Temple and raising it in three days, he spoke of the tabernacle of his body! Oh, how many sayings, which, when spoken by his sacred lips, we understood not, now rush upon us in all their meaning, proving to us that every step of his life was foreknown to him; that he went forward to his death aware of all things whatsoever that were going to befall him!

But his resurrection was also foretold by the holy David, when he said, "Thou wilt not leave his soul in Hades, nor suffer thy Holy One to see corruption therefore my flesh shall rest in hope!" Even his arraignment before Pilate, Caiaphas, and

Herod, was foretold by David, when he said: "The kings of the earth set themselves, and the rulers take counsel together, against the Lord, and against his Anointed:" yet the Lord saith, "Thou art my Son, this day I have begotten thee." Also, my dear father, turn to the Psalm XXII, of King David, and compare the following words, which speak of Messias, with what I have described in my previous letters:

"My God, my God! why hast thou forsaken me!" are prophetic words put into the mouth of Messias when he shall come, and be forsaken of God. You will find that in my letters I have told you that on the cross Jesus uttered these very words.

Again, King David makes Messias, a few sentences further on, to say, "They shoot out the lip at me; they shake the head; they laugh me to scorn. They say, He trusted in the Lord that he would deliver him." Thou best brought me into the dust of death."

All this shows that Messias, if he were to be a king, was also to suffer, to be forsaken of God, to be brought to death! and yet we rejected Jesus as soon as he died! But, my dear father, read the same Psalm of the holy king a little further, and you will see these words, which were put by the royal prophet into the lips of his future Messias:

"The assembly of the wicked have enclosed me. They pierced my hands and my feet. They part my garments among them, and upon my vesture cast lots!"

Read and compare these acknowledged prophecies of Messias with the accounts in my letters, dear father, and you will not only be convinced that Jesus is the Messias of the prophets, and Christ of God, but you will perceive that his humiliation and sufferings before Pilate and Caiaphas, his agony on the cross, his death and burial, instead, as we ignorantly conceived, of being evidences that he was not the Christ, were proof that He was the very Son of the Highest -- the Shiloh of Jehovah foretold by the prophets -- the Anointed King of Israel.

Oh, how wonderful is all this! I saw marvelous these things passing before our eyes! Yet how have we been blinded -- how gross and dark our minds that we could not, until He died, and has arisen again, see in him, all that he was in his sufferings and in his death -- the Divine Messiah. Now all is dazzingly clear! The prophets are unveiled to our sight, and we see that these things must have happened to him! Yet how quickly was He deserted and faith lost in him! How his disciples denied that they ever knew him; and how we all were ashamed that we had ever followed him! Oh, our darkness, our blindness, to have seen in the prophecies of Messias, only the passages which speak of his glory and power, and passed by those which as positively foretold of his humiliation, degradation, and death! Read the prophets no longer, my dearest father, with a veil before your eyes! See, in all you read, Jesus as the end of the prophets, the goal of all their far-seeing prophecies, the veritable and sure realization of their prophetic visions.

But you have said, in one of your late letters to me, "that Elias must first come, ere Messias appear on earth" and then you ask me, where is Elias? Hath he come? Who hath seen him?

This question, my dear father, was also put by some of the Jews to Jesus. He replied:

"Elias truly has come, and ye knew him not, and ye have done unto him whatsoever you list."

"Who was he?" demanded several of the scribes and priests, surprised at hearing this.

"He who came crying in the wilderness before me, and who spake of me, and whom Herod hath slain," He answered.

"But his name was John, master," said they. "But his spirit and power were those of Elias," answered Jesus. "In Elijah's spirit and power he came, and thus was called the Elias that should come. The reality is the man. John was the Elias of Malachi the Prophet -- for prophetic eyes see natures independently of names."

Thus, my dear father, has Jesus in all particulars proved himself to be the subject of all prophecy -- the King of Israel. But you will now ask, "Is He to re-establish the throne of David, and live forever?"

Yes, but not in Jerusalem on earth. Oh, how clear are all things to my apprehension now! His kingdom, which I once believed to be the land of Judah, is to be in a world beyond the skies, which he has created for his followers, and to which they are to pass, like him, through the gates of death. The Jerusalem, in which His Throne is to be placed, is heavenly, and the true Jerusalem, of which the present one is but the material type -- what the body is to the soul of a man.

Jesus has talked with me since his resurrection, and explained all this to me, and much more that is wonderful and full of joy. It is now four weeks since he arose, and during that time, he has been not only seen by all the disciples, but by hundreds of his followers. The seventh day after his resurrection he appeared openly at Nazareth, on the sea-shore, to Peter, John, Andrew, James, and other disciples, to his numerous relatives, and many of the chief citizens of his town, all of whom not only recognized him, but marveled to see his crucified hands and feet. The effect of this recognition, which was made by many, who, being up at the Passover, had seen him crucified, was to bring the whole population worshiping at his knees. The only change in his usual appearance, dear father, to the eye, is a transparent paleness, which gives a soft radiance to his whole aspect, and a certain majestic reserve, which awes all who draw near to him; so that men speak in his presence in subdued whispers. His mother, happiest of women now, as she was before the most wretched, ever sits at his feet, and silently enjoys his sacred presence, seldom speaking, and looking up to him, rather as a worshiper to her God, than a mother upon her son. That He is in the flesh in reality, and not a spirit, He has proven to his disciples, by eating with them; and in a remarkable way to an incredulous disciple, called Thomas, who, not believing that Jesus was risen in his real body from the dead, was told by the Divine Lord to place his fingers into his hands, and his hand into his side which Thomas in fact did do; when, falling at his feet in amazement and adoration, he worshiped him as God.

It would take much time, my dear father, to record the numerous instances in which the risen Lord has been seen and spoken with, by persons who knew him before his crucifixion; so that there is no fact so fully established in the minds of many thousands in Judah, as the resurrection of Jesus from the dead.

And if fuller proof is wanted, it is to be had, as Abram, the learned Pharisee, has been forced to confess to Rabbi Amos, in the conduct of his disciples, after their Master's crucifixion. For they began their defection by denying him, and deserting him; they fled in all directions, and studiously concealed the fact of their former connection with him. They were not only moved by fear to this concealment, but by shame, being sorely mortified at having been led away by him; for they were honest, plain, sensible men, without fanaticism or fanciful vagaries. They had become the followers of Jesus, because they saw in him that moral purity and truth, which formed the elements of their own characters. These plain, homely men -- these poor fishermen, and humble countrymen -- deeply felt how their false position, among judicious folks, would now make them appear, and so they hastened to bury their disgrace and disappointment in the seclusion of the fishing hamlets of Galilee and doubtless desired never more to hear spoken into their ears the name of their crucified Master.

But what do we behold, within a week after the resurrection is made known through the length and breadth of Judah? They who had hidden in dismay, from the face of day, came boldly forth, and once more were with their Lord, forgiven by him, and received by him again into his holy confidence. They went with him wherever He went, even to Jerusalem, from which they had but a few days before fled. They walked with animated steps, and elevated faces, like men no longer serving a defeated monarch, but like men whose Master was Lord of heaven and of earth.

To-day they are with him in the gardens of David, at Bethlehem, where he is holding daily a solemn council with the eleven, unfolding to them the future glory of his kingdom, and opening their understanding to the clear apprehension of all which the prophets have written concerning him. John, who is a member of this divine council, says that the power of Jesus, the extent and majesty of his kingdom, the infinite results of his death and resurrection, are not to be conceived of by those who have not listened to the sublime revelations of his own lips.

"Be hath shown us," said John, "how that his true office as Son of God, and Son of Man, is to be a mediator between both; that by his death he reconciled the race of Adam to his Father, having become our Lamb of sacrifice for the whole world. He showed us that He, himself, was the High Priest; his own precious body was the victim, which He, himself, offered up to appease the wrath at Jehovah against transgressions, and how that the Cross was the Altar of this great world's sacrifice, and the Temple the whole earth and heavens. He showed us how that all the lambs which had bled since Adam's day, typified himself, the one only true and efficient Lamb, which God ultimately looked to, to be sacrificed for sins! How wonderful, dear father, is all this! He further teaches his disciples, that he will shortly ascend from the earth, to enter upon his celestial reign and that his subjects there are to be all who love him and keep his commandments. It is a kingdom of holiness, and none enter there but the pure in heart. He says further, that as we do now confess our sins over the blood of the victim we sacrifice for ourselves in the Temple, so hence-forth, we must look to him (by faith when we see him no longer), slain a sacrifice for us, and confess our sins to the Father for his blood's sake, which the Father has accepted, in the one sacrifice he made on the cross, once for all. Jesus has moreover taught this disciples that the Gentiles are to share equally with the children of Abraham the benefits of his death and resurrection; that this good news shall be proclaimed to them by his disciples, and that they will gladly hear it and believe. That the gospel of redemption, no longer by the blood of bulls and of goats, but by his blood, shall in the progress of ages fill the whole earth when every knee shall bow to his name.

"The foundation of my everlasting kingdom," he saith, "truly shall be laid upon earth in the hearts of men; but the building is with God eternal in the heavens. The tomb through which I have passed is the gate, and all who would come after me, and enter in, must follow in my footsteps."

Thomas then asked his Lord whither he would go, and the way? How he would leave the earth, since he could die no more?

"Thou shalt see for thyself ere many days pass," answered Jesus. "In that I have risen, all whom my Father giveth me shall rise also from the dead; and those whom I raise up, I will take with me the way I go; for where I am they shall evermore be with me also."

Such, dear father, is a brief account of what John has told us, on visiting us, touching the divine teaching of Messiah, the Son of God, respecting his kingdom. Yet much is still mysterious; but we know enough to be willing to trust ourselves to him for this life, and for that which is to come. We know that all power is given into his hands, and that he can save all men who believe in, and accept him as the only sacrificed Lamb, whom the Father hath accepted for the iniquities of men. The sacrifices of the Temple must hence forth cease.

What is remarkable, dear father, not withstanding the Jews have heard that Jesus walks everywhere through Jewry, yet no efforts are made to lay hands on him. At his presence, crowds of his enemies fly like the stricken multitude before the advancing sirocco. His presence in Judea is a present dread, like some great evil, to those who fear him; but like a celestial blessing to more who love him. Pilate, on the eve of making a journey last week to Bethel, before quitting the city, dispatched couriers in advance to ascertain whether Jesus the crucified was on the line of his route! Caiaphas having occasion to go to Jericho, a few days after the Passover, hearing that Jesus had been seen with his disciples on the road made a circuit round by Luz and Shiloh, in order not to meet him. The gates of this city are kept constantly shut, lest he should enter within the walls: some of the chief priests fearing greatly to behold his face, while others imagine that he is engaged in raising an army, to advance upon and take Jerusalem from the Romans. And doubtless, dear father, were the kingdom of Jesus of this world, he would in a few days lead a countless host against the city, and make himself master of Judea. But his kingdom is above; and all who dwell in the true Jerusalem, must follow him thither through sufferings, humiliation and death.

I rejoice to see by your last letter, that you maybe expected to reach here the week after next. Oh,that you were here now, that you might be taken by John to see Jesus: for from what he says he will not long remain visible among us. Whither he goeth or how he goeth away, no man can say. We are filled with expectation of some great event, which will conclude the brilliant and wonderful succession of marvels, that attend his footsteps and presence on earth.

Faithfully, your loving daughter,

ADINA.

LETTER XXXIX

Bethany, Forty Days After the Resurrection.

Dear Father: With emotions that nearly deprive me of the power to hold my pen, and with trembling fingers that make the words I write almost illegible, I sit down to make known to you the extraordinary event, which will mark this day in all future time as the most worthy to be noted among men.

In my last I informed you that Jesus after his wonderful resurrection, which was declared to all men by infallible proofs, gathered once more his amazed and adoring disciples about him, and taught them, with more than mortal wisdom and eloquence, the great truths appertaining to his kingdom, which he now appointed them to extend throughout all the world.

On the fortieth day, my dear father, early in the morning, he left the house of Mary and Lazarus, where he had sat up with us all night. (for none of us thought of sleep within the sound of his heavenly voice), speaking to us of the glories of heaven, and the excellency of heart and purity of life required of all who should enter it.

"Lord," said Martha, as he went forth, "whither goest thou?"

"Come and see," he answered. "Whither I go ye shall know, and the way ye shall know: for where I am ye shall also be, and all those who believe in me."

"Lord," said Mary, kneeling at his feet, "return at noon, and remain with us during the heat of the day."

"Mary," said Jesus, laying his hand gently upon her forehead, "I am going to my Father's house! There thou shalt one day dwell with me in mansions not made with hands. Follow me, and thou shalt know the way thither! Through temptation I have first trodden it, through suffering, through death, and through resurrection from the dead. So also must thou and all who love me follow me. To my friends, the gate of the tomb opens into the world of life eternal."

Thus speaking, he walked slowly onward toward the hill of Bethany, not far from the place where Lazarus was buried. He was followed not only by Mary, Martha, Lazarus, and John, my cousin Mary and myself, each of us expecting from his words and manner, some new and great event to take place; but by all the disciples, who had presently joined him near the cemetery, at the foot of the hill. There were at least five hundred persons in all, moving on with him ere he reached the green hillside beyond the village; for all followed him, expecting to hear more glorious revelations from his lips of the life beyond this.

"He goes to the hill to pray," said one of his disciples.

"Nay," said Peter, "he prays not since his resurrection as before. He has no need of prayer for himself, who has conquered sin, Satan, death, the grave and the world!"

"He goes to show us some mighty miracle, from the expression of power and majesty in his aspect," said Thomas to me, gazing upon the Lord with awe; for each moment as he ascended the hill, his countenance grew more glorious with a certain God-like majesty, and shone like the face of Moses descending from Mount Sinai. We all hung back with adoring fear, and alone he proceeded onward, a wide space being left by us between ourselves and him. Yet there was no terror in the glory which surrounded and shined out from him but rather a holy radiance, that seemed to be the very light of holiness and peace.

"So looked he," said John to us, "when we beheld him transfigured in the mount with Elias and Moses."

The hill, which is not lofty, was soon surmounted by his sacred feet. He stood upon its apex alone. We kept back near the brow of the hill, fearing to approach him, for his raiment shone now like the sun, while his countenance was as lightning. We shaded our eyes to behold him. All was now expectation, and looking for some mighty event -- what we knew not! John drew nearest to him, and upon his knees, with clasped hands looked toward him earnestly for he knew, as he afterward told us, what would take place; Jesus having informed him the night before. Joy and yet tears were on his face, as he gazed with blinded eyes, as one gazes on the noon-day sun, upon his Divine Master. It was a scene, dear father, impressive beyond expression. The hill-top was thronged with an expectant, awe-stricken multitude, which knew not whether to remain or fly from the glorious majesty of the presence of the Son of God. The blue sky spread out its illimitable concave above the hills without a cloud. At the foot of the eminence toward the holy city, slept the gardens of Gethsemane, where Jesus loved to walk, and where he was arrested. Jerusalem, with its towers, pinnacles, palaces, and gorgeous Temple, glittered in the distance; and Calvary, studded with fresh Roman crosses, stood out boldly in view, in the transparent air. The tall cypresses which grew above the tomb of Joseph, where he had lain, were also visible. Jesus seemed for a moment to survey these scenes of his suffering, of his ignominy and death, with the look of a divine conqueror. He then turned to his disciples and said:

"Ye have been with me in my sorrows, and you now shall behold my glory, and the reward which my Father doth give me. Today I take leave of you and ascend to my Father and your Father. Remember all things which I have taught you concerning my kingdom. Go forth and teach the glad tidings of salvation to all men, and baptize all nations in the name of the Father, and of the Son, and of the Holy Ghost; and lo, I am with you always, even unto the end of the world."

Thus speaking, in a voice that thrilled every bosom with emotions indescribable, he extended his hands above their heads and blessed them, while we all fell upon our faces to the ground, also to receive his blessing.

He then lifted up his eyes to the calm blue depths of heaven, and said:

"And now, O Father, glorify thou me with thine own self, with the glory which I had with Thee before the world was!"

As he spoke, we raised our faces from the ground, and saw him leaving the earth, rising from the hill-top into the air, with a slow and majestic ascension; his hands out spread over us beneath, as if shedding down blessings upon us all. The loud burst of surprise which rose from five hundred voices at seeing him soar away into the atmosphere, was followed by a profound and awful silence, as we watched him rise and still rise, ascending and still ascending into the upper air, his whole form growing brighter and brighter, as the distance widened between his feet and the earth!

Upon our knees, in speechless amazement, we followed his

ascent with our eyes, not a word being spoken by any soul and hearts might have been heard beating in the intense expectation of the moment.

Then in the far off height of heaven, we beheld appear a bright cloud, no larger than a man's hand, but each instant it expanded and grew broader and brighter, and swift as the winged lightning, it descended through the firmament downward, until we beheld it evolve itself into a glittering host of angels, which no man could number, countless as the stars of heaven. As these shining legions descended, they parted into two bands, and sweeping along the air, met the ascending Son of God in the mid sky! The rushing of their ten thousand times ten thousand wings, was heard like the sound of many waters. Surrounding Jesus, like a shining cloud, they received him into their midst, and hid him from our eyes, amid the glories of their celestial splendor.

While we stood gazing up into the far skies, hoping, expecting, yet doubting if we should ever behold him again, two bright stars seemed to be descending from the height of heaven toward us. In a few seconds we saw that they were angels alighting on the place Jesus had left, they said to the eleven, "Why gaze ye up into heaven, ye men of Galilee? This same Jesus whom ye have seen go into heaven, shall so come in like manner as ye have now seen him ascend!" Thus speaking, they vanished out of our sight!

The above account, my dear father, of the ascent yesterday into heaven of the Christ, our Blessed Lord Jesus, I wrote the same evening, while all the circumstances were present and vivid upon my mind. Oh, what a sublime spectacle! What human language can describe it! But one thing I have presented clearly to you, dear father, and that is the fact that Jesus has ascended into the heaven of heavens! Oh, amazing reality! Overwhelming truth! What, oh what is earth? What is Judea? -- What is man? -- that God is mindful of Him -- that He should so have visited him! And when He has visited us when His Divine Son, the brightness of the glory of the Father, has descended to earth, and assumed our nature, to reconcile us to God, and obtain an eternal life for us, how has He been received? Shunned for his voluntary poverty -- despised for his humble human parentage -- hated for his holiness -- tried before tribunals for crimes unknown to him -- scourged and spit upon, mocked, and buffeted, and crucified with thieves, as if his enemies would render his death as ignominious as it was capable of being made!

But behold the issue! See, when he had paid the debt of death for us, the change in all things! He awakes to life! He bursts the tomb! He walks forth from the sepulcher! Angels are his servants! After forty days on earth, unfolding to his disciples the mysteries of his gospel and the splendor of his kingdom, he ascends visibly to heaven at mid-day from Bethany, in the sight of many hundreds, and is escorted by armies of angels to the right hand of the majesty on high!

Such, my dear father, is the appropriate crowning event of the extraordinary life of Jesus, both Lord and Christ! His ascent from this earth into the heaven of heavens, not only is proof that He came from God, but that God is well pleased with all that He has done in the flesh. If in any one thing He taught, He spoke what was not true, either concerning the Father or concerning himself, he would not have received such a welcome back to the heavenly abodes! All that Jesus said of himself is therefore true! Jehovah attests it! We must then believe, or we can have no interest in the kingdom which He has gone to prepare for us, and which we can enter only as He has traveled through it, through humiliation, suffering, death, the tomb, resurrection, and also ascension! Thus did he truly say, "The way I go ye shall know."

His kingdom is therefore, my dear father, clearly not of this world, as he said to Pilate, the Procurator; but it is above. To it he has triumphantly ascended, attended by legions of Cherubim and Seraphim, an ascent which David clearly foresaw in vision, when he wrote:

"God has gone up with a shout, he has ascended on High!"

Doubt, then, no longer, dearest father! Jesus, the son of Mary in His human nature, was the Son of God in His Divine nature; an incomprehensible and mysterious union, whereby he has brought together in harmony the two natures, separated far apart by sin, by sacrificing His own body as a sin-offering, to reconcile both in one Immaculate body upon the cross. There is now no more condemnation to them who believe in Him and accept Him; for in His body He took our sins, and with his precious blood, as that of a lamb without blemish, cleansed them forever away.

But I cannot write all I would say to you, dearest father. When we meet, which you rejoice me in saying, will be on the first day of the week, at Jerusalem, I will unfold to you all that the divine and glorified Jesus has taught me. Doubt not that He is Messiah. Hesitate not to accept Him; for He is the end of

Moses, and of the Law, and of the Prophets, the very Shiloh who should come and restore all things, to whom be glory, power, dominion, majesty, and excellency evermore.

Your loving daughter,

ADINA.

Here terminates the series of letters of the Jewish maiden to her father, written during the Procuratorship of Pontius Pilate, under the reign of Tiberius Caesar, the Roman Emperor. They cover a period of three years and six months, embracing all the events of the life of John the Baptist, and of the Holy Jesus of Nazareth, to the day of His ascension into heaven.

The Roman Centurion, Aemilius, it would appear from history, became Procurator of the Island of Britain in the West, and with Adina, his noble lady, was the first to entertain the Christian Apostle, Saul of Tarsus, otherwise Paulus, on his visit thither to proclaim at those ends of the earth the gospel of Jesus the Crucified, in obedience to the command left by Him with His disciples, that they should preach His gospel to every creature.

The history of the first establishment of the faith of Jesus in this remote Roman barbaric Province by the Jewish Apostle, and of its spread throughout the island, is to be found written in detail in certain letters, which the daughter of Aemilius and of Adina wrote to her brother, a Roman knight at Rome].

Endorsement upon the original letters of Adina by the Roman Jewish Scribe,

ELIAS BEN EZRA.

THE END